Democracy's Blameless Leaders

Democracy's Blameless Leaders

From Dresden to Abu Ghraib,
How Leaders Evade Accountability
for Abuse, Atrocity, and Killing

Neil James Mitchell

NEW YORK UNIVERSITY PRESS
New York and London

NEW YORK UNIVERSITY PRESS
New York and London
www.nyupress.org

References to Internet websites (URLs) were accurate at the time of writing.
Neither the author nor New York University Press is responsible for URLs that
may have expired or changed since the manuscript was prepared.

Library of Congress Cataloging-in-Publication Data

Mitchell, Neil J. (Neil James), 1953–
Democracy's blameless leaders : from Dresden to Abu Ghraib, how leaders
evade accountability for abuse, atrocity, and killing / Neil James Mitchell.
p. cm.
Includes bibliographical references and index.
ISBN 978–0–8147–6144–1 (cloth : alk. paper)
ISBN 978–0–8147–6337–7 (ebook)
ISBN 978–0–8147–6338–4 (ebook)
1. Political leadership—Moral and ethical aspects—Case studies.
2. Democracy—Moral and ethical aspects—Case studies.
3. Civilians in war—Crimes against—Case studies.
4. Criminal liability (International law)—Case studies.
5. Atrocities—Case studies.
6. Government accountability—Case studies.
I. Title.
JC330.3.M57   2012
303.3'4—dc23   2011040796

New York University Press books are printed on acid-free paper,
and their binding materials are chosen for strength and durability.
We strive to use environmentally responsible suppliers and materials
to the greatest extent possible in publishing our books.

Manufactured in the United States of America
10 9 8 7 6 5 4 3 2 1

For Colin and Kate

Contents

Acknowledgments

I have people to thank for help with the research and the preparation of the manuscript. What success I have had in writing a book for both a general and an academic audience I owe to Eric Prentice and his infallibly polite nudges on matters of style and usage and to the editors at New York University Press, who also came up with the book's title. Thanks to Rhoda Howard-Hassmann, Hank Jenkins-Smith, Grant Jordan, Jim McCormick, David Pervin, Sabine Carey, Chris Butler, and the reviewers for New York University Press for very useful comments on drafts of the manuscript. For help obtaining courts-martial documents, thanks to Liz Mackie, Law Librarian, University of Aberdeen Library. For help at the UK National Archives, thanks to Liz Evans. For research assistance and data collection, thanks to Bronia Flett, Catriona Webster, Alex Arktos, and Colin Mitchell. Thanks to Ilene Kalish, of New York University Press, for her guidance, enthusiasm, and encouragement with the project. Finally, thanks to Agnes and other Mitchells for their encouragement, advice and support. The blame for any errors in style or substance better belong to the author.

Preface

When they meet with policy disasters, leaders in democracies are likely to behave in expedient rather than principled ways. Like most of us, they seek a positive balance of credit over blame for their actions. While we associate accountability with democracy, we have failed to recognize the significance of the problem of evasion and, therefore, to think about the forces at work. In this book, I describe the techniques democratic leaders use to evade accountability for human rights violations and the killing of civilians and argue that leaders frequently behave in expedient rather than principled ways. This proposition is examined in the context of well-known cases of abuse and the killing of civilians from Dresden and before to Abu Ghraib and afterwards in Iraq. Winston Churchill's words in the Amritsar debate in the House of Commons in July 1920 capture the scale of the policy implications and the drama of these events.

> There has not been, I suppose, for many years a case of this kind, which has raised so many grave and wide issues, or in regard to which a right and wise decision is so necessary in the general interest. There is the intensity of racial feeling which has been aroused on both sides in India. Every word we speak ought to have regard to that. There are the difficulties of military officers who, in these turbulent times, have been or are likely to be called upon to handle their troops in the suppression of civil disturbance. There are the requirements of justice, and fair play towards an individual. There are the moral and humanitarian conceptions which are involved. All these, combined, make the task of the Government and of the Committee one of exceptional seriousness, delicacy, and responsibility.[1]

Surprisingly, given the interest in the subject matter and the conflicts and drama involved, the management of blame is an undeservedly understudied subject. Guiding the way is the work of Niccoló Machiavelli and, perhaps less obviously, David Hume, as well as the research of contemporary historians, political scientists, and economists. This book offers an explanation of why accountability proves such a tough test. It finishes with an assessment of what might be done to improve things.

1

Introduction

The gravitational theory of accountability has one central proposition: blame falls to the bottom, to the fall guy. When things go wrong with a policy, people try to shift the blame. Those best placed to do this are those at the top. Even when there is evidence of complicity at the highest levels of government, blame will find its lowest plausible level. When the news of abuse or atrocity hits the front page, leaders faced with managing the blame are likely to react in a self-interested and opportunistic way and seek to deny and evade accountability. It is a rare leader who acts differently. Despite our reflexive association of democracy with accountability, our institutions provide poor compensation for such human failings and blame-shifting forces. In arguing for this simple proposition, this book places political and military leaders at the center of the explanation of how democracies manage the blame for atrocities. It has modest expectations about their motives as they adapt to the demands and pressures of their political environment.

Individual motivation is more complicated than is assumed here. This explanation has, for example, no place for some internal moral compass setting leaders on a course for truth and responsibility. All the same, it is worth seeing how far such a simplification can take us. If an explanation of this sort works anywhere, it is going to work in the less sentimental sectors of human interaction, the for-profit or for-power sectors, and when the expected consequences are very serious, which is the case with a government's use of violence and killing of civilians.

The central concern of the book is how leaders in democracies have managed the blame for killing civilians and for violations of human rights and humanitarian law committed by their armed forces. The argument that democratic leaders behave in an opportunistic rather than a principled way and manipulate the institutions designed to deliver accountability is counter to the conventional wisdom. If accountability is to be found in any country's politics, it is to be expected in a country with stable democratic institutions and free and independent media. Accountability is the guiding principle of a representative democracy. At elections, voters can hold leaders accountable for their performance in office. Between elections, internal systems are in place for monitoring and punishing decision makers. These systems either separate power among institutions so that each watches the other or fuse power so that government decision makers are routinely responsible to their colleagues in parliament. As one of the foremost scholars of political leadership says, "a democratic process is a pragmatic way to ensure that modern leaders enter their position with a firm claim of legitimacy and can be held accountable once they get there."[1] It does not happen with human rights violations.

With either a presidential or a parliamentary design, this book argues, political leaders manage the blame for doing wrong in armed conflict in a similar way. They do not submit an honest account of what happened. If they are forced to acknowledge the action, they shift blame for it to the lowest plausible level. As a consequence, and despite the general claim that accountability is a central feature of democracy, it is not delivered when it is most needed and where it might be most expected—where the rule of law and long-held moral prohibitions against killing and abusing civilians are at issue.

The failure to deliver accountability must have been apparent to Baha Mousa's father when he received the news of the one-year prison sentence given to one soldier for beating his son to death. In September 2003, Baha Mousa was taken into custody by British soldiers in Basra, Iraq, and beaten over a prolonged period, apparently out of earshot of the officers in charge.[2] The failure of accountability was evident to survivors of a massacre in Beirut by an Israeli-armed militia in 1982, to the families of the British citizens shot to death in Londonderry in January 1972, and to the survivors of a protest in the Punjabi city of Amritsar in the spring of 1919. All must have harbored doubts about democratic promises concerning the rule of law.

Hypocrisy aside, these types of events tell us a lot about how things work. They are difficult to foresee and have a galvanizing effect on political actors. As a consequence, when they make the headlines, they put decision makers and political systems under sudden, extreme stress, yielding information on the performance of individuals and processes. The process of accountability normally includes information on what happened, an evaluation of wrongdoing if any, and consequences for those responsible.[3] Yet, despite the academic and political significance of this topic, there is surprisingly little work on violations of human rights and the subsequent processes of accountability in full democracies. There is a literature on truth commissions that other political systems have employed to resolve conflicts.[4] There are accounts of democracies imposing accountability on others, as at Nuremberg, and there is work on apologies and the treatment of the past.[5] There is some general literature on how politicians manage the blame or the placement of responsibility for the harm done by their decisions or actions. The literature includes work by the philosopher J. L. Austin and the political scientists Morris Fiorina, Christopher Hood, Kathleen McGraw, and Kent Weaver, but there is not much to be found on blame management in the areas of armed conflict and human rights violations.[6]

There are other ways to think about these issues. There is a strong tradition in the study of international politics for using ideas and values as a starting point. We might assume that politicians in democracies are motivated by liberal and democratic values and that they are responsive to concerned organizations such as Amnesty International.[7] The fact that war crimes tribunals and inquiries take place may be pointed to as evidence of the impact of these liberal democratic values. The Israeli judicial inquiry that followed the massacre of Palestinians in Beirut in 1982 and other similar cases may be interpreted as suggesting the power of principled ideas.[8] The literature on human rights protection is broadly consistent with this emphasis.

This literature is more attentive to the causes than to the political consequences of killing civilians or using torture on prisoners. In the effort to explain why countries display marked variation in their observance of human rights standards, this literature points to the presence of mechanisms of accountability and the importance of democracy. Research shows how important it is to have states committed to protecting human rights and to have citizens active in support of those commitments.[9] The presence of elections and an active set of voluntary associations mobilized around human rights and civil liberties issues reduce the chances of torture and killing carried out by government agents. This combination of institutions and activity is what is meant by a mature liberal democracy. The most robust finding of this literature is that these types of democracy—not just systems that hold elections—are substantially less likely to commit violations. The interpretation of this statistical finding suggests the importance of accountability as a defining feature of such democracies: "Accountability appears to be the critical feature that makes full-fledged democracies respect human rights."[10] This book explores the limits of this assumption.

To take the ideal case as illustrative, a leader most firmly in the grip of principle would not explicitly or tacitly consent to abuse or atrocity in the first place and would take action to stop it and punish those responsible as soon as she knew of it. Such a leader would not require the goad of public outrage. The timing of the process of accountability is significant. With gravitational theory, the assumption is that it is the public's knowledge, rather than the leader's knowledge and commitment to the rule of law, that triggers inquiries and the downward shifting of blame. Blame for policy disasters becomes an issue only when there is pressure on public support and when the news of the event threatens to damage careers and reputations. In cases of human rights violations, it is a rare leader who acts to put his or her reputation at risk in advance of public exposure and on moral calculation alone. Yet, on occasion, I expect that gravity (not a technical term here) fails in the political world. After all, here we deal with individuals and choices, not with Newton's apple. In the political world, gravity is a resistible, rather than an irresistible, force. Candidly admitting responsibility for the abuse or for failing to control those who committed the abuse and so inviting the blame is an option.

The political scientist Christian Davenport has disentangled the different aspects of accountability and examined their impact on human rights violations. One aspect is the dependence of politicians on public support in competitive and participatory political systems. This factor ("voice") is more important than the particular institutional checks or constraints on the executive ("veto") in the political system. Davenport says that "when authorities are accountable . . . they are less inclined to use coercion against them because they could lose mass support, be removed from office, or face . . . some form of investigation."[11] These are important findings about what is likely to reduce the incidence of violations. My question concerns what happens under conditions where there are "voice" and "veto"—that is to say, under the condition of full democracy—in the unlikely event that violations do occur. Is accountability delivered? While a commitment to protect human rights and the presence of mechanisms for accountability matter in terms of reducing the likelihood of violations in the first place, after violations occur, expediency, not principle, dominates. It may be that leaders take responsibility for other types of policy disaster. Some scholars suggest they do: "In the end, buck passing only undermines one's authority, whereas proactive and well-communicated responsibility taking serves to reinforce it."[12] It is an empirical claim. I suppose it depends on what they are taking accountability for and the precise meaning of these management concepts. There is no evidence that leaders submit timely and honest accounts ("proactive and well-communicated responsibility taking") for policy disasters involving the security forces and the killing of civilians and the abuse of prisoners. And they tend not to be corrected by the electorate. Voters may punish politicians for their performance in other areas, for example, their management of the economy. But, at least according to President George W. Bush's campaign strategist, the issue of war crimes was more of a liability for John Kerry in the 2004 election than for the president.[13] Rather than the president being punished for violations committed by American soldiers, Kerry was punished for raising the issue of American war crimes as a Vietnam veteran.

So how do we sort out responsibility and punishment? What evasive tactics do we employ, and what signal do we send about our values and standards of conduct? How do we meet this test of national character? The argument in this book applies to democratic governments' use of force, their adherence to human rights and humanitarian obligations, and the treatment of civilians and prisoners. It may extend to other sorts of policy disasters and other hierarchical institutions, such as corporations and churches and their unlawful activities. The concluding chapter discusses the limitations and extensions of the argument.

Shocking Events in Amritsar, Dresden, Londonderry, Beirut, and Baghdad

The overall aim of this book is to understand how leaders in democracies manage the blame when their agents commit violations. Examining the forces at work and thinking about why leaders let us down spark analytical curiosity. Analysis and an appreciation of the challenge that delivering accountability represents are the basis for reform and an antidote to the human rights hubris of countries like America and Britain. Recognition that democracy's promise of accountability has systematically exceeded its performance in this area is important in itself. Only by considering a series of cases across time and political space is this recognition possible. Such recognition points the way to informed and perhaps more authoritative participation in the progress of the idea of human rights. At the same time, it is also helpful to say what the aim is not. The aim of the book is not to suggest that we should remain silent on human rights—or to make an argument that no one is good enough to speak to this issue. Nor is it to suggest moral equivalency. To take the most extreme example, Dresden does not bring into balance the inhumanity of the other side. Remembering rather than forgetting our own inhumane acts and the inadequacy of the response to these acts does not truncate all points on the worldwide scale of inhumanity to one value.

The cases considered in these pages stretch from the early twentieth century to the early twenty-first century. They presented leaders in the United States, the United Kingdom, and Israel with choices in accounting for what happened. This book examines the choices that they made and how accountability was delivered. These cases allow an initial empirical assessment of my argument and an understanding of the forces at work in managing the blame. Because they are relatively rare events and seem so extraordinary at the time, they have been left largely to historians. They are regarded as accidental to democracy. After the Beirut massacre, the Israeli government was said to be "still treating the entire affair as a freak historical accident or a matter of abominable luck."[14] There is, then, room to think about whether there is a connecting pattern of political behavior left by these "freak" events. Like the events themselves, the failures of accountability tend to be seen as isolated failures in an imperfect world, rather than as indicative of a systemic weakness.

The book does not include all possible cases of violations committed by the armed forces of stable, liberal democracies. Were this study part of a large collaborative research project, its empirical scope could be more extensive. Instead, the book pursues a case study approach appropriate for a theory-building effort. Case studies have the advantage of allowing more in-depth consideration of the forces at work. A disadvantage is that such an approach is necessarily selective, rather than exhaustive. That said, the criteria for selecting the cases are described, and, the theoretical argument, like any other, is subject to the collective efforts of the research process and to the identification of counterexamples.

I used several criteria in selecting cases. First, the cases are limited to what seemed at the time extraordinary violations involving killing civilians and mistreating prisoners that might be expected to result in calls for accountability. What was done by liberal democracies in Amritsar, Dresden, Londonderry, Beirut, and Baghdad violated long-established liberal norms against killing and abusing civilians and prisoners. These cases raise issues of humanitarian and human rights law. Whether a violation has occurred is contested, at least by the perpetrators. The cases concern the safety of the person as described in Article 3 of the United Nations Universal Declaration of Human Rights, on "right to life," and in Article 5, on "prohibiting torture or cruel, inhuman or degrading treatment or punishment." Two of the cases predate the 1948 Universal Declaration. Yet, when those cases occurred, there were already in existence established principles of international law that prohibited killing civilians and abusing prisoners. The United States and the United Kingdom were state parties to the 1907 Hague Convention on the Laws and Customs of War. This convention prohibited killing, unnecessary suffering, and attacks on undefended towns, villages, or dwellings. It provided for the humane treatment of prisoners. Furthermore, the London Agreement of 1945, with its Charter of the Nuremberg International Military Tribunal, reinforced Britain and America's principled commitments to the treatment of civilians and prisoners. The London Charter provided the standards for evaluating the actions and policies of Nazi Germany in its use of armed force. This Charter, using principles from the existing Hague and Geneva Conventions, took the important step of individualizing criminal responsibility for war crimes. Government office and purpose did not protect an incumbent from criminal charges. These crimes included "wanton" attacks on cities. The Charter's description of crimes against humanity protected the state's own civilians from the state. These crimes included "murder, extermination . . . and other inhumane acts committed against any civilian population, before or during the war."[15] The Charter extended cover for the civilian population against inhumane acts for wartime and peacetime.

Beyond international agreements, the cases were shocking at the time. The Amritsar massacre was an appalling event even by the standards of colonial rule. As a cabinet minister, Winston Churchill condemned the inhumane act at Amritsar in what is regarded as one of his great speeches. His word was "frightfulness."[16] At the time of Dresden, Churchill was prime minister. These two cities provided quite different contexts for killing civilians. Suppressing colonial unrest inspired by saintly nonviolence is not the same as fighting a war for national survival against an enemy capable of anything. Yet, before Dresden, Churchill's government concealed the nature of the bombing campaign from the British public. After Dresden, the prime minister used the London Charter's word "wanton" to describe the Royal Air Force's bombing of that city.[17] Then he left Bomber Command and its commander to shoulder the blame.

The number of fatalities that occurred in the cases under study ranges from relatively few at Bloody Sunday in Londonderry to hundreds at Amritsar and in Beirut and up to perhaps twenty-five thousand in Dresden. Yet, all are of a scale sufficient to have been described as conscience-shocking at the time. While the cases under study do not include all possible conscience-shocking cases, those included are the ones that tend to come to mind in this regard (and not just my mind). For example, in discussing Bloody Sunday, journalists remarked that "on English soil the only parallel is the so-called Peterloo Massacre when demonstrators seeking parliamentary reform were charged down by cavalry in Manchester, in August 1819. In the annals of atrocities committed by the state against its own people, Bloody Sunday takes its place alongside India's Amritsar, South Africa's Sharpeville."[18] To be clear, India's Amritsar was an exercise of colonial power.

Second, the cases provide variation in the political status of the victims. Bloody Sunday differs from the other cases in that the victims were citizens of the state. In the other cases, it was Indians, Germans, Palestinian refugees, or Iraqis who were killed or abused by the British, Israelis, and Americans. On this criterion, of all the cases, then, accountability would be expected for what happened in Northern Ireland on January 30, 1972. Here the victims' families had the right of representation. Members of Parliament were present at the march and the shooting. And the event unfolded on the pages, recordings, and screens of an independent media.

Third, these cases are selected to represent both state violations, where political leaders decided on a policy of killing or abuse, and violations initiated by individual soldiers. They extend from situations where there was evidence of an individual violation (Amritsar) and where accountability should be relatively easy for those in leadership positions to deliver to those where there is substantial evidence of centralized state complicity at the highest level (Dresden, Baghdad). There are other cases where the evidence remains difficult to classify (Londonderry, Beirut), despite high-powered, judge-led inquiries. In these cases, it is difficult to know whether it was an issue of *can't control* (where leaders lose control of their followers) or an issue of *won't control* (where they refuse to take control). This distinction in the role of leaders is examined at length in the next chapter.

Fourth, the cases are restricted to the use of armed force by established liberal democracies. The weaknesses of the theoretical argument are most likely to be revealed in cases where the accountability of leaders and high officials is a defining feature of the political system.[19] Britain and the United States are selected as leading examples of parliamentary and presidential systems of accountability. They are widely emulated models.[20] While there are a number of other presidential systems, in Latin America for example, and there is a hybrid presidential system in France, the United States is "the most famous presidential system in the world."[21] Britain's parliamentary democracy has historically been "widely admired," even by American political scientists.[22] Both of these democracies have a lengthy history of conflict and therefore of violations. Importantly, these democracies have a history of policing other countries' observance of human rights standards. They have taken a prominent role in making individuals of other states accountable for violations. The effort to make leaders of other states individually accountable for their inhumane acts includes the London Charter and the Nuremberg Tribunal. As such, if we are to find gravity defied anywhere and accountability delivered, then we would expect it to be in London and Washington. Israel meets the stable-democracy criterion and has a lengthy history of conflict. It has a parliamentary system and a doctrine of ministerial responsibility, but there are some notable differences in its electoral system and the likelihood of coalition government. Importantly, it shares with Britain and America a commitment to individualizing responsibility for violations.

Fifth, the cases provide some variation in the consequences. Across the cases, there was variation in punishment for ordinary soldiers and the agents who carried out the violations. Those involved at Abu Ghraib got prison time. Those who shot people in the camps in Beirut, on the streets of Londonderry, or in the square at Amritsar did not.[23] An important factor in explaining the variation, this book argues, is the perceived motives of the perpetrators. Assuming the perpetrators are subject to disciplinary measures (it is less clear with Beirut and the use of a foreign militia), whether or not they are seen to derive private benefits from the violation influences the likelihood of punishment. At the top of the hierarchy, Israeli leaders came closest to political accountability and loss of office. Although its Christian militia agents, based and operating in Lebanon, went unpunished, Israel acquired a reputation for accountability for the way it dealt with what happened in Beirut. In news accounts and in the research literature, Israel's subsequent handling of the event was praised. From these accounts, this case seems to offer a counterexample to my theoretical argument. It is important to include it in the analysis. On the release of the report of the inquiry into the massacre in Beirut, the

American secretary of state, George Schulz, commented that Israel provided a "model" for other democracies.[24] The Harvard professor Marshall Goldman pointed out that the Germans had had tribunals imposed on them and that, in contrast to Israel, Britain and America were unwilling to hold inquiries into My Lai and similar events.[25] The Beirut case is cited as an example of the power of principle and the rule of law in the research literature.[26] Such counterexamples of political leaders responding to an atrocity in a principled way or of self-regulating democratic institutions delivering accountability would be diagnostic. But, as shall be clear, my understanding of the Israeli case differs from these interpretations.

Sixth, the cases cover a substantial period of time. They allow for generalization but also for the possibility of learning and the diffusion of learning across political systems. Finally, the cases involve a range of more or less well-regarded leaders. The influence of leaders as well institutions is important to the analysis. A strong leader such as Winston Churchill provides a stiffer test for the theory. If he could defy the tide of events in May 1940, when the only realistic option appeared to be negotiation with Hitler, presumably he could defy anything. One might be less surprised to find gravitational theory at work in President Bush's administration. He could be depicted as readily shifting blame to subordinates. He did so after Hurricane Katrina when he shifted blame for the government's response to the head of the Federal Emergency Management Administration, Michael Brown. He did so with Lynndie England and the others for the events at Abu Ghraib. For another example, given the low regard accorded to President Richard M. Nixon, an argument resting on his administration's handling of massacres such as at My Lai in Vietnam might be less persuasive. My Lai seems to support the argument; efforts were made to evade accountability, and blame was ultimately made to rest on one soldier, who received a light punishment. If gravitational theory is going to work anywhere, it is going to work with overtly opportunistic leaders.

It is certainly possible to come up with other examples of civilian killings committed by democracies, ones that received somewhat less attention and so posed less of a test for political leaders than those one finds in this book. Britain's suppression of the Mau Mau insurgency in 1950s Kenya yields examples of such killings. But, again, no Conservative politician at the time took responsibility for any wrongdoing. Or, for Israel in the 1950s, one could look at the massacre of Jordanian villagers in Qibya. Over his foreign minister's objections, after the massacre, Prime Minister

David Ben-Gurion denied his army's involvement. He blamed the slaughter on settlers.[27] The action did not, at least in an obvious way, handicap the career of the commander who led the operation, Ariel Sharon. It is a case that would likely support the argument.

The next chapter presents the theoretical argument. Chapter three examines the repertoire of evasive techniques, from denial to finding a fall guy, the effectiveness of these techniques, and the hard and soft forms that accountability might take. The later chapters provide the analysis of the cases and compare democratic promise with performance in the management of the blame for human rights disasters. In each chapter, the material is organized by the theoretical argument. The key components include a synopsis of the violent event and the type of violation, the evidence concerning the motivations for the violence, audience pressures, the expected and observed responses of leaders, and an assessment of whether accountability was delivered. The expected responses to reports of abuse or atrocity are denial, delay, diversion, or delegation. An honest account of what happened from the leaders involved is not the expected response. Condign punishment for those responsible for what happened is not the expected outcome. Chapter four analyzes the management of the blame for the shooting of unarmed Indian protesters by the British at Amritsar in 1919. Chapter five is about the bombing of the citizens of Dresden. The perennial context for British policy toward insurgency is Ireland, and chapter six examines the 1972 Bloody Sunday killings in Northern Ireland. Israeli leaders' responses to outrages committed by their Christian allies are the focus of chapter seven. Chapter eight examines events at Baghdad Central Confinement Facility (Abu Ghraib prison).

In a departure from the other chapters, which focus on a single well-known event, chapter nine provides a comparison of the investigation and proceedings taken against American and British soldiers over allegations of killing and abuse in Iraq. The invasion of Iraq by the United States and Britain provides a common arena for comparing performance and the outcome for accountability. There are some fine accounts of the invasion of Iraq, including *Fiasco*, by Thomas Ricks, and of the abuse and torture, such as *Torture and Truth*, by Mark Danner, *Torture Team*, by Philippe Sands, and *Standard Operating Procedure: A War Story*, by Philip Gourevitch and Errol Morris, but there is no systematic analysis of blame management. The information on allegations of unlawful killing and abuse by coalition forces was collected from media reporting and open sources. The chapter analyzes these data from the vantage points offered by the theoretical argument. The argument has implications for the patterns of convictions and sentencing. The chapter examines the treatment of troops accused of unlawful activities, with particular attention to the influence of the different human rights commitments of the leaders (Blair and Bush), the role of the private interests of those committing the violation, and the influence of rank on the severity of punishment. The book finishes with a discussion of the gap between democracy's promise and performance, the extensions and limitations of the argument, and the implications for how to strengthen accountability. Do we find better leaders, better institutions, or a better audience?

2

The Theory of the Fall Guy

Britain's top soldier at the time of the invasion of Iraq, General Sir Mike Jackson, told the inquiry into the death of Baha Mousa, who was beaten to death by British soldiers in 2003, that "it is absolutely bedrock to the British Army's philosophy that a commanding officer is responsible for what goes on within his command."[1] Yet no British officer was held responsible for Baha Mousa's death, for any other case of unlawful killing or abuse in Iraq, or for the deaths in Londonderry on Bloody Sunday in 1972. No minister was held responsible, either. The Israeli and American records are similar. The gravitational theory of accountability offers an answer to the puzzle of why, despite the presence of democratic mechanisms of accountability, despite democratic folklore about where the buck stops and ministerial responsibility, and despite military claims of a doctrine of command responsibility, accountability is so difficult to deliver. This chapter describes the logic underlying the management of these shocking and, at the time, seemingly unique events. It identifies the general incentives at work. The argument applies to individuals in hierarchical institutions and draws on the insights of economists' principal-agent theory as modified for the political world.

The way blame is attributed for violations is connected to the underlying motives. There are three general motives for violations.[2] There is Machiavelli's motive, namely to get and secure power. The leader is willing to use violence and deception to deal with threats from opponents.[3] There is the Inquisitor's motive (after Dostoevsky's tale of the Grand Inquisitor) and the atrocities that follow from the logic of the leader's intolerant belief system. For such leaders, violence is directed at those on the wrong side of the political argument, whether or not they represent a threat. Be it about dogma or power, as the violence is usually carried out by someone else, there is a third motive to consider. The agent who administers the violence may bring his own selfish motive to the encounter with polemical or political threats.

These motives lead to violations committed either on the initiative of government leaders or on the initiative of individual agents. There are state violations of humanitarian standards, where government leaders motivated by power or dogma identify some strategic goal to be achieved by the use of violence and cruelty. There are also individual agent violations, where agents may have a taste for revenge or an enjoyment of violence or may simply misunderstand their duty. Individual violations committed on the initiative of the agent suggest a breakdown of control by the leaders; these leaders have failed to adequately instruct and supervise their agents. In any large organization there are control problems.[4] Those giving orders cannot observe how their orders are carried out at all times. Agents may misunderstand their mission or improperly take advantage of their own position for selfish purposes. Security forces are no different. Recruitment standards, monitoring, and enforcement mechanisms are set up to address these familiar problems.[5] Other things being equal, these individual violations are expected to be the easiest type of violation for which to deliver accountability. Leaders are assumed to have an interest in correcting breaches of discipline.

Can't Control, Won't Control, and the Unscrupulous Principle

Complicating things, in addition to individual and state violations, there are violations initiated jointly by the state and by individual agents. In some circumstances, leaders choose not to control their selfishly motivated agents. In 1415, Shakespeare's Henry V extracts tactical advantage from the mere threat that he might lose control of his happy few at the siege of the French town of Harfleur.[6] He addresses the people of the town and warns them: "The gates of mercy shall be all shut up / And the fleshed soldier, rough and hard of heart . . . With conscience wide as hell, mowing like grass / Your fresh fair virgins and your flow'ring infants."[7] The agents' desire to commit selfish violations is so powerful that it outweighs the efforts at command of the victorious commander. Henry knows the wickedness of his men but says that he will not have command. He pleads "vain command." Vain command is a convenient claim for an accountability-evading principal to make. Of course, a few weeks later, he shows he can control his men's fear at Agincourt but not apparently their greed at Harfleur. Shakespeare's Henry V goes so far as to say that it is for the besieged to take pity on themselves. He has no responsibility: "What

YBP Library Services

MITCHELL, NEIL J. (NEIL JAMES), 1953-

DEMOCRACY'S BLAMELESS LEADERS: FROM DRESDEN TO
ABU GHRAIB, HOW LEADERS EVADE ACCOUNTABILITY FOR
ABUSE,...   Cloth   263 P.
NEW YORK: NEW YORK UNIVERSITY PRESS, 2012

TITLE CONT: ATROCITY, AND KILLING. AUTH: UNIV.
COLLEGE LONDON.
 LCCN 2011-40796
  ISBN 0814761445   **Library PO#** FIRM ORDERS
                                    List   39.00 USD
   8395 NATIONAL UNIVERSITY LIBRAR   **Disc**   14.0%
   App. Date 3/26/14 GOV   8214-08 **Net**   33.54 USD

SUBJ: POLITICAL LEADERSHIP--MORAL & ETHICAL
ASPECTS--CASE STUDIES.

CLASS JC330.3   DEWEY# 303.4   LEVEL ADV-AC

rein can hold licentious wickedness / When down the hill he holds his fierce career?"[8] Even with the best will in the world, it will not be possible to control the men. No commander has the means to check this behavior. Blame falls on his enraged soldiers, though they cannot really help themselves, and on the governor for not surrendering. As it happens, the governor of Harfleur finds the threat credible and surrenders. His people are spared. Henry's motivation in making threats about the individual violations his agents will commit is tactical. He wants to take the objective efficiently, minimizing his casualties. In this way, the threat of the agency problem and individually initiated violations contributes a tactical benefit. It may have saved the loss of civilian lives, as well. Two centuries later, as his Walloons and Croats stormed the city of Magdeburg in 1631, the victorious commander, Count Tilly, was alerted by officers that these troops were committing atrocities. He is reported to have said, "Return in an hour, I will see what I can do; the soldier must have some reward for his dangers and toils."[9] If Friedrich Schiller's history is correct, Tilly refused rather than lost control of his men.

The argument is that leaders may see a tactical or strategic benefit in the agents' private violence. Such violence may send a stern message to the unruly inhabitants of the region, drive out undesirable population groups, extract information from civilians or detainees, or serve as an incentive for agents. At the same time, leaders will perceive fewer costs if the violence is not attributable to them as a deliberate act or policy. Rather than give specific direction, they may simply provide the opportunity for their agents' "hidden action." Then they turn a blind eye to their selfishly motivated agents. In other words, there are both leaders who *can't control* and leaders who *won't control*. In instances of *can't control* violations, where the agent takes advantage of his position to realize some private benefit, the violence is initiated by the individual agent. In cases of *won't control*, the violence is initiated by both. The power-seeking or dogma-following leader entraps the self-seeking and violent agent. The implication for the placement of the blame is straightforward. If there is to be any accounting for the violation, the *won't control* leader anticipates that the bad acts will be treated as an instance of the more familiar control problem. The damage to reputation and punishment will be done to others: blame will fall to the bottom, to the individual and independently motivated agents involved.

Delegation is a relationship entered into to save us from doing the task ourselves. The disadvantage we accept is that delegation is a relationship characterized by self-interest and unequal information.[10] Those charged with carrying out the policy, the agents, are likely to know more about the task than the principal, and they have their own self-interested goals that, if they get the opportunity, they will prefer over the principal's goal. This divergence of goals or goal variance is the true source of the rot in a bad apple. At their worst, the agents may be more interested in earning bribes than in enforcing regulations. They may wish to secure a future career with a defense contractor, which may influence how they perform their duties at the ministry. They cannot be trusted. But there are protective measures to prevent the rot. The likelihood that agents will do these sorts of things is linked to how much they value their position, how much they are paid, and what they think they can get away with. If the position itself becomes more valuable to the agent, it is more likely that the agent will see her interest in faithfully carrying out the mission.[11] The need for monitoring may also be reduced if the principal chooses the agents carefully and then trains them well.[12]

The scrupulous principal seeks knowledge about the characteristics and otherwise hidden actions of the agents. Faced with the knowledge advantage that agents customarily enjoy, the principal is expected to respond by redressing the imbalance in information through monitoring. She then tries to arrange incentives and recruitment strategies appropriately. But, in the political world, the leader may have the imagination to convert the problems of information asymmetry and goal variance into an opportunity and may see some strategic benefit in not knowing and in leaving agents to their selfish devices. In the common situations that economists tend to think about, this is an absurd tactic. It would be strange indeed for a manager to recruit lazy workers and leave them to themselves. In the administration of violence, on the other hand, there may be occasions when otherwise risky prospects are recruited or are chosen to be deployed and left to get on with it, that is, when an agent's self-interested violent activity serves a strategic purpose. The thrust of the analysis of delegation is to show the problems that principals encounter in exercising control. In contrast, in the policy area of repression, delegation may afford opportunities to unscrupulous principals, as well as to self-seeking agents.

By recruiting bad apples and those with "conscience wide as hell," the leader anticipates creating terror and a fearsome reputation in order to achieve a strategic objective. And when some accounting is to be had, the violence can be blamed on these "hard of heart," as Shakespeare's

Henry V says, and minimized if not dismissed as a control problem. The issue is the authenticity of his claim of "vain command." The question is whether the principal *can't control* or *won't control*. When the principal *won't control*, the self-interested agent is present, but there is no information asymmetry.[13] The leader knows that the agent is likely to pursue selfishly motivated violence, yet chooses to do nothing about it. He knows the character and actions of the agents as well as they do. Should the need arise, they are likely fall guys. If the action is exposed and accountability sought, the problem becomes a problem for the agents—an "agent-principal" problem, if you like, as the principal pleads vain command.

To restore the integrity of the model (if not the leader), one can stretch back the chain of delegation. Theories simplify reality, and the "policy stage" relationship between the leader and those who carry out policies is one segment of a larger political process that can be thought about as a chain of relationships. If we stretch the chain back from the "policy stage" to the "representation stage" of the process, where leaders are chosen and governments originate, then the leader is now an untrustworthy agent of an ultimate principal. The principal-agent model returns to a more familiar form. In democratic politics, voters are the ultimate principal.[14] Political leaders are agents entrusted with the task of governing.

Stephan Poth and Torsten Selck provide an insightful analysis of the links among the ultimate principal, the leader, and the agents. They suggest the usefulness of the effort to distinguish between cases of *can't control* and *won't control* and between genuine information asymmetry and the pretense of it. They use Elizabeth I as an example. She blamed "subordinate authorities" for Mary Stuart's execution: "Respect among peers and possibly her own conscience counterbalance Queen Elizabeth's personal and political rationale to rid herself of a dangerous troublemaker." Poth and Selck suggest that, in cases like this, psychological factors "might effectively take the role of a principal."[15] It is appropriate to recognize the length of the chain of delegation. We could dispose of the unscrupulous leader in this way. He is conceived as an untrustworthy agent of some ultimate principal. But we are left with the need to describe how he hid his action from the ultimate principal, the fraudulent assertion of a simple agency problem, and his relationship with his agents in the policy stage. The idea of *won't control* is meant to capture the leader's temptation to evade accountability.

Political scientists have appreciated some of the blame-shifting benefits of delegation. Morris Fiorina observed that, in addition to the benefits economists emphasize, there is a political incentive attached to delegation: "By charging an agency with implementation . . . legislators not only save themselves the time and trouble of making specific decisions, they also avoid or at least disguise their responsibility for the consequences of the decisions."[16] The recognition of the political advantages of delegation extends the analysis of delegation beyond its economic and administrative implications.[17] The conventional preoccupation with the untrustworthy agent and with the measures available to deal with him has largely set the research agenda. In contrast, Fiorina directed attention to the political opportunities presented by institutional delegation. Beyond the application of this way of thinking to the question of why democracies do so poorly in coming to terms with their own violations of human rights, there is a more general contribution to be made to do with the distinction between *can't control* and *won't control* and with attention to delegating to individuals, not just shifting responsibility between bureaucratic organizations.

In Fiorina's analysis, policy is implemented faithfully. The agents are expected to do what the legislator wants: "I assume that delegation only places added political daylight between legislators and those who feel the incidence of legislative actions."[18] If the policy fails, unhappiness will be directed at the organization to which responsibility has been shifted. On the downside, in shifting responsibility, as Fiorina noted, the legislator risks losing credit for actions that turn out well. The loss of credit may be less keenly felt than the desire to avoid blame. Kent Weaver discusses a "negativity bias" among legislators. Generally, they have greater sensitivity to blame than desire for credit. They are not "credit maximizers" but "blame minimizers."[19] Timidity prevails. Out of fear of the blame, legislators shift responsibility for a policy to an agency.

But there is a step beyond Fiorina's blame-shifting understanding of delegation that is evident when one examines the use of political violence. What if the legislator is unscrupulous and not simply averse to risk as Fiorina assumes? Beyond straightforward delegation, in the tension between principal and agent there lie opportunities for the leader who, with a nod and a wink, has the Machiavellian wherewithal (Machiavelli referred to it as *virtù*) to exploit them. The leader may be tempted with a more decisive shift in responsibility, appropriate for the most controversial of high-cost policies, such as the use of violence. We can compare Fiorina's legislator in his shifting responsibility model with a *won't control* legislator. While both Fiorina's legislator and a *won't control* leader exploit delegation to deflect blame, the latter combines delegation with the false claim of a "runaway" agent.[20] In other words, Fiorina's legislator *avoids* blame. The *won't control* leader *evades* blame. The *won't control* principal exploits the internal mechanics of delegation. Simple reference to the well-known problems associated with delegation insulates the leader from blame. It makes the nastiness of the actions the agents' responsibility, should it have to come to that. All that is required is slack in the reins of control, followed by a plea of vain command. The leader claims a lack of information and an inability to monitor all agents all of the time. The agents' actions are attributed to the agents' private goals and deviant nature, not to the leader's goals.

We have taken our analytical eye off the *won't control* leader to focus on the untrustworthy agent. The assumption is that a selfishly motivated agent has a goal that necessarily conflicts with the principal's goal. The goals of agent and principal may be different—but they are not necessarily in conflict. One may be in search of revenge, selfish pleasure, or peer approbation in the violation of human rights; the other may desire some strategic end, such as the extraction of information. They may have different reasons for deciding on the usefulness of the violation.

Delegation is a notably available technique to evade accountability in the area of armed conflict and when there are allegations of abuse and atrocity. Agents in conflict conditions are inevitably left with discretion, proverbially under the "fog of war," required to exercise judgment under stress and have the means of abuse at hand. Under these conditions, the general role for central authority is to be inactive in the control of the agents. States refuse rather than lose control of their agents in order to minimize political costs. When blame needs assigning, it falls not on the principal but on his agents.

There are horrifying examples of *can't control*. Five soldiers from the United States 101st Airborne Division were charged with raping an Iraqi girl and then killing her, her parents, and her younger sister in March 2006.[21] The ringleader had joined the army a year earlier. By that time, the United States was having problems finding the numbers of soldiers necessary for the task. Indeed, it lowered entry test standards and made exceptions for recruits with criminal records in an effort to increase recruitment. (The test scores of the soldiers in the case are not known.)[22] The rape and murder did strategic harm to the United States. By 2006, leaders were well aware of the need to actively develop public support for the war effort. They no longer assumed that the invasion was self-justifying, as they seemed to do in the first phase of Operation Iraqi Freedom. Relaxing selection requirements heightens the likelihood of picking bad apples.[23] More selective recruitment reduces control problems. Commanders have long known this wisdom. In the seventeenth century, the English civil war commander Oliver Cromwell said that he carefully chose soldiers who had a "conscience" about their task. He boasted that they were never beaten.[24]

Some cases of violence committed by security forces appear singularly attributable to out-of-control agents. They carry significant strategic costs for the principal. In contrast, in other cases, the principal may refuse to control in pursuit of the strategic goal of terrorizing the population, as leaders are alleged to have done with armed militias in the former Yugoslavia and in Sudan.[25] Disentangling whether a principal *can't control* or *won't control* is a thorny problem, which is what the unscrupulous leader relies upon.

If we classify violations by who initiates them, we have state violations, individual violations, and joint *won't control* state-individual violations. The type of violation has implications for the management of blame. An insistence on flawless administration of any government policy, including security policy, is unrealistic. Recognizing that all agents cannot be monitored all of the time—for that would begin to undermine the time-saving rationale for delegation in the first place—individual violations will happen. Accountability is most likely to be delivered with this type of violation. When individual violations occur, blame belongs to, rather than falls on, the individual who actually carried out the activity. Furthermore, the universality of the simple agency problem is readily acknowledged. But there are inherent characteristics of the power relationships involved that are likely to confound accountability even for individually initiated violations of human rights.

The Theory of the Fall Guy

When the costs are high, and they are very high with the misuse of violence, it is an exceptional leader who keeps to principles. Accountability is a more severe test than we are led to believe. Accountability requires a timely and accurate account of actions and policies and an assessment of how they met or fell short of expected standards. The relevant standards that inform our expectations in the government's use of violence are provided by human rights and humanitarian law and longer-standing moral inhibitions about killing civilians, as Schiller and Shakespeare made clear.

Beyond an honest account, the ordinary use of the term "accountability" requires that consequences follow for those responsible for wrongful actions or policies. Ruth Grant and Robert Keohane provide a definition: "Accountability . . . implies that some actors have the right to hold other actors to a set of standards, to judge whether they have fulfilled their responsibilities in light of these standards, and to impose sanctions if they determine that these responsibilities have not been met."[26] On hearing a call for accountability, we expect something to happen to those whose conduct has fallen short of accepted standards. But, when the stakes are high, honest accounts are rare, and people try to place responsibility for the harm done—the blame—on others.[27] Those best placed to do this are those up the chain of delegation. If there is punishment, it falls to the lowest plausible level. Some punishment may belong there. The fall guy in gravitational theory is not necessarily innocent. In this respect, he differs from his biblical antecedent, the scapegoat. But both pay for the sins of others.

The argument assumes that the action has taken place within hierarchical organizations. In other words, there were leaders and followers, and blame has a place to fall. Both leaders and followers are self-interested. Neither can be trusted. The simple agency approach does not capture the insincerity of the leader. In the language of analysis, that approach assumes both an information asymmetry and, if you like, an insincerity asymmetry. But both assumptions are shaky. There are *won't control* as well as *can't control* leaders. Both sides of the principal-agent relationship are sometimes staffed with self-interested and untrustworthy individuals. Machiavelli knew this. He teaches us to distrust both leader and follower. As described, Machiavelli and the analysis of delegation also help us understand why human rights violations and atrocities happen in the first place.[28] In applying the same general theoretical argument, the claim is that it helps us understand the political cleanup process after violations and even the pattern of sentencing should it come to courts-martial or legal proceedings.

Alternatively, if one extends the accountability claims of the democracy literature, one would expect leaders to oversee a robust accountability regime. To assume that a leader is in the grip of principle is also to suggest something about the timing of his or her actions. The rule-of-law leader will act on knowledge of the policy disaster, whether or not the public knows or cares. She will select a course of action on a bearing from her moral compass. She will hold to it despite the hazards to reputation that may lie ahead. In contrast, the opportunist responds only once the abuse or violations are visible to the public eye and in fear of an impending storm of public outrage. Rather than hold to the rule of law, the opportunist adjusts and trims to the demands and pressures of a suddenly harsher political environment.

These demands and pressures are generated by those groups and organizations, external and internal, that observe and evaluate a leader's performance and potentially influence the opinions of voters. It is in democracies that the leader's actions are most visible and that leaders are likely to be most sensitive to issues of trust. It is in an environment where media watchdogs have freedom and citizens have the opportunity to mobilize that governments are most likely to meet human rights treaty obligations, for example.[29] It is fear of what the political scientist James Fearon terms "audience costs." His analysis is of international crises in which audiences have had an opportunity to evaluate the performance of their leaders. If the leader backs down after mobilizing troops and engaging national honor, he or she is likely to pay a cost in public support. Audience effects are strongest in democracies, he argues.[30] Similarly, atrocities and violations provide a particularly dramatic opportunity for audiences, domestic and international, to evaluate leaders.

It was neither treaties nor the confidential reports on conditions in American military prisons in Iraq by the International Committee of the Red Cross, the monitoring organization for the Geneva Conventions, that persuaded the U.S. government to initiate investigations and courts-martial for what happened at Abu Ghraib. It was quite simply that the abuse was visible to the electorate. CBS television broadcast the images of the fearful victims of abuse and their tormentors at Abu Ghraib. It is, then, in the leader's interaction with the audience that we can expect to discern some conscience-guiding events—provided, of course, that the audience is good enough. Repression, black lists, and other violations can be popular.

The leader in a democracy faces the demands and pressures of domestic politics and is attuned to changes in public support. Pressure from an international audience of foreign leaders, foreign media, and concerned organizations may be on the horizon. Below is the internal audience of officials, potentially mutinous and likely expecting encouragement and support. If audiences force the issue of accountability for a violation, the democratic leader will choose to secure his own position and let blame fall on the agent, which, granted, is more than is likely to happen under authoritarian rule. But, even at this stage, when the disgrace and punishment have come down on those who carried out the shooting or the bombing of civilians, the priority is not values and principles. The leader will seek to confine and contain the consequences for the agent in order to minimize the wider impact on the morale of other agents, because he depends on their continued support in order to govern effectively. Accountability is not delivered. There is neither an honest account of what happened nor condign punishment for those responsible.

There are two components to a leader's perceived self-interest that conflict with accountability: a personal component and a governance component. Leaders seek to evade any personal blame for initiating violations or for failing to prevent them. They fear their reputations will suffer and their political support will decline or that they may even have to face legal proceedings. They seek to avoid charges of negligence or worse.

The second component is the desire to continue to govern and to be able to implement policies. In order to do so, leaders seek to avoid blame for their agents for fear that accepting blame might weaken commitment to the task. As a way of maintaining loyalty, they deny the culpability of agents and impose only token punishment so far as that is within their control. While the benefit of personally evading blame is readily appreciated, the costs to overall agent commitment associated with punishment are not clearly recognized.

In the analysis of delegation, punishment, sometimes referred to as "reactive strategies," is understood to deter misbehavior by agents. Agents "can be removed from office, and even prosecuted, if their actions stray too far from the grey areas surrounding the mandate and power of their agency."[31] As a result of punishment, agents learn compliance. Yet, there are two further features of punishment that are of particular relevance to the management of blame.

First, punishment may create noncompliant action as well as correct it. It has unintended effects on the willingness of other agents to perform their tasks. For one thing, in satisfying domestic and international demands for accountability, the leader is faced with immediate counterpressure from the fall guy's coworkers, whose continued cooperation he wants. The opinions of the military or security agents require attention, leadership, and persuasion. David Hume's "first principles of government" are worth remembering. He wondered how it is that the many can be governed by the few:

> When we inquire by what means this wonder is effected, we shall find
> that . . . the governors have nothing to support them but opinion . . .
> this maxim extends to the most despotic and most military govern-
> ments. . . . The soldan of Egypt or the emperor of Rome might drive
> his harmless subjects like brute beasts. . . . But he must, at least, have
> led his *mamalukes* or *praetorian bands*, like men, by their opinion.[32]

In order to effect the wonder of the many being governed by the few, leaders need, at a minimum, to have the confidence of their security forces.
Leaders want to protect agents because they fear the impact on morale
of punishing one of their number and even worry about generating mutinous impulses among a group trained to value intragroup loyalties of a
"one for all, all for one" variety.

Under conflict conditions and given the risks agents run, loyalty and
support may be harmed by the exposure of abuse and may also be damaged by the administration of punishment. Political and military leaders are concerned about the effects of delivering accountability on the
general loyalty and obedience of their agents and on their own political support. As they have responsibility for placing soldiers in the difficult conditions of conflict, then norms of loyalty to the soldiers may
conflict with the human rights and justice claims of organizations that
support civilian or detainee victims. Leaders are expected to "back their
men and women." To avoid the perception that they do not support the
troops, leaders are generally reluctant to admit that abuse has occurred
in the first place and then to administer punishment. Under most conditions, the agent confidence factor associated with the internal audience creates pressure not to satisfy the minimum definition of accountability by providing an honest account of violations. If such violations
are exposed, this factor can also serve to encourage leaders to accept the
imposition of a light punishment.

The second feature of punishment that the analysis of delegation
neglects is its use as a mechanism for shifting blame for a violation. From
a leader's perspective, if a serious violation is exposed and there is any
suggestion of complicity, the potential costs of the violation rise sharply.
It is prudent that some punishment be administered, notwithstanding
any cost to the confidence of agents. This act of leadership distinguishes
the violation as individually initiated, rather than a matter of state policy.
If punishment involves not merely loss of office or demotion (General
Karpinski in the prisoner abuse scandal at Abu Ghraib, for example) but

prosecution, it may be difficult for even independent courts to counteract this process in the absence of clear orders linking the leader to the violation. Punishment may provide the political benefit of putting distance between the unlawful act and those higher in the chain of delegation. Of course, even severe punishment may disguise undeclared state policy. If punishment is administered, it will fall not on all those responsible, as adherence to democratic norms would suggest, but on those at the lowest plausible level.

Although he did not use the same terms, Machiavelli was well aware of the underlying logic. He knew that the relationship between principal and agent is ripe for exploitation and manipulation from both sides. He had no faith in agents and knew the control issues and the difficulties caused by mercenaries in Italy in his day. But Machiavelli was alert to how bold leaders seized opportunities to secure power. They used and abused their agents. He describes Cesaré Borgia's employment of his Spanish minister, Remirro de Orco: "He determined to make plain that whatever cruelty had occurred had come, not from him, but from the brutal character of the minister. Taking a proper occasion, therefore, he had him placed on the public square of Cesena one morning, in two pieces. . . . The ferocity of this scene left the people at once stunned and satisfied."[33] Cesaré's ultimate principal was the stunned and satisfied people of Cesena.

Not all exercises in the management of the blame are so successful. But it follows that punishment is not a clear or "noiseless" signal that the violations were inconsistent with state policy. Even if, as with Cesaré's Spanish minister, the punishment is more than token punishment, it may still obscure the hidden intent of the state authorities. The intent is to evade blame. It is not to deliver justice.

If the media, nongovernmental organizations, and political opponents do sustain some pressure for adherence to human rights standards, leaders are likely to let blame fall on the agent. And they are likely to equate the example of punishment with their own exoneration, as if the load of blame is finite and of a zero-sum character (i.e., the more blame is given to one, the less blame is left for the other). We will see how this use of punishment is practiced in later chapters.

The leader's motives of evading blame and maintaining agent confidence initially converge. They account for the general reluctance to admit abuse even in established democracies. This reluctance likely extends to opposition political parties, suggesting that the formal mechanisms of accountability in democracies, strong in structure and design, are weak in operation. The assertion of democratic accountability for human rights disasters confuses the presence of these mechanisms with their operation. There is little electoral incentive for opposition parties to risk embarrassing members of the armed forces.

Yet, once abuse or atrocity is exposed and there is the suggestion of leader complicity in the abuse, the leader's personal motive to avoid or evade blame and the desire to maintain agent confidence are more difficult to reconcile. The benefit of using punishment, as far as it is within the leader's control or influence, to put distance between the agent and those higher in the chain of delegation comes at the expected cost of alienating agents more generally. To reduce this cost, the leader's interest is to let blame fall but then tokenize the punishment. The fall guy is allowed a soft landing. A second method to reduce this cost is to clearly isolate the agent to be blamed from other agents and to present him as deserving of punishment. The leader's interest is to identify a bad apple. If the violence can be attributed to very clear goal variance and to an agent who was seeking some purely private or personal benefit, then harsher punishment is likely.

Democratic and despotic leaders are alike, as Hume made clear, in their worry about the agent confidence factor. They differ in the costs they face for maintaining it. The costs of maintaining agent confidence are higher for leaders in democracies. Democracies are distinguished from nondemocracies by the presence of formal mechanisms of accountability and civil liberty, allowing the media and other organizations to sustain at least some pressure to attribute blame for wrongdoing. So leaders in democracies have a dilemma. Do they prioritize the confidence of their agents or the conscience-nagging elements of their public? Punishment of agents is by no means certain, but it is more likely in democracies than in "despotic and military governments," as leaders seek a way out of the dilemma posed by the exposure of a shocking event.

In short, accountability in the sense of appropriate punishment for those responsible is unlikely. Leaders, concerned about the effects on the general loyalty and obedience of their agents and, above all, about their own political support, are most likely to be thinking of denials, excuses, inquiries (if necessary) to buy time, and other ways to dissipate the pressure for accountability. Where offenses are punished, punishment will fall to the lowest plausible level. Chapter three looks at the repertoire of available evasive techniques and the alternative forms that accountability might take.

3

Evading Accountability

When things go wrong in politics, people seek to deflect the blame. No matter how well designed a constitution, we are dealing with individuals, with power, with selfishness and human failings. There may be examples of leaders who courageously do the right thing, but one should not expect it, any more than Napoleon expected instantaneous courage—"I have rarely met with two o'clock in the morning courage: I mean instantaneous courage." In general, leaders do not individually and openly face the press at dawn, regardless of the consequences. Instead, in order to rebuild public support, they resort to techniques of evasion, which are quite predictable in their various forms.

These techniques are suggested by the components of accountability. In democracies, lines of accountability run from government leaders to legislatures and to voters in more or less complex patterns. The relative simplicity of parliamentary models of accountability offers a contrast with the more complex presidential model.[1] In both systems, the media generally trigger accountability processes. An item in the news prompts questions in the legislature and a demand for accountability, though what exactly is entailed in this demand is quite complicated. A minimal definition of accountability requires providing a timely and accurate account of actions and policies and how they met or fell short of the relevant standards for assessment. Information is a key component of accountability, yet is insufficient on its own. A fuller definition of accountability adds to the submission of an honest account the requirement that consequences follow for those responsible for wrongful actions or policies.[2] The fuller definition accords with the ordinary use of the term. On hearing a call for accountability, we expect something to happen to those whose conduct fell short of accepted standards. Given these components of accountability, it follows that evading accountability can be achieved in three ways. First, it can be evaded by manipulating the flow of information about events, actions, and policies. Second, it can be evaded by manipulating the standards used for evaluating the action or policy. Third, it can be evaded by manipulating the consequences for wrongdoing.

The Techniques of Evasion

The evasive techniques comprise four main types: denial, delay, delegation, and diversion.[3] Denial, delay, and delegation are techniques that reject or at least do not admit responsibility for what happened. Diversion admits responsibility but then questions the standards applied to evaluate the action. This technique either redirects attention to the benefits of an act that is usually deplored or points to the ordinariness of the act and to the actions of others. Diversion might involve the claim that similar violations or worse occur elsewhere or the assertion that they represent a tragic choice necessitated by extremely hazardous conditions. With the tragic-choice argument, once normal standards are suspended and the context is set appropriately, the leader takes responsibility for an action that becomes, under the specific circumstances, creditworthy, rather than blameworthy.[4] General Reginald Dyer used this defense and referred to his "horrible duty" in justifying his action at Amritsar.[5] With the "elsewhere too" argument, everyone shares the blame. The exculpatory idea is that, in fairness, no one should be singled out. The term sometimes used is *tu quoque*. Diversion means accepting responsibility, while preparing the context within which the audience views the violation. In this way, one accepts responsibility for the action but not at its "face value" moral weight.

Of all the techniques, delegation is the most dramatic and the most theoretically interesting, with the distinction between *can't control* and *won't control* that was discussed in the previous chapter. Whereas the other techniques simply reject or accept responsibility, delegation shifts responsibility to others. It creates the drama of division and conflict among individuals in the hierarchy and offers an opportunity for the various audiences to the conflict to choose sides.

Denial and Delay

Denial takes various forms in relation to atrocities. The action may be denied, the existence of the victims themselves may be hidden or denied, or the victims may be denied status as victims and turned into combatants.[6] With denial, there is no official abuse and zero accountability. In Argentina's "Dirty War" against domestic opposition in the late 1970s, prisoners were without names and their cells were without numbers, according to the journalist and political prisoner Jacobo Timmerman.[7] To voice opposition was to expose yourself to the risk of anonymous death. Your grandmother might have noticed that you were missing—grandmothers of the disappeared courageously protested against the actions of the government in the capital—but no Argentine official could find a trace of you.

Unnumbered cells and unnamed prisoners are not confined to the southern hemisphere. During the administration of George W. Bush, the CIA transported "ghost detainees" to the overseas locations of their secret prisons. These prisons were operated by CIA personnel and their perimeters protected by local security forces. The local forces were not allowed to enter the prisons or to know what was happening inside.[8] Amnesty International described it as a program of "enforced disappearances."[9] A Council of Europe investigation under the auspices of the European Convention on Human Rights, drawing on testimony from government and intelligence officials in the United States, Poland, and Romania, collected information about the operation of these secret prisons in those countries. According to its report, the United States "intentionally created a framework enabling it to evade all accountability."[10] In Poland, Abu Zubaydah and Khalid Sheikh Mohamed were subjected to "enhanced interrogation techniques."[11] The Romanian site was used for captives from Afghanistan and, later, from Iraq.[12] The report repeatedly draws attention to how this policy is directly contrary to the normative foundations of democratic countries and to the obligation of accountability. According to anonymous testimony collected by the Council of Europe, on arrival, "ghost detainees" were stripped naked and kept that way for weeks. Solitary confinement, temperature, light, and noise were used to make conditions hard.[13] Human rights groups identified a total of thirty-nine detainees who were likely to have been taken to these prisons and who remained missing.[14] The United States admitted to holding three of these detainees. The disappeared were from Pakistan, Morocco, Somalia, Egypt, and elsewhere and were beyond the reach of the rule of law and even the International Committee of the Red Cross.

Under the policy of "rendition," American officials transferred prisoners to prisons in other countries, often countries with quite poor records of human rights protection and even those known to practice torture systematically. Maher Arar, a Canadian and Syrian citizen, was arrested in New York and sent to Syria. He was there for a year. Syrian military intelligence personnel beat Arar, and "he was confined in a coffin-like cell, with rats and cats, stifling hot in summer and freezing cold in winter."[15] The Canadian government inquiry stated that "there is no evidence that Mr. Arar has committed any offence or that his activities constitute a threat to the security of Canada."[16] The Canadian inquiry found that Maher Arar's treatment by the Syrians amounted to torture as defined by the Convention against Torture.

International law provides a common standard by which to evaluate a policy of disappearances. It is contrary to international law and to the United Nations International Covenant on Civil and Political Rights, which the United States ratified in 1992. Articles 9, 10, and 14 prohibit arbitrary detention and require humane treatment and "respect for the inherent dignity of the human person" and a public hearing in accordance with the rule of law for detainees. It is also contrary to the assurance provided by the U.S. Department of State that protecting human rights and the values enshrined in the Universal Declaration of Human Rights motivate American foreign policy.[17] The U.S. Department of State releases, each year, country reports describing human rights conditions around the world. A recent report on Syria states that "methods of torture and abuse included electrical shocks; pulling out fingernails; burning genitalia."[18] The State Department reports are detailed and generally reliable, standing up quite well to a comparison with, for example, Amnesty International reports on human rights conditions, at least since the end of the Cold War.[19] On the release of these reports in March 2007, Assistant Secretary of State Barry Lowenkron showed some awareness of the glass house that the United States had built for itself. He recognized that U.S. practices had been criticized. He then went on to claim that "our democratic system of government is not infallible, but it is accountable. Our robust civil society, our vibrant free media, our independent branches of government and a well-established rule of law work as correctives."[20] No doubt this was said sincerely. Lowenkron's claim is the conventional wisdom on democracy and accountability. It underlines the importance of examining the delivery of accountability.

If denial is difficult and the news is out, *delay* may allow time for other events to crowd the agenda. There may be a genuine need for an inquiry. But inquiries serve to delay any further action with respect to the event. They may buy some time, but there is little evidence that they are effective in putting off the media.[21] Examining how tight a rein government leaders hold over the composition of the inquiry suggests whether the goal of the inquiry is accountability. A significant number of members and a willingness to appoint outsiders, as was the case with the second inquiry into Bloody Sunday but not the first (which was a one-person inquiry), suggest that a high priority is being given to accountability. The multiple inquiries that followed Abu Ghraib extended the period of delay and helped to generate a confusion of details, rather than a clear picture of what happened. With delay, the hope is that other events will dissipate the negative attention.

Diversion

Attention to the abuse or atrocity can be distracted and diverted with the reminder that it is equally bad and probably a lot worse elsewhere. The assumption of *diversion* as a technique is that everyone gets his hands dirty when repressing insurgencies or fighting wars. The implication is that no one should be held to account. This type of claim has considerable force. In her discussion of "how to blame people responsibly," the philosopher Marilyn Friedman says that "a responsible blamer should be committed to those norms to which she is prepared to hold others."[22] It is an appeal for consistency and a dislike of hypocrisy. Admiral Karl Dönitz, who commanded Germany's U-boats during World War II, was tried at Nuremberg. One of the charges he faced was that he had waged unrestricted submarine warfare against enemy and neutral merchant shipping. His defense was that the British and the Americans were waging unrestricted warfare, as well.[23] Dönitz was convicted on other charges and served ten years.

In 1948, hundreds of thousands of Palestinians fled their homes, gripped by the fear created by the conflict that erupted at the birth of the State of Israel and perhaps expecting to be able to return home when the surrounding Arab states defeated Israel. Israeli officials were concerned about international reaction to the issue of displaced Palestinians. One approach was to point out how widespread this practice was: "We will be able to give every respectable nation its list of crimes in this sphere."[24] And, clearly, with large parts of Central and Eastern Europe subject to violent and forceful population transfers in the postwar period and with Europe's retreat from Empire, the Israelis had some evidence. Here the violation is conceded, rather than denied. Then it is placed in a context that makes it acceptable.

The tragic-choice justification causes officials to do things they ordinarily abhor. The use of repression is explained in means-and-ends terms: it is necessary to preserve the political community as a whole. Leaders tend to understate the repressiveness of the measures taken and to overstate the level of threat. This is understandable, as the potential costs of misjudging the situation and not responding vigorously enough are high.

Under the condition of an exceptional threat to security, countries reserve the right to modify their commitments (some articles in the international conventions, such as the prohibition of torture, are defined as nonderogable). Critics claim that the "tragic choice" between security and the protection of human rights and civil liberties is a false choice. They point out that the information yielded by torture could have been gathered in other ways, that the information is of poor quality and is unusable, and that, by damaging rights and liberties, leaders actually damage security by alienating groups and populations. Not convinced, leaders in Israel, the United States, and the United Kingdom generally see a trade-off between rights and security needs.

President Bush employed the tragic-choice technique when he conceded the existence of secret detention after the policy had been exposed by the media and subjected to judicial examination in *Hamdan v. Rumsfeld* (June 6, 2006). This U.S. Supreme Court decision found against the military commission system used to deal with foreign detainees and decided that the Geneva Conventions and the prohibition of humiliating and degrading treatment covered the detainees. Before his chosen audience of administration officials, congressional representatives, and the families of the victims of the attack on the World Trade Towers, President Bush began by recalling the events of September 11, 2001, the dawn of a dangerous new world, and the responses of his administration.[25] The president and his officials had consistently asserted that the war that they were fighting was different from other wars. The enemy was willing to escalate to any weapon available and would use it against civilians. There is little reason to doubt the administration's anxiety, whether or not the strategic decision to define its actions as a war in the first place was correct. The president pointed out that, thanks to the policies of the administration, there had been no subsequent attacks on Americans in America despite a determined, stateless, out-of-uniform enemy. President Bush stated that those policies included holding some detainees secretly, where they could be questioned by experts and asserted that the information obtained from them had saved American lives, just as Israel had justified its legally sanctioned torture regime in the 1990s by the quality of information received and the attacks thwarted. The president used the example of Abu Zubaydah for illustration. This individual, who was captured in Afghanistan, was "defiant and evasive" and eventually stopped cooperating with his interrogators. According to the president, the CIA then switched to other methods, which the administration's Department of Justice said were lawful, and soon began to get what it wanted from Zubaydah, leading to further arrests. The president went on to assure his audience of the value of the information received. He maintained that the interrogators and their methods had been thoroughly vetted by the U.S. Justice Department and reiterated that the United States does not use torture. He also drew attention to the issues of degrading treatment. Worried that his agents in the CIA might be at risk of war crimes prosecutions "simply for doing their job in a thorough and professional way" and asserting that "America is a nation of law," he described legislation, the Military Commissions Act of 2006, with which Congress could protect the interrogators from war crimes charges.[26] The administration had been concerned about immunity from war crimes prosecutions from the start of its war on terror, and this concern had led to the infamous Department of Justice memo that mentioned pain at the intensity of organ failure as the definition of torture. It is also consistent, as Amnesty International has pointed out, with the Bush administration's policy of securing bilateral agreements with other countries to immunize American personnel from prosecution by the International Criminal Court (ICC). The state parties to the Rome Statute of 1998, the treaty that set up the ICC, agreed to procedures to put on trial those accused of war crimes, crimes against humanity, and genocide.

The tragic choice is not self-evidently a false choice. The claim of a trade-off between liberty and security is not necessarily spurious. There is force to the argument that, without a secure political community, there would be no meaningful human rights whatsoever. These concerns over security may be legitimate, the repression proportionate, and the justification less evasive, but officials' aversion to security risks tends to be high. They are susceptible to authorizing increasingly repressive behaviors and to blacklists and witch hunts. In this way, the implementation of tragic choices may impair security by creating an additional sense of grievance among the affected population and increasing the chances of backlash violence. An analysis of the repressive measures employed by the British in Northern Ireland, including detention without trial and the use of the Special Air Service, shows that these measures had a backlash rather than deterrent effect (only Operation Motorman to retake "no-go areas," launched in July 1972, had a deterrent effect).[27]

With tragic choice, the political authorities more or less take responsibility for the repressive measures. They then point to a larger harm that would result if they did not take these measures. In practice, officials tend to exaggerate the level of threat. By resorting to this technique, they may compound the tragedy by equipping all other nations with a similar defense. There may be tragic choices to be made, yet policymakers are quite capable of both tragically choosing security and then tragically generating greater insecurity.

Delegation

Abuse or atrocities may result from a temporary breakdown in control over those delegated to carry out a policy, or, evasively, they may be attributed to such a breakdown. There are "bad apples" in any organization. While it is perfectly possible that principals may lose control, it is also possible that they may cynically not bother to take control of their agents. They may ignore warnings of control problems when it suits their purpose of incentivizing their troops, deterring opposition, obtaining information, or other strategic goals. With *won't control*, private selfishness delivers strategic goods. The key question, of course, is whether the private selfishness is beyond the control of government, as it sometimes is, or whether it is encouraged by a government that *won't control*, as it also sometimes is. This question is at the heart of assessing accountability for Abu Ghraib. Was it Lynndie England's sense of fun or Donald Rumsfeld's priority of actionable intelligence that was the real driver of events at that prison? The question is also at the heart of the Beirut massacre. Did the Israelis know what they were doing in letting the Christian Phalange militia through their lines? Or were they surprised by the conduct of their allies? If it is a question of deciding not to control, government leaders expect at least a residue of exculpatory doubt about their responsibility to be sufficient to sustain what in practice is a very generous presumption of political innocence.

Where atrocity and abuses are concerned, political leaders use *delegation* to hold on to office and to act opportunistically. What is more, while much is made about the design of constitutions—whether or not they are written, whether or not they invoke separation of powers—we find similar behavior across democracies. Political leaders manipulate institutions, norms, and the public in order to achieve their objective. Instances of leaders with a steadfast adherence to the rule of law who have overridden this sequence of maneuvers and turned into the impending political storm are difficult to find. Political survival, which rests on public support and the loyalty of agents, leads democratic leaders to resort to evasive measures and to seek shelter from events that threaten their reputations. Doing the right thing for the victims of some atrocity turns out to be a profound test of political leadership.

The Effectiveness of Evasion

In discussing blame and what to do about it, Austin distinguishes between excuses and justifications. He argues that when you are accused of something, you have options. You can admit to it but explain why it wasn't such a bad thing to do under the circumstances—in our terms, the "tragic choice" and "everyone has dirty hands" sort of justification. Alternatively, you can admit it was a bad thing but claim that in fact someone or something else caused it to happen and that it was not your responsibility. Austin describes these alternative strategies: "In the one defense, briefly, we accept responsibility but deny that it was bad: in the other, we admit that it was bad but don't accept full, or even any, responsibility."[28] The former are justifications; the latter are excuses. He did not expect that any defense would be very effective.

The political psychologist Kathleen McGraw used experimental methods to investigate whether justifications or excuses are more effective. As she points out, with justification the effort is to shift the evaluation of the policy outcome and to explain why the outcome is in fact desirable.[29] It is the bolder strategy of credit claiming. Her experiment involved exposing subjects first to a hypothetical vote by a politician on a budget that cut services or increased taxes and then to a subsequent public meeting where the politician explained his vote to concerned citizens. She presented one group with a set of justifications and excuses for the vote, while the control group received no additional information defending the vote. The most interesting finding in this experiment was that, in general, offering no defense, neither excuse nor justification, worked best. The control group's level of satisfaction with the politician and his vote was systematically higher than that of the group exposed to blame management strategies. This finding, McGraw argues, is likely qualified by the prior reputation of the politician, which provides a context for the accounts and defenses offered. If, at the beginning of the management of the event, there is at least a pocket of good will for the politician, that may help retain some buoyancy in public support and may help in weathering the outrage.

If one examines the specific excuses and justifications employed, one finds that there were some clear differences in performance. The excuse of ignorance ("I voted for the budget bill but did not foresee that it would result in the police and fire safety cuts") worked least well. Excuses that diffused responsibility (blamed a higher official or other participants) were assessed as less satisfactory than excuses claiming mitigating circumstances ("I had to vote for the budget bill because the freewheeling spending of the previous administration had crippled the state's economy") or justifications that appealed to normative principles ("I had to follow my conscience . . . and therefore I did what I believed was in the best interests of the community").[30] Overall, the message seems to be that if you choose to offer a defense, you're best off choosing justifications that involve accepting responsibility but reset the context, rather than making excuses, at least in this experimental environment.

Austin anticipated the poor service excuses often provide: "Because it has always to be remembered that few excuses get us out of it completely: the average excuse, in a poor situation, gets us only out of the fire into the frying pan."[31] While pleas of ignorance and scapegoating might not sound convincing to subjects in an experiment and might not have great resonance with the public, they may serve to keep political leaders free of formal charges. The evasions may not appear convincing, but they may be sufficient to permit leaders to survive in office. President Ronald Reagan and Vice President George H. W. Bush managed the blame for the Iran-Contra scandal that preoccupied them during Reagan's second term of office in this way, while some of their agents were indicted. The scandal involved the secret sale of arms to Iran in exchange for the release of hostages held in Lebanon. The arms deals violated the Arms Export Control Act requirement that the administration notify Congress of possible violations of the act and contradicted President Reagan's repeated claim that the United States did not negotiate for hostages. The proceeds from selling arms to the Iranians were then used to evade a congressional prohibition against military assistance to the Contras, a violent U.S.-supported armed group opposed to the Sandinista government of Nicaragua.

When the news of the arms-for-hostages deal appeared in a Lebanese newspaper, President Reagan found a fall guy in the basement of the

White House, Lieutenant Colonel Oliver North. Others indicted included two national security advisers, Robert McFarlane and John Poindexter.[32] An independent counsel, Lawrence Walsh, was appointed to investigate the affair. He said the president had tried "to get Congress to give immunity to Admiral Poindexter and Colonel North in the hopes that they would exculpate him and take the fall. Congress decided to go after the scapegoats, and Colonel North and Admiral Poindexter were terrific as scapegoats . . . they denied informing the President of the diversion of the proceeds of the arms sales."[33] Reagan saw out his term. He left a reputation big enough for him to have an airport renamed in his honor. If those are the measures by which we are to judge, the president suffered little lasting damage from the affair. His vice president went on to become president, North's and Poindexter's convictions were reversed on appeal, and even Secretary of Defense Caspar Weinberger managed a soft landing. Weinberger had claimed poor recall, but Walsh describes how he was caught with detailed notes showing that both he and the president had knowledge of the affair. Weinberger was indicted for lying to Congress and to the independent counsel but was pardoned by President George H. W. Bush. According to the independent counsel: "President Bush stood by while other people . . . had been convicted of felonies. For these others he did not lift a finger; it was only when the political upper crust was reached that this extraordinary act of clemency was taken."[34] President Bush's son, George W. Bush, found positions for others involved in the scandal, including Elliot Abrams, who had been pardoned by his father, as well as John Negroponte and Poindexter. Lawrence Walsh's main conclusion was that the scandal and the consequences for those involved were an affront to the rule of law.

A minimal definition of accountability requires the submission of an honest account. It was not the constitutional system of checks and balances but a Lebanese newspaper that exposed the unlawful activities and began the submission of such an account, despite the obstructions of democratic leaders. If we think about accountability as involving sanctions, then it was a case of failed accountability. Sanctions fell on those on the lowest plausible level and then were eased by pardons and reappointments. The political scientist James McCormick titles his analysis "The Iran-Contra Affair: A Case of Failed Accountability."[35] The outcome seems to defy the constitutional design of democracy. It also puts us in search of better leaders.

Democratic Institutions and the Hard and
Soft Forms of Accountability

Long gone are the days of the Emperor Trajan. This Roman emperor set up a simple system of accountability. He instructed one of his Praetorian Guard: "Take this drawn sword to use for me if I reigne well, if not, to use against me."[36] Accountability is more complicated in democracies. It takes various forms, as does punishment. Legal accountability is imposed by the courts, where loss of liberty is the likely punishment.[37] Political accountability is imposed by the voters or by confidence votes in parliamentary systems, where loss of office is the punishment. Reputational accountability is imposed by the media and the public, where loss of image is the punishment. Finally, personal accountability is imposed by one's conscience, where loss of sleep is the punishment. Across democracies the courts, voters, legislatures, the media, and individual consciences are more or less well set up to extract an honest account of wrongdoing and then to impose consequences.

For legal accountability, the standards for deciding the wrongfulness of actions are provided by international and domestic laws. These standards describe unlawful actions and even attempt to define leaders' responsibilities. The United States, Britain, and Israel are party to the Geneva Conventions, the International Covenant on Civil and Political Rights, and the Convention against Torture and also have domestic constitutional provisions protecting life and liberty. The U.S. Constitution provides for citizens' rights to free speech, association, timely trials, and legal representation and includes prohibitions against "cruel and unusual punishments." These principles inform public expectations about how leaders should behave.

Traditionally, judges and the common law in the United Kingdom going back to the Magna Carta have provided protection for free speech and association and against arbitrary imprisonment. In 1998, the Labour government's Human Rights Act moved in the direction of a written constitution and of allowing judges to review government actions in this area. The Human Rights Act made the European Convention on Human Rights British law, although the Convention had been drafted by the Council of Europe, signed by the United Kingdom in 1950, and ratified the following year. It provides for the right to life, freedom of expression, and freedom of association and prohibits torture and inhuman or degrading treatment or punishment, forced labor and servitude, and detention without trial. Under the 1998 Act, British courts can declare government actions incompatible with the Human Rights Act. Then it is up to the government and parliament to address the issue.

The State of Israel is seven months older than the Universal Declaration of Human Rights. The May 14, 1948, Declaration of the Establishment of the State of Israel describes a country committed to freedom, justice, and peace and pledged to the principles found in the United Nations Charter. Israel's Basic Law: Human Dignity and Liberty, which sets out the values of the State of Israel "as a Jewish and Democratic state," provides for rights to life and liberty. In Israel, as in the other democracies, there are standards by which to assess the violent actions of security forces and a foundation of principles from which to exert pressure on leaders for accountability.

Legal accountability has been imposed by domestic and military courts for killing or abuse. Those convicted lie at the bottom of the chain of command. In other countries, there are a few cases of individualizing responsibility for torture in which former leaders faced trial. Chile's former dictator General Augusto Pinochet was arrested in London in 1999, following a Spanish extradition request and under the United Kingdom's obligations as a party to the United Nations Convention against Torture, which was ratified by the United Kingdom in 1988. As Geoffrey Robertson says, "the most remarkable feature of the Torture Convention is that it applies the universal jurisdiction principle—either you extradite or you punish—to any person suspected of committing a single act of official torture."[38] Pinochet eventually returned to Chile for health reasons. He faced trial but died unpunished. In 2009, the former president of Peru, Alberto Fujimori, who had been extradited from Chile, was convicted by Peru's Supreme Court for the Peruvian military's killing of twenty-five civilians in the early 1990s.[39] Fujimori was found responsible for actions taken by his armed forces during his authoritarian rule.

Under the doctrine of command responsibility, a commander is held legally responsible if he knew or should have known of violations and did nothing to prevent or punish them. While the focus of this book is the self-regulating claims of democracies, international courts have applied this doctrine, as well. The Statute of the International Criminal Tribunal for the Former Yugoslavia holds that a commander is criminally responsible for acts of his subordinates if he "knew or had reason to know that his subordinates were about to commit such acts or had done so and . . .

failed to take necessary and reasonable measures to prevent such acts or to punish the subordinates."[40] In this way, the court recognized explicitly the significance of the relationship between commanders and subordinates. It included the actions of militias as relevant to assessing state compliance. President Slobodan Milosevic was held responsible for acts committed by Arkan's Tigers, an informal armed group that fought against the Bosnian Muslims. In another, recent case targeting a political leader, the prosecutor for the International Criminal Court (ICC), Luis Moreno-Ocampo, has sought the arrest of the president of Sudan, Omar Al-Bashir, charging that he masterminded the tribal slaughter in the Darfur region of that country. According to the prosecutor, the president of Sudan, although he denied having control over the militias that did the killing, is criminally responsible for their acts. As many as 300,000 people died in the Darfur region of Sudan over the five-year period from 2003 to 2008, and Moreno-Ocampo points to evidence of systematic killing and raping. His account suggests that what happened in Sudan was a case of *won't control*, not *can't control*: "They all report to him, they all obey him. His control is absolute."[41] In March 2009, the ICC issued an arrest warrant for the Sudanese president, but he continues in office. Leaders in less powerful states are more exposed to external legal constraints, whereas powerful democracies with resources, military forces, and "strong internal legitimacy . . . may be largely immune from sanctions" and external accountability.[42]

In democracies, the self-regulating political mechanisms of accountability are expected to be robust. Democracies differ in the arrangement of their institutions and in the specific mechanisms of accountability. But all promise accountability in the sense of producing an honest account of what happened and imposing consequences on those responsible for negligence or wrongdoing. There is evidence that the presence of mechanisms of accountability reduces the likelihood that wrongdoing will occur.[43] We can even begin to be specific about the types of mechanisms. The political scientists David Cingranelli and Mikhail Filippov found that differences in electoral rules influence the likelihood of human rights violations. Particular forms of proportional representation (open-list systems with small numbers of seats in a constituency) provide individualized incentives for elected officials to improve human rights protection.[44] In contrast, proportional representation systems that have large numbers of seats per district and that do not allow voters to choose among individual candidates encourage competition between parties, rather than individuals. Under these conditions, where the individual reputations of candidates are not at stake, politicians are less concerned with protecting human rights.

The fear of accountability instilled by the presence of these electoral mechanisms may encourage good behavior. The question for this book is what happens after things go wrong. We must not confuse the presence of mechanisms with their operation. How do these systems exact accountability? In considering the general problem, James Fearon and others point out that, at elections, voters may not be paying much attention. They may lack the incentive to be informed about politics.[45] As a rule, multiple issues and priorities characterize election campaigns; if a single issue dominates, it is likely to be the economy. Knowing this, politicians manipulate the economy coincident with the electoral cycle (or vice versa in cases where the government has control over the timing of elections), manipulate the release of information about the economy, and manipulate the standards used to evaluate economic performance; public attention may be focused on inflation, rather than on unemployment, for example. Sometimes it works: "if there ever was a sure case of a government doomed by economic performance, the first Thatcher government should have been it."[46] Political parties are thoroughly engaged in the competition over the interpretation of economic performance.[47] In contrast, in both parliamentary and presidential systems, party competition has not produced accountability in the area of armed conflict and human rights violations.

Even in the 2004 presidential election in the United States, which took place just months after the stunning news from Abu Ghraib, what happened at that prison was not a campaign issue. The mechanism for accountability was in place, but it takes the political opposition, the media, and voters to engage it. Opposition parties monitor government performance for voters and sound the alarm. But they are particularly unreliable where human rights violations are concerned. One may not often find President Bush's campaign strategist, Karl Rove, in the company of French philosophers. Yet he seems to have shared Ernst Renan's view that nations prefer to forget their own abuses and atrocities when he argued that John Kerry was politically vulnerable because he had reminded Americans about U.S. war crimes in Vietnam.[48] Rove's analysis of the 2004 presidential campaign raises the specter of an ultimate principal that *won't control.*

In a presidential democracy such as the United States, voters directly elect both an executive (through the mechanism of the Electoral College) and a legislature. Powers are separated between the two. In a parliamentary democracy, voters elect a legislature or parliament, and that body selects the executive. The executive in a parliamentary democracy controls a voting majority in the parliament and most of the parliamentary agenda. The dependence of the executive on a majority in parliament strengthens the emphasis on discipline within political parties. Members of political parties in parliamentary systems are more cohesive ideologically, and there are stronger career incentives not to dissent from the party leadership. The governing party is more predictably supportive of the executive. The concentration of power in the prime minister and the cabinet in these systems makes responsibility for policy more straightforward. In contrast, given the separation of powers between a legislature and an executive in presidential systems, the responsibility for policy is less clear. Each branch has its mandate from the voters and has the capacity to set the policy agenda and influence policy. In presidential systems, there is more opportunity to shift the blame to another branch of government; the executive can blame the legislature, and the legislature can blame the executive. In contrast, as Kent Weaver notes, a parliamentary system "makes it particularly difficult for these governments to dodge blame for losses they have imposed or acquiesced in, because it concentrates authority and accountability in the government-of-the-day and provides regular opportunities to hold government accountable . . . There is no one to whom the buck can be passed."[49] It is easier for voters to disentangle who is responsible for policy in a parliamentary system than in a presidential system. Between elections, parliamentary systems have oversight mechanisms. Parliamentary question time, where individual ministers have to respond to members' questions, can be lively. But the House of Commons too often accepts "the substitution of wit for confession."[50] In some circumstances, public inquiries are appointed to look into particular issues of high public concern, such as the Iraq war. But the government sets the terms of inquiries. The reports may be criticized for having too little or too much detail, and their findings are often viewed as part of the process of managing blame. All of the events investigated in this book except for Dresden triggered some form of public inquiry.

More independent of control by the executive, congressional committees in the United States have the power to compel members of the executive to testify at their hearings. While in some policy areas—notably budgetary control and the economy—the separation of powers between legislature and executive permits shifting of responsibility, the more complex lines of accountability provided by this constitutional principle, with officials responsive to both president and legislature, likely result in making more information available.[51] The separation of powers and the weaker party discipline in presidential systems give the executive less control over the legislative branch, even when the president's party controls Congress. The question of which system delivers more accountability is complex, as illustrated by the combination of greater openness and greater opportunity to shift responsibility associated with the separation of powers.

In practice, accountability in the very minimal sense of an honest account is difficult to achieve under either system. Leaders will not volunteer one. And they are unlikely to cooperate with the legislative committees and public inquiries that seek to amend, correct, and supplement known accounts of the event and improve the quality of information. Whether it is President Reagan on Iran-Contra or former prime minister Edward Heath responding to questions about Bloody Sunday, memory loss is an affliction of leaders in both systems.

Ministerial responsibility is a celebrated feature of British parliamentarism. It is a convention that holds ministers responsible to Parliament for department policy, their officials' actions, and their own conduct. Ministers are expected to inform Parliament of these actions, apologize for errors, and take steps to correct the error. A minister's loss of office through resignation is "the ultimate accountability action and sanction."[52] In this way, ministerial responsibility, like command responsibility, institutionalizes incentives for leaders to exercise supervision and control.

Yet, this convention works unpredictably. The evidence suggests that it does not work at all with respect to abuse and atrocity. A distinction between policy and the administration of policy is made by those who wish to limit the responsibility of ministers, usually ministers themselves. The claim is that they cannot be held responsible for all that is done by civil servants, the exceptional minister of agriculture, Sir Thomas Dugdale, notwithstanding (this minister did resign for the actions of civil servants in his department in the 1954 Crichel Down case). The former Ulster Unionist member for Down South, Enoch Powell, derided the distinction between policy and implementation when it was used to defend the Northern Ireland secretary, James Prior, after an escape from the Maze Prison in Northern Ireland in 1983: "What happened was an immense administrative disaster. . . . If the responsibility for administration so central to a Department can be abjured by a Minister, a great deal of our proceedings in the House is a beating of the air."[53] Beyond this distinction between policy and control of those who administer it, the backing of the prime minister and media coverage are thought to be critical to whether a minister receives punishment for his own actions or for the actions of his subordinates.

Ministers other than ministers of agriculture resign. But where control is a resignation issue, it has to do not with delegation. It has to do with self-control. Most resignations result from scandal in private lives, where there is little joy in delegation and no place else for the blame to fall. In cases of collective cabinet responsibility, ministers resign over issues of principle (e.g., Munich in 1938 or the Iraq war in 2003) and over policy disagreements with the government. But, in these cases, resignation is a preference, not a punishment. Lord Carrington resigned over the Argentine invasion of the Falklands, after which Prime Minister Margaret Thatcher observed a "visceral desire that a disaster should be paid for by a scapegoat. There is no doubt that Peter's resignation ultimately made it easier to unite the Party and concentrate on recovering the Falklands. . . . Having seen Monday's press, in particular the *Times* leader, he decided that he must go."[54] Fifty years ago, Professor S. E. Finer reviewed the practice of individual ministerial responsibility and the application of the punishment of resignation.[55] He was skeptical about the existence of a convention, noting that the rare incidences of resignation were often followed by reappointment to another office after a decent interval. A more recent analysis by Keith Dowding and Won-taek Kang came to a similar conclusion. Department error is rarely a reason for resignation, they maintain, and point to the Dugdale and Carrington cases. Other than policy disagreements between a minister and the government, sex scandals and financial scandals are most likely to produce resignations.[56]

Reviewing the cases from 1855 to 1954 that Professor Finer identifies, as well as more recent ones, we find that not one case of abuse or atrocity has resulted in resignation. No minister has taken individual responsibility for abuse and atrocities. For example, despite atrocities committed during the suppression of the Mau Mau insurgency in Kenya in the 1950s, which involved both regular army and nonstate actors such as the pro-colonial government Home Guard, no minister took responsibility and resigned. None took responsibility for Bloody Sunday on January 30, 1972, in Northern Ireland, the worst episode of its kind since 1819. The record since Professor Finer's analysis suggests that his verdict on ministerial responsibility remains safe. He says that if "charges of incompetence were habitually followed by the punishment, the remedy would be a very real one. . . . In fact, that sequence is not only exceedingly rare, but arbitrary and unpredictable. Most charges never reach the stage of individualization at all."[57] His statement applies to charges of abuses and atrocity involving the police and armed forces. If there is "individualization" of charges, the penalty is exacted at the level of the soldier.

Israel adopted the convention of ministerial responsibility and a similar practice in applying it: "In Israel, as in England—whence it came to us—the principle prevails that a member of the Cabinet is responsible to the elected assembly for all the administrative actions of the apparatus within his ministry, even if he was not initially aware of them."[58] The experience with the convention is similar: "even the English experience shows that . . . the question of which cases . . . require him to resign from his ministerial office; this varies . . . from one case to the next. The main reason for this is that the question of the possible resignation . . . is essentially a political question."[59] As we shall see, in the wake of the massacre of civilians in Beirut in 1982, Defense Minister Ariel Sharon, after being forced to resign, was reappointed to another cabinet office without even the decent interval Professor Finer would expect.

Soft Forms of Accountability

The political scientist Joseph Nye's analysis of leadership distinguishes between the use of hard power and soft power. Hiring or firing and offering financial incentives are exercises of hard power. Hard power is more likely the resort of those with formal authority, though Nye argues that if they are smart they will mix it with soft power. Persuasion, in contrast, is a soft approach to getting your own way.[60] We can think about the forms of accountability in a similar way. Legal and political accountability are the hard forms of accountability in the sense that they bring formal and tangible consequences. Reputational and personal accountability are softer forms of accountability, and the type of loss is more indeterminate with these forms. You may retain formal authority but find that damage to reputation or to your conscience takes a toll. You may lose influence and personal effectiveness. Your future prospects may be dimmer.

Reputational accountability is imposed by the media and the public.[61] Unfavorable publicity may not result in loss of office but may limit employment options. Former prime minister Tony Blair had an interest in the new European Union office of president in 2009. A Belgian candidate was preferred. Although he had led the Labour Party to a third successive general election victory in 2005, Blair reportedly found that his candidacy for the EU post suffered because of his willingness to join the American invasion of Iraq and the questionable status of that decision in international law.[62] Reputational accountability as demonstrated here is a soft form of accountability. It is of unpredictable duration and effect. As reputation is "Oft got without merit," the fear of its loss is more or less bearable, depending on the individual.[63] "Keep calm and carry on" may work.

There is, in American politics, the phenomenon of the "Teflon presidency." Some individuals, President Reagan for example, seem able to emerge unscathed by scandal and incompetence. Christopher Hood observes that some leaders have "teflon blame-resistant qualities" that allow them to avoid "public excoriation even over outcomes for which they could hardly escape the most personal kind of responsibility. Well-known examples include US President Bill Clinton's high popularity during his 1998 impeachment over the Lewinsky affair or the continuing high popularity of Japanese Prime Minister Kakuei Tanaka after his implication in Japan's greatest post–World War II bribery scandal."[64] Either as reward for good deeds or as punishment for bad deeds, the pain or pleasure of a good or bad reputation may be strongly felt. A concern for reputation may restrain some leaders from violating human rights or from associating with those with a questionable record in this regard. But it did not deter the Reagan administration's support of the armed forces of El Salvador or the Nicaraguan Contras in the 1980s, nor did it deter Israeli Prime Minister Menachem Begin from using the Lebanese Christian Phalange militia in 1982. Without dismissing the importance of reputation, its fickle and often fleeting nature makes it a poor foundation for claims that accountability is a central feature of democratic politics. What is more, even where a leader's reputation suffers, that damage is likely seen as inadequate compensation by the victims of abuse.

We might be tempted to dismiss what seems the softest form of accountability too lightly. For it is clear that we do, at times, make ourselves pay: "Macbeth shall sleep no more." For some, the pain of personal accountability is likely to be real enough. For one close student of incentives and rational calculation, the "horror of blameworthiness" allows "neither quiet nor repose . . . from which no assurance of secrecy can protect them, from which no principle of irreligion can entirely deliver them, and from which nothing can free them but the vilest and most abject of all states, a complete insensibility to honor and infamy."[65] Granted, personal accountability is not to be depended on. The insensible may be in control. And, as with reputation, depending upon personal accountability to operate is not democracy's particular gift, as Macbeth reminds us, and does not sit well with victims' families. But, as we shall see, it is most likely to be what they are left with.

The United States, the United Kingdom, and Israel are countries with long histories of holding elections and a public commitment to the rule of law. The ethos in these countries is that individual abuses will be addressed by holding agents to high standards and imposing sanctions on both leaders and followers when warranted. We do not expect strategic abuses, cover-ups, and evasions. But, as democratic values create a demand for accountability, the North Star of political survival makes resort to evasion a likely course even for the best of leaders.

4

Amritsar

The killing of more than three hundred civilians in the city of Amritsar took ten minutes on April 13, 1919. It was a ten-minute turning point in the long relationship between Britain and India. With Gandhi's non-violent protests forcing the issue, Prime Minister Lloyd George's coalition government was preparing the ground for Indian self-government. The year before, Britain had reformed its own democracy, extending the franchise to women more than thirty years of age. Yet, reaction, not reform, marked that spring day in the Punjab, with disastrous consequences for the Indian victims and for British authority in the subcontinent. Afterwards, efforts to manage the blame failed to restore the damage done to imperial legitimacy and did not correct the injustice done to the people of the city. A lone Sikh gunman did that in London in 1940, taking his revenge on the man who had served as lieutenant governor of the Punjab at the time of the massacre.

There is a wealth of information available about the Amritsar massacre. There are official reports, parliamentary proceedings, newspaper coverage, and historical accounts. The key pieces for the accountability argument include the individually initiated nature of the violation, the motivations at work, the contradictory pressures on the flow of information and the imposition of punishment, and the techniques used by politicians in London to relieve these pressures. Exerting pressure on the politicians were Indian nationalists, the domestic audience in Britain, and the internal audience of officials.

If any atrocity was an easy one for politicians to deliver accountability on, then the shooting at Jallianwala Bagh, the place in Amritsar where it happened, should have been that case. Responsibility came down to one individual, Brigadier General Reginald Dyer. Dyer made a point of keeping his responsibility "to the fore." He volunteered self-incriminating information in support of his assertion of responsibility. The action clearly violated not just regulations but also the very standards of decency that Britain had set itself to champion during and after World War I. The shooting was widely described, even by Indians, as "unBritish." Discussing whether it prevented rebellion, Viscount Milner, secretary of state for the colonies, was willing to concede that the approach taken by Dyer might have been effective in suppressing a population, "but that does not conclude the case. Do not let us forget that it was the persistence in such methods, shocking the conscience of mankind, which caused Prussia and Germany . . . to find three-quarters of the civilized world united against them."[1] Finally, in addition to the presence of an individual who owned up to the act and in addition to what was a clear violation of standards, the political leaders in London were not complicit in the massacre and so had a reduced a stake in biasing the distribution of the blame. Presumably, with shocked conscience, they could let it fall, full force, where it belonged and in a timely manner. Yet, the question of what to do with the soldier responsible presented leaders with a dilemma. It was a choice between loyalty to their man and justice for his victims. They wanted it both ways.

Despite broad agreement on the facts of the Amritsar massacre, at the time it provoked very different, intensely held opinions. The Houses of Parliament were divided; reform carried the lower and reaction the upper. Parliamentary consideration of the massacre drew contributions from Irish Protestant politicians fearful of anyone else's mutinies against British imperial power and from former and future prime ministers. The speech by Edwin Montagu, secretary of state for India, before the House of Commons reads better than it was received at the time. Despite the nature of the massacre, Montagu faced a tough audience in the Commons. The debate was distinguished by Winston Churchill's contribution. Seated in the gallery of the House of Commons was General Reginald Dyer, the soldier who had ordered and, strange as it seems, then sought credit for a mass killing of civilians.

The Event

Around 5 p.m. on April 13, 1919, Brigadier General Dyer's force of twenty-five Gurkhas and twenty-five Baluchis armed with rifles, plus a further forty Gurkhas with their distinctive knives, filed into position in the city of Amitsar.[2] They faced a crowd of Indians, unarmed and unthreatening. Some were lying down, others squatting to play cards. A speaker, the editor of a local paper, was addressing the public meeting held to protest restrictions on the rights and liberties of Indians and the crackdown on leaders of the civil disobedience campaign. Two resolutions had been passed reasserting the peaceful nature of the campaign against the "despotic conduct" of the colonial authorities.[3] Without asking the crowd to disperse or otherwise warning them, General Dyer ordered his riflemen to fire.[4] He ordered aimed fire at chosen targets. His troops did not fire a warning volley over the heads of members of the crowd. They continued firing for ten minutes. In this time, his small force, always under control, shot dead 379 unarmed civilians and wounded an estimated 1,200 more. That was the official count.[5] Fatalities were fewer than they might have been. Dyer said that he could not squeeze his two armored cars with machine guns through the narrow entrance to the square, and he was constrained by the amount of available ammunition. He withdrew his troops when they had only enough ammunition remaining to safeguard the withdrawal.[6] It was a methodical operation, by Dyer's account.

He had issued a warning earlier in the day. He had marched his men through the city announcing a prohibition on meetings: "any gathering of four men would be looked upon and treated as an unlawful assembly and dispersed by force of arms if necessary."[7] One issue, raised by the committee of inquiry, was how far this warning reached. On arriving at the unlawful assembly, Dyer did not question the necessity of force of arms. He said later that he had decided to fire before arriving at the meeting place and that the crowd might have dispersed without the shooting.[8] But if it had dispersed, an opportunity to give a lesson in the rule of law would have been lost.

In the days before the massacre, there had been protests against Britain's suppression of Gandhi's civil disobedience campaign. There were arrests, and Gandhi was sent back to Bombay. There was strong opposition among Indians to new legislation (the Rowlatt Acts) permitting trials without juries and imprisonment without trial. In the city, buildings burned, and Europeans were killed. A missionary, Miss Sherwood, was assaulted. She was, however, "afterwards picked up by some Hindus by whose action she was enabled to receive medical attention in time . . . to save her life."[9] Following the massacre, Dyer flogged some schoolboys he thought had assaulted the missionary. He issued an order requiring Indians to crawl past the spot where the assault happened, which was marked by a triangle on the street. The Hunter Committee, a joint British and Indian committee of inquiry set up under the Scottish justice Lord

Hunter to investigate the massacre, estimated that General Dyer had fifty citizens of Amritsar crawling in the street. The Committee stated that, "from an administrative point of view, in subjecting the Indian population to an act of humiliation, it has continued to be a cause of bitterness and racial ill-feeling long after it was recalled."[10] Dyer explained that the order was meant to show that the spot on the street was now "holy ground." It seems to have been the missionary's gender, rather than her calling, that moved Dyer. The crawling order was lifted after a week.[11]

The evidence is that the killing of civilians at Amritsar was an individual rather than a state-initiated action. It was a result of a decision taken by Dyer. It reflected his view of how law and order should be established. It went no higher. There is no evidence of that he had received direction from his superiors: "it was a clear and well-documented violation of explicit British rules regulating the use of fire power against civilians."[12] Responsibility does not belong lower; Dyer was consistent that his soldiers were disciplined. They did not fire recklessly in rage or in panic. It appears to have been a straightforward case. Despite the available information, at first Dyer went on with his career, only to have his employment taken from him a year later. The timing and the relatively light sanction suggest the importance of pressure and other policy concerns, rather than principle, in guiding the government's actions.

Motives

Dyer's rationality came into question because of the crawling order. It showed "a lack of balance of mind and of soundness of judgment on the part of General Dyer," according to Lord Curzon, the foreign secretary and former viceroy of India, in stating the government's position in the House of Lords.[13] An important factor in establishing accountability is the degree to which the selfish nature of the agent and the private benefits that he derived from the action are perceived to have influenced events. If the agent's selfishness can be exposed as the primary motivation at work in the violation, the government has less to fear in punishing the agent. Disciplining an obviously "bad apple" is less likely to damage the confidence of other agents and the public in their leaders. In contrast to the killing, which was attributed to some misguided conception of duty, the nonlethal crawling order seems more borderline and vindictive. It is more easily connected to selfish gratification for the individual agent than to the fulfillment of some strategic purpose. The lieutenant governor of the Punjab, Sir Michael O'Dwyer, may have seen this distinction; he approved the killing but stopped the crawling.[14]

Information about the shooting quickly passed up the chain of command. The British deputy commissioner in Amritsar had his report delivered to Sir Michael O'Dwyer, thirty-five miles away in Lahore, at 3 a.m. the following morning. He made clear that he had not been at Jallianwala Bagh. He said he had no prior knowledge of what was going to happen. His message referred to a "meeting," not to a "mob." It stated that no warning had been issued to those who had assembled: "the Military found a large meeting of some five thousand men, and opened fire without warning, killing about two hundred. . . . I much regret that I was not present, but when out previously with the Military the greatest forbearance had been used in making people disperse. I had absolutely no idea of the action taken."[15] The deputy commissioner seems to have realized the seriousness of the event, that it had been unnecessary and avoidable. He understood the urgency of establishing his distance from it as precisely and as quickly as possible.

Dyer reported his action to his superiors the day after. He took responsibility. His thinking was that "to hesitate might induce attack. I immediately opened fire and dispersed the crowd . . . between 200 and 300 of the crowd were killed. My party fired 1,650 rounds."[16] He did not say the crowd was behaving in a threatening way. He did not refer to his victims as a "mob." In his later official report of August 1919 and in testimony to the Hunter Committee, Dyer went into detail. He stressed his duty and his use of force to maintain order: "the responsibility was very great. If I fired I must fire with good effect, a small amount of firing would be a criminal act of folly. I had the choice of carrying out a very distasteful and horrible duty or of neglecting my duty, of suppressing disorder or of becoming responsible for all future bloodshed."[17] As Rupert Furneaux comments, "Dyer made no suggestion in his report of there being an emergency or anything in the demeanor of the crowd . . . which compelled him to fire at once without warning."[18] The killing was designed as a lesson to protestors and to the disobedient Punjab. In Lahore, Dyer's immediate military and civilian superiors endorsed this justification. They approved his action. In London, the secretary of state for India, Edwin Montagu, was to come to see it differently. Informed by the committee of inquiry, he believed that Dyer had violated the principle of minimum force, had not issued a proper warning, and had not aided the wounded after the shooting. Dyer "displayed honesty of purpose and unflinching adherence to his conception of duty. . . . But his conception of his duty . . . was so fundamentally at variance with that which His Majesty's Government had a right to expect."[19] For Montagu, it was goal variance arising from an erroneous conception of duty, not from some private selfishness on the part of the agent.

Explaining his action, Dyer said that "it was no longer a question of merely dispersing the crowd, but one of producing sufficient moral effect, from a military point of view, not only on those who were present, but more especially throughout the Punjab."[20] In its majority report, the Hunter Committee stated that General Dyer had "a mistaken conception of his duty . . . continued firing upon that crowd cannot be justified because of the effect such firing may have upon people in other places. The employment of excessive measures is as likely as not to produce the opposite result to that desired."[21] The minority report, signed by three Indian members of the committee, describes Dyer's action and his "adopting this method of frightfulness" as "inhuman and unBritish."[22] In his testimony before the Hunter Committee, Dyer admitted that he might have dispersed the crowd without shooting. But he thought that "I could disperse them for some time, then they would all come back and laugh at me, and I considered I would be making myself a fool."[23] Coexistent with Dyer's sense of duty, this statement suggested a less high-minded concern. He was concerned about what kind of figure he cut.

Dyer took pains to clarify that he had lost neither his nerve nor control of his men in the shooting of hundreds of unarmed civilians. He told the Committee that the firing was directed at all times by him. He was asked whether "your men continued to fire on these people who were lying on the ground?" He responded, "I cannot say that. I think that some were running at the time, and I directed them to fire and sometimes I stopped firing and re-directed the firing on other targets. The firing was controlled."[24] His unambiguous assertion of total control meant that vain command was unavailable as an excuse. He could not shift blame to his Gurkhas and Baluchis. But neither did he want to. He was not trying to evade blame for a "horrible" act. He anticipated receiving credit for making a tough choice. The justification lay in the argument for the larger security benefits that the British would derive from the killing. So Dyer gave evidence to this effect: "I fired and continued to fire until the crowd dispersed, and I consider this is the least amount of firing which would produce the necessary moral and widespread effect it was my duty to produce if I was to justify my action. If more troops had been at hand the casualties would have been greater in proportion."[25] If delegation and the excuse of out-of-control soldiers was now precluded as an evasive technique by his justification and soldierly vanity, then he might have tried to deny, despite the evidence, the peaceful nature of the crowd and have suggested that they were advancing, were armed, or were acting in a threatening way. He did not resort to this evasive technique, at least until the seriousness of his personal situation became clear to him after the report of the Hunter Committee was published, in May 1920. Only then did he retain legal counsel.

The Hunter Committee's majority report disputed the justification that "the action taken by General Dyer . . . saved the situation in the Punjab and . . . averted a rebellion on a scale similar to the Mutiny." Instead, the majority argued: "It does not, however, appear to us possible to draw this conclusion, particularly in view of the fact that it is not proved that a conspiracy to overthrow British power had been formed prior to the outbreaks."[26] In the face of this skepticism, Dyer looked for an alternative explanation for his action. He needed one that fit with military regulations. With legal assistance, he now prepared a different version of his story and, in July 1920, submitted a written statement to the secretary of war in which he responded to the Hunter Committee. He now emphasized the threatening nature of the crowd. He said he might have been attacked from the rear and stated: "after some firing two groups appeared to be collecting as though to rush us. . . . I directed fire specially to the two points in question and dispersed the groups."[27] Until his July 1920 statement, he must have counted as sufficient the rule-of-law justification and his tragic choice to kill civilians in order to avoid future bloodshed. This nearly was. It went further than expected in a democratic country that condemned "Prussianism." The justification was sufficient for his immediate civilian and military superiors in India. It was sufficient for the House of Lords and for readers of the *Morning Post*, who sponsored a whip-round for the "Saviour of India." It was not sufficient for the cabinet and the Commons.

There is broad agreement that General Dyer's action was an individual violation and not state policy. According to an historian, Derek Sayer, "no previous use of military force, in the United Kingdom or colonies, against an unarmed and peaceable crowd had resulted in a remotely comparable loss of life. . . . There is no evidence that the Amritsar massacre was an act of deliberate policy. . . . It appears, on the face of it, a tragic aberration in British imperial history, and Dyer's individual responsibility alone."[28] The sociologist Helen Fein says that there "has never been any substantive proof that it was calculated by the British-appointed imperial government of India as were many pogroms in Russia" and that it was "a clear and well-documented violation of explicit British rules regulating the use of firepower against civilians."[29] Complicating her interpretation, Fein says that Dyer's action "was a potentiality endemic in the class division created by the empire."[30] Fein's view is similar to that of Gandhi and the Labour Party, which blamed the "system" or the "failings of civil government" for the massacre.[31] Ramsay MacDonald, at the Labour Party conference, "had warned that Dyer must not be allowed to be made the scapegoat for the broader failings of civil government in India."[32] This position was consistent with Indian nationalist sentiment. Gandhi stated that "we do not want to punish Dyer. We have no desire for revenge. We want to change the system that produced Dyer."[33] This perspective, that Dyer was a fall guy for a system, is not meaningful to an understanding of specific events that seeks to allocate blame, or credit, for that matter. Blame requires action by individuals who could have done otherwise. It does not belong with individuals subsumed and so exonerated in more abstract constructions—historical, sociological, economical or imperial.

There are no grounds to claim that it was the central political authorities who had instructed Dyer to give a moral lesson in the Punjab. He did not make this claim. He was not a fall guy for carrying out a "frightful" policy designed by Montagu or by Winston Churchill, secretary of state for war, or by the viceroy of India, Lord Chelmsford. General Dyer initiated the action himself. He anticipated receiving credit for averting a larger rebellion, not blame. He boasted of his firm control of his soldiers. He believed he was doing the right thing and that the authorities should have thanked him. He was questioned by an Indian member of the Committee about whether he realized what "a great disservice to the British Raj" he had done "by adopting this method of frightfulness—excuse the term." Dyer replied that "it was a merciful act, though a horrible act, and they ought to be thankful to me for doing it."[34] Dyer was encouraged to get legal assistance for his appearance at the inquiry. He refused.[35] When outrage attracted the intervention of politicians, it became clear to Dyer that he had taken responsibility for a blameworthy, not a creditworthy, act, and the timing suggests that he was punished or, as his supporters saw it, "sacrificed" to dissipate the pressure.

Audience Pressures

The internal audience of government officials and soldiers circled protectively around Dyer. With both his military superior in Lahore, General Beynon, and his civilian superior, Sir Michael O'Dwyer, approving his action in shooting at the crowd at Amritsar, the immediate consequences for Dyer were opportunities for further active service and promotion. Sir Michael shared General Dyer's view of the net gain to general safety from killing those who had, knowingly or unknowingly, made themselves available to be killed by gathering that afternoon at Jallianwala Bagh. Years later, Sir Michael would pay the highest price for his approval.

The senior commander in India, General Sir Charles Monro, and other officials opposed an inquiry. They worried about the effect on the military's reputation.[36] In India, one official wrote, "Gandhi and others were trying to force the enquiry. . . . I spoke to His Excellency [the viceroy, Lord Chelmsford] about this, urging very strong reasons against an enquiry, but he said the Secretary of State had already promised one."[37] In the aftermath of the government's handling of the massacre, the association of former officers expressed its outrage at Dyer's treatment.[38] At the Army Council, the chief of the Imperial General Staff "insisted, against cabinet pressure, upon Dyer being given the opportunity to submit a statement" and complained to his diary about "the soldier being thrown to the winds."[39] General Monro, concerned about the agent confidence factor, opposed the prosecution of Dyer. He thought punishing Dyer would "arouse the sentiments of the services."[40] There was press speculation that the Army Council might go so far as to reject the inquiry's findings, and so there was a reminder in the *Times* that, in Britain, the military was subordinate to civilian rule.[41] The most forceful spokesman for the internal audience was the Irish Unionist MP and the founder, in 1913, of the loyalist paramilitary group the Ulster Volunteer Force, Sir Edward Carson. In berating the secretary of state for India in the House of Commons, he described General Dyer as a scapegoat. He argued that politicians should not belatedly question the decisions of the soldiers that they put in such difficult situations.

Montagu set up the Hunter Committee's inquiry following public agitation in India and pressure from Indian representatives in London. Amritsar had interrupted his policy agenda of self-government for the subcontinent. Scholars agree on the importance of Indian pressure.

According to Derek Sayer, "Montagu . . . under pressure in the Commons and from Indian nationalists, had promised in May 1919 to set up an inquiry."[42] According to Helen Fein, Montagu "was pressed by the Indian delegation in London whose support he also needed for the reforms he had spent three years in developing."[43] Adding to the pressure on the British government to be seen to do something, the Indian National Congress began its own inquiry. In July 1919, Montagu explained to the viceroy that an inquiry "would sooth the Indian delegation."[44] Despite the soldiers' misgivings, at this stage in the process of blame management, the balance tipped in favor of the external audience.

The choice of Lord Hunter to head the committee was Montagu's. But he left the appointment of other members to the viceroy. Montagu, according to V. N. Datta, "warned that the selection of safe and prejudiced men ought to be avoided."[45] In addition to Hunter, there were both British and Indian members. Overall, says Datta, "both the Indians and the British were dissatisfied with the composition of the committee. . . . Barrow was a hardened soldier, Rice a Bengal civilian. . . . The British officials had felt particularly sore about the inclusion of Jagat Narayan, who behaved like a prosecuting counsel." As the Indian National Congress decided to boycott the inquiry in an effort to get the government to release Punjab leaders from prison, the witnesses were almost all British, and so, "from the Indian point of view, it was entirely a one-sided affair."[46] Appointing judges "in one's own case" leads inevitably to disputes. But, as committees of inquiry go, the joint-nationality Hunter Committee compares favorably with, for example, the one-man inquiry undertaken by Lord Widgery into Bloody Sunday fifty years later.

Montagu revealed his sensitivity to public opinion on the issue in oral answers in the House of Commons on December 23, 1919: "I can quite appreciate the profound disturbance which must have been caused in public opinion by the evidence published, but I trust . . . the House will agree with me that we are right in waiting until an impartial, authoritative pronouncement on all the facts is made by Lord Hunter's Committee . . . the evidence as published in the newspapers is profoundly disturbing."[47] Colonel Wedgwood, a Liberal, then Labour member of Parliament who had fought with distinction in the Boer War and the First World War, told the House that "the whole country has been horrified at what took place . . . and when we tell the Turks 'You massacred the Armenians,' they will say 'yes, we wish we had the chance of getting 5,000 of them together, and then of shooting straight.'"[48] The British newspapers, with the exception of the *Morning Post*, expressed outrage at the massacre.[49] The *Observer* complained of the national humiliation of keeping company with the likes of Lenin.[50] The Hunter Committee issued its report in March 1920. Parliamentary debates followed in July of that year.

Techniques of Evasion

In London, the first response to the event was obfuscation and delay. The initial government account was a brief and misleading statement from the India Office. It was issued on April 18 and reported in the *Times* four days later under the headline "Defiant Crowd at Amritsar: Looting and Incendiarism." The statement read: "At Amritsar, on April 13, the mob defied the proclamation forbidding public meetings. Firing ensued, and 200 casualties occurred."[51] Between Amritsar and London, the account lost clarity. The "crowd" or "meeting" of Dyer's and the deputy commissioner's reports had become a defiant mob. Who was doing the firing and the dying was now more ambiguous. And, the "killed" had been reincarnated as "casualties," their number fixed at the lowest estimate.

The following month, Montagu spoke to the House of Commons, muddying more than clarifying. He described the prevailing political conditions and identified the serious threat to law and order. His was a supportive message to the authorities in India. There was no criticism of the use of force at Amritsar. Instead, there were hints of dark conspiracy: "There are . . . in India some men, opponents of all government, who are incurably evilly disposed." He distinguished Gandhi, "a man of the highest motives," from "the real revolutionary, the man who lurks in dark corners . . . men who are a danger to any country, and against whom the Government of India are determined to do unceasing battle until they have been extirpated." He also gave credence to Dyer's claims about the threat of rebellion. He went on to mention the need for an inquiry, deftly shifting responsibility to the viceroy, though, according to historians, Montagu wanted an inquiry to placate agitation in India.[52] But, in preparing the way for an inquiry, Montagu conciliated his internal audience, as well. He described the inquiry not as an investigation into the casualties but as a means to deal with "libellous charges which have been made against British troops." He stated that "the only message which we send from this House today to India is a message of confidence and sympathy with those upon whom the great responsibility has fallen to restore the situation."[53]

It was an inquiry not into Amritsar but into the Punjab disturbances. In May, he denied that the soldiers had behaved unlawfully. He framed the inquiry as a device to defend their reputations.

Dyer's account of his actions at Amritsar became public in December 1919. In the House of Commons that month, the secretary of state for India had intimated that he had just learned the details of what had happened. He was asked the question dreaded by politicians implicated in cover-ups: what did you know, and when did you know it? Montagu said he "knew of no details of the circumstances until I saw the report in the newspapers." He was asked why it took eight months to hear about the massacre. Montagu replied that statements were published as they were received. He was asked if there was any "censorship to prevent the telegraphing of the evidence before Lord Hunter's Committee." Montagu replied that "the wires are very much congested, and it may have been for that reason that none of this evidence was telegraphed."[54] His claims were refuted by Lieutenant Governor O'Dwyer.

The lieutenant governor had informed the secretary of state in person and in detail in June 1919. In a letter to the *Observer* in 1925 and after pursuing a successful libel suit concerning Amritsar, O'Dwyer wrote that the "legend of the Amritsar massacre" was the result of misleading information from "Indian extremists," the government's failure to report the facts when it had them, and the Hunter Committee's failure to consider all the evidence.[55] He claimed that Montagu withheld information. He claimed that the Committee did not give proper credence to Dyer's justification of deterring a general rebellion and the counterfactual speculation that, but for the shooting, there would have been such a rebellion. He pointed to the external audience pressures on the government.

Even in this case, where the violation was an individual violation without the complicity of political leaders, the initial response was not to provide a timely and accurate account. The research literature, from different theoretical vantage points, agrees with this assessment. The historian Derek Sayer notes "Montagu's evasiveness on when he first learned the details of the massacre."[56] Helen Fein observes the "questionable belated knowledge of Montagu" and suggests that Montagu "had concealed his own cognizance of the massacre—probably to avoid charges that the Dyer censure was biased by his own pre-judgment as well as to conciliate both Indian politicians and the imperial class."[57] The minister was cross-pressured by his own officials and by the external audience, which shaped the incentives for evasion and the eventual punishment.

Consequences

General Dyer was removed from employment and put on half pay by the army. It was the most lenient of the options available. The House of Lords "deplored" even this mild treatment as "unjust." Dyer, who heard the debate in the Lords, was "pleased."[58] The calls for legal accountability and a court-martial were ignored. Despite its leniency, the government was challenged to defend its management of the blame for the Amritsar massacre in the House of Commons.

The motions for debate concerned reducing the salary of the secretary of state for India, Edwin Montagu. These motions were put by both Labour Party members who thought that the blame spread far wider than Dyer and by defenders of Dyer, who saw him as a loyal officer used as a scapegoat to buy off Indian nationalist opinion. The defenders of Dyer gave the government the harder time.

The Commons' debate began with Montagu framing the issue as a choice between rule by terror and "frightfulness" and rule by cooperation. He advocated generating goodwill rather than relying on terror and humiliation. He explained that embarking on terror as a method of rule would entail continued resort to this method and that it would be ultimately counterproductive because it would generate further hostility and protests from both the British and the Indian peoples and lead to the end of the Empire. He recommended an alternative policy "which I assumed office to commend to this House . . . a complete free partnership in the British Commonwealth. . . . We want to safeguard British honour by protecting and safeguarding Indian honour too." Jeered by Dyer's supporters, Montagu pared the issue to the essentially different conceptions of governance that underlay the debate. It was a choice between reaction and reform. He pointed out that, to his critics, "an Indian is a person who is tolerable so long as he will obey your orders, but if once he joins the educated classes . . . if once he imbibes the ideas of individual liberty . . . why then you class him as an educated Indian and as an agitator. What a terrible and cynical verdict on the whole!"[59] At which point a member shouted, "What a terrible speech." The next to his feet was Sir Edward Carson, the Irish Unionist MP.

Carson feared for Ireland. He bitterly opposed any action against Dyer and chided Montagu, as a minister of the Crown, for not approaching the matter in a "calmer spirit." Carson himself then had to suffer interruption. As Carson reviewed Dyer's gallant service, Colonel Wedgwood, a veteran of both the Boer War and the First World War, interjected that "five hundred people were shot." Carson pointed out how difficult it was for a soldier to come to the aid of the "civil power" and, under stressful conditions, judge precisely and instantly the necessary amount of force. After the soldier did act, along came "the armchair politician in Downing Street" to "break him." Soldiers could not operate in a situation where they had to ask themselves "what will the House of Commons say to us when they have been stirred up six months afterwards." He saw Dyer as a scapegoat used by politicians to appease critics and quell public agitation: "You have to deal with human nature in the men you put into all these difficult places. Do not let them suppose that if they do their best . . . that they will be made scapegoats of and be thrown to the wolves to satisfy an agitation such as that which arose after this incident. You must back your men."[60] Carson's words are important. He appreciated the position of the agent and spoke for the internal audience, concisely capturing the pressures on the politician. The soldier serves in a "difficult place," but one chosen by the politician, not by him. If he is trying to do his "best," you have to support him, not make him a scapegoat, and therefore not give in to the external audience. Carson noted that the military and political authorities on the spot did obey this injunction. They did back their man. Sir Michael O'Dwyer was Irish, and Carson said, in passing, that "it is not an Irishman who has thrown over his subordinate."[61] He drew attention to the government's failure to submit an accurate account. He pointed out that Montagu met with O'Dwyer and claimed that he acted only when pressured to do so by Indian opinion, identifying the point at which Montagu might have taken a bearing from his internal moral compass but chose not to. Carson argued that justice for Dyer and the Indians required immediate action. Only when, six or seven months later, in an effort "to placate these people," did ministers throw the scapegoat to the wolves. Sir Edward was right about the timing but wrong about the wolves. They were innocent in the case of the scapegoat. A version of the biblical story has the goat going over a precipice. It was gravity that got that goat.

Sir Edward was willing to concede that Dyer might have made an error of judgment but insisted that he was dealing with a conspiracy to end British power in Asia. He finished by saying that to "break a man under the circumstances of this case is un-English."[62] He had already noted that it was un-Irish, as well. Churchill's biographer, Martin Gilbert, says that Carson's un-English remark was intended to remind the House that Montagu was Jewish. Gilbert quotes Lloyd George's parliamentary secretary, who reported back that "Montagu got excited when making his speech and became more racial and more Yiddish in screaming tone and gesture, and a strong anti-Jewish sentiment was shown by shouts and excitement among normally placid Tories of the back Bench category."[63] In beginning by telling Montagu to calm down, and with his final remark, Carson diverted attention from what was a cogent analysis of the basis for British rule in India—a similar analysis to that which underlay Churchill's much praised contribution.

Churchill began by acknowledging the importance of a calm discussion and the singularity and sensitivity of the case.[64] As Churchill pointed out, these cases are rare events; attention must be paid to multiple audiences, including the government's own agents, and the moral and political stakes are high. He moved on to the options that were available in disciplining an officer. Officers could be removed from employment and put on half pay, and Churchill noted that during the war many officers were dealt with in this way. More severely, judicial procedures may be followed, and cashiering, a prison sentence, or the death penalty may be applied. As Churchill described, Dyer received the least severe option, removal from employment. He spelled out to Dyer's supporters that things could have been a lot worse for their man.

Carson had spoken of the difficult situations soldiers find themselves in when policing disturbances. Churchill accepted this point but, in doing so, added that there were simple tests and guidelines available to officers who found themselves in these situations. First, officers needed to ask themselves, "Is the crowd attacking anything or anybody?" Second, "is the crowd armed?" He then pointed out that "at Amritsar the crowd was neither armed nor attacking." Third, "no more force should be used than is necessary to secure compliance with the law"; last, the officer should "confine himself to a limited and definite objective."[65] However difficult the situation, according to Churchill, officers should be able to observe these tests, especially in view of the far more difficult tasks they had accomplished in trench warfare during World War I, where, under the most trying circumstances, they had demonstrated the restraint to protect prisoners and the wounded. He then went on to identify one general prohibition: "I mean a prohibition against what is called frightfulness. What I mean by frightfulness is the inflicting of great slaughter or massacre upon a particular crowd of people, with the intention of terrorizing not merely the rest of the crowd, but the whole district or the whole country." He was interrupted with the question "Was not the frightfulness started three days before? Was not the frightfulness on the other side?" Churchill replied:

> We cannot admit this doctrine in any form. Frightfulness is not a remedy known to the British pharmacopoeia. I yield to no one in my detestation of Bolshevism, and of the revolutionary violence which precedes it . . . . But my hatred . . . is not founded on their silly system of economics, or their absurd doctrine of an impossible equality. It arises from the bloody and devastating terrorism which they practice . . . the august and venerable structure of the British Empire, where lawful authority descends from hand to hand and generation after generation, does not need such aid. Such ideas are absolutely foreign to the British way of doing things.[66]

He then described the "fusillade at the Jallianwallah Bagh" in Amritsar, a place smaller than Trafalgar Square, and recited Macaulay's words: "and then was seen what we believe to be the most frightful of all spectacles, the strength of civilization without its mercy."[67] Churchill continued by arguing that British rule in India did not rest on what we might now refer to as hard power alone. He reminded the House of Commons of Montagu's insistence on the importance of cooperation and closed by saying that Dyer deserved more severe punishment. However, the cabinet's hands had been tied by the approval that Dyer had received for his acts at Amritsar from his immediate superiors.

Martin Gilbert accords Churchill's speech the highest praise: it was "unanswerable." It was "a personal triumph, and seemed to all who listened to have saved the Government from the danger of a serious setback."[68] The evaluation is to Montagu's disadvantage. Montagu's political career never recovered from the Amritsar debate and he resigned from the government in 1922. Churchill's contribution was to show that Dyer was well treated, that his actions failed the tests for officers in these situations, and that British rule could not rest on hard power alone. He adopted Montagu's point and language in condemning terrorism and frightfulness and said that they were un-British. Following Churchill, the former Liberal prime minister Herbert Asquith rose to dismiss Dyer's justification, pointing out that there was no immediate threat of rebellion in the Punjab.[69] Others followed Asquith in a debate that continued for some hours.

These arguments worked in the House of Commons but fell on deaf ears in the House of Lords. In the unelected chamber, Carson's encomium to the agent and Dyer's justification, not the pressures from external audiences, won the day. On July 20, 1920, the House of Lords adopted this motion: "That this House deplores the conduct of the case of General Dyer as unjust to that officer and as establishing a precedent dangerous to the preservation of order in the face of rebellion." From the Bishops' Bench, the Archbishop of Canterbury argued that the motion was contrary to the policy of self-government. He was conscious of his temporal audience and was concerned about public reaction.[70] Lord Sumner, speaking for the motion, also drew attention to the audience, saying that it was the "tragic misfortune of General Dyer that the stage upon which he had to play out this terrible scene has been so conspicuous. I cannot help thinking that it is because of it in public discussions in India and here that it has become necessary to treat him in a manner different."[71] He saw the forces at work and what shifted the position of the government.

Detailed information about the massacre became available to the public despite the early evasions of the government. The government's immediate response to the massacre was to release a brief and misleading statement that denied the peaceful nature of the crowd. The government was then pressured by Indian nationalists into the tactical concession of an inquiry. Once the information gathered by the inquiry was available, much of it thanks to Dyer's alarmingly frank admissions, the government had little choice but to act. His punishment was, as Churchill pointed out, the least severe option, and it was decided by the military leadership and then accepted by the government. These were, as the secretary of state for the colonies, Viscount Milner, put it, "the lightest possible consequences in the circumstances."[72] Even these consequences were to some extent undone by the vote deploring them in the House of Lords.

Churchill said the government was not willing to lift the blame from General Dyer: "I do not think it is in the interests of the British Empire or of the British Army, for us to take a load of that sort for all time upon our backs."[73] The government did, however, place as light a load as was available on Dyer's back. It took action against Dyer in response to public outrage in India and in Britain, balanced against internal pressure from officials and the army. It wanted to safeguard Britain's reputation and its commitment to advance the policy of Indian self-government. And these were the terms that Churchill and other politicians used to explain the treatment of Dyer. The secretary of state for foreign affairs, Lord Curzon, was aware of the harm done in India by the failure of the British Parliament to send an unequivocal signal of accountability. He stated, "I agree with Lord Meston that we shall deal a blow at our reputation in India, we shall lower our own standards of justice and humanity, we shall debase the currency of our national honour. I cannot believe that your Lordships wish to undertake this course."[74] The treatment of Dyer did not placate Indian opinion. According to the historian A. J. P. Taylor's widely quoted assessment of the massacre, it was "the worst bloodshed since the Mutiny, and the decisive moment when Indians were alienated from British rule."[75] As it was, government ministers faced serious criticism from supporters of the coalition government for not backing their man. The House of Common's defeat of Sir Edward Carson's motion to reduce the minister's salary was expected to be closer than 230 votes to 129.

General Dyer initiated and took responsibility for the killing of civilians at Amritsar. Blame could go no higher. There was no policy, order, or indirect signal from his superiors to commit the violation. He sought approval after the killing. Because Sir Michael O'Dwyer gave this approval, albeit after the fact, a lone Sikh assassin shot him in London, in 1940. Blame could also fall no lower. Dyer represented the lowest plausible level for blame, as his candor and perhaps his soldierly vanity precluded a *can't control* excuse. Instead, he took responsibility, thinking that he was doing the right thing, apparently unaware of the moral and political consequences of his decision. He offered a justification and an alternative standard to evaluate his conduct in claiming credit for preempting wider rebellion. In the aftermath, dealing with blame took a personal toll on Dyer. He "suffered in the long years when he had nothing to do but go over and over the events in Amritsar until he could not sleep."[76] He died in 1927.

The process of managing the blame by the British government followed public exposure and responded to cues from both internal and external audiences. Derek Sayer observes that the general outrage at the treatment of Dyer was comparable to the outrage at the massacre. He asks, "how could the perpetrator of the . . . massacre come to be so widely perceived as its principal victim?"[77] He says that viewing Dyer as "a victim of shoddy political expediency was plausible" given Montagu's evasions and the delay in doing anything, as well as the immediate approval of Dyer's action and the government's intervention, precipitated by pressure from Indian nationalists.[78] The actions of the British government, then, were not the result of the operation of the internalized moral values of its political leaders on being informed of the disaster, though they eventually found strong moral voice. When the efforts to restrict and muddy the flow of information failed, they initiated the investigation and punishment of Dyer in response to pressure from Indian nationalists and in order to deliver on policy commitments and their reformist agenda in India. From the first drips of information to the initiation and composition of the inquiry to the final consequences for Dyer, British leaders balanced the pressure exerted by their external audience against the need to maintain the confidence of their own officials and soldiers. If the sanctions served political expediency, they were not severe. They prompted a Sikh to take justice into his own hands. The reports of the Hunter Committee, thanks in part to Dyer's unusual willingness to cooperate, helped meet the minimal of standard of delivering an accurate account of what happened.

Perhaps Montagu does not emerge as well as he might from this analysis. To speak for him, accountability, even in the minimal sense, turns out to be a very severe standard that democracies have set for themselves. As David Hume noted, the most tyrannical of regimes have to lead praetorian guards "like men." To get the inquiry off the ground, Montagu had to sell it to the colonial administration in India and to the army. While the Indian National Congress criticized the Indian members of the committee, its composition was not "safe," and both the majority and minority reports rejected Dyer's action and justification. When Montagu's critics offered him the opportunity to address the issue in the Commons debate, he defended his actions robustly, if not as effectively as he might. Meanwhile, Churchill established a clear and compelling position against British use of frightfulness. In doing so, he gave a hostage to fortune.

5

Dresden

Dresden, taken altogether, is a clean cheerful city, and strikes the stranger on his first entrance as a place in which men are gregarious, busy, full of merriment, and pre-eminently social. Such is the happy appearance of but few towns either in the old or the new world, and is hardly more common in Germany than elsewhere. Leipsig is decidedly busy, but does not look to be social. Vienna is sufficiently gregarious, but its streets are melancholy. Munich is social, but lacks the hum of business. Frankfurt is both practical and picturesque, but it is dirty, and apparently averse to mirth. Dresden has much to recommend it.[1]

What could recommend the destruction of this city? In contrast to the massacre at Amritsar, the mass killing of civilians in Dresden and the destruction of urban and residential Germany was government policy. How could frightfulness become the policy of a government led by a man who, as secretary of war twenty-five years earlier, had given an "unanswerable" denunciation of that remedy? Or, for those more interested in the relationship between political systems and policies than in biographical riddles, how could the killing of civilians that culminated in the bombing of Dresden become a sustained policy of a democratic government? Beyond inconsistencies between declared principles and subsequent conduct, the political consequences of the bombing and the individual leader involved in managing the blame make Dresden an important case for analysis. We expect ordinary political leaders to jump ship, but not Winston Churchill. Dresden is a case where one of the more immovable of political leaders encountered a potentially resistible force.

He was immovable in May 1940, and, as he demonstrated in the management of the Amritsar massacre, he understood the moral issue. Not at his best in the spring of 1945, he let blame fall.

The Event

Dresden's prewar population was about 600,000. Noticeably rich in culture, the city was not entirely lacking in what could be considered military targets.[2] It was a transportation center and important to communications with the Eastern Front. But the claim that it was a military objective was undermined within weeks by the prime minister's sudden disillusion with the pretense about targets and his characterization of the policy as terror bombing. On the night of February 13, 1945, the incendiary and other bombs dropped from about eight hundred Lancaster and Halifax bombers of the Royal Air Force (RAF) created an inferno. Daylight brought four hundred Fortresses and Liberators of the American Eighth Air Force. The day after, two hundred more American bombers struck, and another four hundred returned to Dresden on March 2. The night bombing by RAF Bomber Command did most of the damage, according to the official history.[3]

The effect of a firestorm on residential areas is described in an account of the bombing of Hamburg in 1943 by the police president of that city. He reported that the mix of high explosive, land mines, and incendiary bombs dropped on Hamburg forced the firemen into the cellars, allowing the fires to spread. The high explosive turned houses and blocks of flats into kindling, which was lit by the phosphorous and liquid incendiary bombs. The draught from the larger fires "acted as a bellows" on the smaller fires, drawing them together. The firestorm involved an area of twenty-two square kilometers on the night of July 27, 1943. According to the police president's report, "women, especially, hesitated to risk flight from the apparently safe shelters . . . until the heat and obvious danger compelled some immediate action." He says that "in many cases they were no longer able to act by themselves. They were already unconscious or dead from carbon monoxide poisoning." Some survived by jumping into the canals. Or they drowned. Though much else was destroyed, according to his report, morale remained intact. There was no general panic.[4] The police president pointed to the difficulties in establishing the number of deaths, as all that was left was ash.[5]

It is difficult to number the dead at Dresden. As with other mass killings the numbers are a political issue. The most plausible estimate, based on burial records, archaeological research, and witnesses, is between eighteen thousand and twenty-five thousand and was provided by a 2008 investigation by a panel of German historians.[6] Some estimates have been far higher.

It was arguably within the rules of war to bomb a city, if the city was defended and if military targets were identified.[7] There was no international convention on aerial bombing. There was a draft of one from the 1920s. Yet, the 1907 Hague Convention Respecting the Laws and Customs of War on Land seems clear in the protection it gives to civilians. In article 23, it prohibited the use of "arms, projectiles or material calculated to cause unnecessary suffering." Article 25 prohibited "the attack or bombardment, by whatever means, of towns, villages, dwellings, or buildings which are undefended." And article 27 stated that "in sieges and bombardments all necessary steps must be taken to spare, as far as possible, buildings dedicated to religion, art, science, or charitable purposes, historic monuments, hospitals." These articles did not restrain the Luftwaffe. They did not restrain Churchill's cabinet and RAF commanders, either. They privately agreed on the destruction of German civilian morale as a strategic objective. They then pursued this undeclared policy for four years.

Just weeks after Dresden, Churchill condemned the bombing as an act of terror. He abruptly distanced himself from the bombing campaign. The RAF used the term "terror" in an indiscreet briefing for journalists. The Associated Press reported that "the Allied Air Chiefs had made the long awaited decision to adopt deliberate terror bombing of German population centers as a ruthless expedient to hastening Hitler's doom." The bombing of "residential sections" was for "the avowed purpose of heaping more confusion on Nazi road and rail traffic, and to sap German morale."[8] In contrast, Churchill's predecessor, Prime Minister Neville Chamberlain, had a clear view that international law standards applied to bombing policy, at least before the conflict started. He thought that a policy of terror bombing was illegal and would be ineffective.[9] But that is the policy that Britain adopted.

Motives—"The Title Deed of That Controversial Operation"

The relevant motives are those of members of the political and military leadership who chose to destroy cities, not the individual motives of those who flew and crewed the bombers over their targets. Soldiers or policemen mistreat civilians or prisoners in their custody for selfish reasons. Air crews are removed from such temptations. They are less likely to create simple agency problems motivated by self-interest. Yet, a principled objection to compliance with orders to kill civilians creates a different sort of agency problem. The possibility of such a problem was raised by the RAF and by policymakers, who discussed whether the bomber crews would feel ashamed. But the pretext of military targets, the invisibility of the victims, and the stakes involved in fighting a total war may have provided peace of mind for the bombing crews. In comparison to Amritsar, where the soldiers had to aim at individual victims, for the bomber crews there was more detachment. Psychologists tell us that detachment affects the compliance of agents when given orders to harm others.[10] Proximity to human suffering reduces compliance. At one stage in the bombing offensive, leaders considered having fighter planes strafe civilians. Such a policy and the increased visibility of victims might have led to more compliance problems, although that was not the reason offered for rejecting that option.

For the political and military leadership, area bombing of cities had strategic, technical, and punishment motives. Strategically, it was claimed to be Britain's only way of fighting back after France fell. Fighting back was important to bolstering public support for the war effort, beyond its potential destructive effects on the enemy's will and means to fight. Technically, even if the air crews had wanted to protect civilians, the inaccuracy of the equipment and the decision to bomb at night in order to minimize risk to the flight crews would have made that difficult to achieve. As historians point out, Britain decided early in the war to make a huge material and technological commitment to producing large numbers of bombers. Having produced them, it used them. As far as Arthur Harris, air officer commander in chief of Bomber Command, was concerned, the bombers were designed to destroy industrial centers. In his view, daylight bombing was too risky. The main British bombers could not fly high enough and had light armor and guns, and the crews had not had training for formation flying. These deficiencies precluded daylight raids. Even after an attack on some French railroad targets provided a demonstration that the British bombers could bomb with some precision, Harris stuck to his own perception of his command's operational strengths and weaknesses.[11] He was convinced of the priority of area bombing. Finally, punitively, the Blitz and the bombing of Coventry required reprisal. But, by February 1945, many German civilians had been bombed in many other cities, and there were strategic alternatives to area bombing.

The issue of bombing civilians was long the subject of interservice debate. In the 1920s, the chief of Air Staff was at odds with his counterparts in the army and navy. The chief of the Imperial General Staff referred to the draft regulations on aerial warfare of the Commission of Jurists, which prohibited indiscriminate bombing of civilians, and wanted interservice consistency, meaning that bombing undefended towns would by analogy permit the sinking of merchant ships. Most important for our purposes, he finished by clarifying the responsibilities of politicians: "as regards the ethical aspect . . . it is for His Majesty's Government to accept or refuse a doctrine which, put into plain English, amounts to one which advocates unrestricted warfare against the civil population of one's enemy."[12] The chief of Naval Staff added his opposition to the air force's doctrine and feared that the enemy would see it as justification for unrestricted submarine warfare. He also saw it as an unprecedented extension to the threat to civilians.[13] Come the war, the air force doctrine prevailed. His Majesty's Government accepted the policy but not the ethical burden or the willingness to clearly communicate what it was doing. For the lifetime of the policy of killing civilians, and afterwards, the government abjured plain English.

The case for applying the doctrine of warfare against civilians in the war with Nazi Germany rested on national prejudices. The RAF argued that Germans were less able to tolerate attacks on civilians than were the British. In May 1941, Lord Trenchard, marshal of the Royal Air Force, provided the prime minister with his thinking on strategic bombing. His first major point was that Britain, historically, had shown that it could put up with casualties better than other nations. He identified German civilian morale as the enemy's chief vulnerability. Noting the technical constraints on bombing and observing that all but 1 percent of bombs miss their military targets, he argued that these technical factors were themselves further reason for a policy designed to attack civilian morale. He argued as follows: if "our bombs are dropped in Germany, then 99 percent which miss the military target all help to kill, damage, frighten or interfere with Germans in Germany and the whole 100 percent of the bomber organization is doing useful work, not merely 1 percent of it."[14] The overall objective was to bring home the costs of war to the civilian population. Beyond the appeal to history, Trenchard offered some observations on behavior in air raid shelters in support of what he had to say about German morale. He reported that Germans in air raid shelters were not very cheerful. He said that they were "passive and easy prey to hysteria and panic. . . . There is no joking in the German shelters as in ours . . . this, then, is their weak point compared with ourselves, and it is at this weak point that we should strike and strike again."[15] It is improbable that this memorandum served as a basis for policy. Were civilian lives to depend on Trenchard's (not Trollope's) impressions of German cheerfulness? Nevertheless, the prime minister circulated Lord Trenchard's memorandum to the chiefs of staff.

Sir Charles Portal, chief of Air Staff, concurred with the estimation of Germans' ability to stand casualties and Trenchard's argument that Germany's weakness "is the morale of her civilian population under air attack . . . the main weight of our air attack should be directed against objectives in Germany, so situated that bombs which miss their target will directly affect the morale of the German civilian population."[16] In July 1941, the RAF was directed to concentrate on transportation and on German civilian morale as the most vulnerable targets.[17] At that time, commanders saw benefits from targeting a number of small towns in order to have a broader effect on morale. In May 1942, Arthur Harris was informed by Air Vice-Marshal Bottomley that the main aim of bombing operations remained civilian morale.[18] In January 1943, the "Casablanca directive" for bombing policy reemphasized that "your primary objective will be the progressive destruction and dislocation of the German military, industrial and economic system, and the undermining of the morale of the German people to a point where their capacity for armed resistance is fatally weakened."[19] On August 1, 1944, Portal sent a memorandum on bombing and German civilian morale to the chiefs of staff of the other services. The memorandum, backed by the Foreign Office, identified the potential benefits of an attack on civilians. A major attack might induce rioting and strikes and absenteeism from work and divert German resources from other priorities. The memorandum weighed the methods of delivering the attack. Using fighter planes to strafe civilians would cause "uneasiness" but not a "calamity." Obliteration of small towns with populations of fewer than twenty thousand would require greater precision and would not affect a large enough proportion of the German population. Berlin as a target had more to offer. Alternatively, selecting a city that had largely escaped bombing up to that point might have a dramatic effect.[20] The official history notes these proposals were approved by the chiefs of staff on August 5 1944. It observes that "when the blow of catastrophic force came to be delivered it fell not on Berlin, but on Dresden." It describes this memorandum as "if only indirectly . . . the title deed of that controversial operation."[21] Beyond the anticipated effect on morale, bombing an East German city, if not Dresden specifically, addressed the expectations of the Soviet Union. A raid on Dresden would show that the Allies were actively trying to relieve some pressure on the Eastern Front, clog communication lines with civilian refugees, and provide a bargaining item for Yalta.

On January 25, 1945, Arthur Harris identified the cities of Chemnitz, Leipzig, and Dresden, as well as Berlin, as possible targets for raids.[22] That same night, the prime minister asked the secretary of state for air, Sir Archibald Sinclair, about bombing policy. In a written response, Sir Archibald said that Berlin and some other large cities in Eastern Germany (Leipzig, Dresden, and Chemnitz) were possible targets, and the next day Winston Churchill set in motion the destruction of Dresden. He testily pressed the secretary of state for air to have Bomber Command bomb East Germany.

I did not ask you last night about plans for harrying the German retreat from Breslau. On the contrary, I asked whether Berlin, and no doubt other large cities in East Germany, should not now be considered especially attractive targets. I am glad that this is "under examination." Pray report to me tomorrow what is going to be done.[23]

The prime minister's intervention produced "precipitate action."[24] In addition to its size and its relatively undamaged status, which met the targeting criteria, Dresden was in the east, and so bombing that city might contribute to the Soviet effort. The key decision makers in the selection of Dresden were the prime minister and Harris: "Thus, as a result of the Prime Minister's insistent intervention, Sir Arthur Harris was, on 27th January, formally instructed to carry out the policy which he himself had informally suggested on the previous day."[25] The prime minister was informed on January 27 of the bombing targeted at Berlin, Dresden, Chemnitz, and Leipzig.[26] As promised to the prime minister, Dresden was destroyed about two and half weeks later. On February 14, there was also an attack on Chemnitz, and one thousand bombers attacked Berlin on February 26.

Harris was a strong advocate for Bomber Command. Winston Churchill's chief of the Imperial General Staff, Field Marshal Lord Alanbrooke, observed Harris and other leading allied commanders at close quarters and made the following entry in his diary for May 15, 1944:

"Monty made excellent speech. Bertie Ramsay indifferent, and over-whelmed by all his own difficulties. Spaatz [U.S. VIIIth Army Air Force] read every word of a poor statement. Bert Harris [Bomber Command] told us how well he might have won this war if it had not been for the handicap imposed by the existence of the two other services!"[27] Harris was on good terms with the prime minister: "Never, indeed, in British history had such an important Commander in Chief been so continu-ously close to the centre of government power as Sir Arthur Harris was to Mr. Churchill."[28] When Harris quarreled with his air force superior over bombing policy and offered to resign, Portal gave in. The historian Max Hastings says that, "by the spring of 1944, it was quite clear that Harris's area bombing campaign had failed to bring Germany even within dis-tant sight of defeat. That winter, when Harris made clear his continuing commitment to the area offensive despite the major reservations of the Chief of Air Staff, he should have been sacked."[29] Portal had advocated bombing German cities. He then shifted his priorities toward target-ing Germany's oil supply, in part as a result of military intelligence sug-gesting that Germany was vulnerable in that regard.[30] This vulnerability was confirmed by the Reich minister of armaments and war production, Albert Speer. On June 30, 1944, Speer had finished a report to Hitler in which he stressed the problems with protecting fuel.[31] Under interroga-tion by the Allies, Speer credited the oil attacks as the "first heavy blow" on industry and acknowledged the difficulties created by attacks on tank production. On the other hand, the "purpose of the night attacks directed exclusively against city centers had been incomprehensible."[32] Speer said that the American daylight bombing of industrial targets was more effec-tive than the night bombing of the civilian population. He thought the German people had been underestimated, as was the "fatalistic frame of mind which a civil population finally acquires." In contrast, and if we needed reminding that Nazis were not without their national prejudices, the Italians "would have certainly collapsed," Speer said.[33] While no doubt as important as a tank engine, morale is an elusive and ideologically con-structed target.

Subsequent analyses of bombing civilians have not supported war-time RAF doctrine. Empirical analysis of aerial bombing over the period 1917–1999 by the political scientists Michael Horowitz and Dan Reiter concluded that military targeting was more effective than punishment attacks or terror bombing.[34] A. C. Grayling provides a moral analysis of allied bombing, focusing our attention on the bombing of Hamburg, rather than Dresden. Among other things, the outcome of the war was less certain when Hamburg was bombed in 1943. As he points out, if Hamburg can be shown to be a poor choice, then Dresden was yet more so.[35] Others have come to a similar evaluation. The political philosopher Michael Walzer says that "the British bombing of German cities might have been defensible in 1940 and '41 . . . the bulk of the bombing that actually took place is certainly not defensible, for it took place after it had become clear that Germany could not win the war."[36] Bomber Command's raid on Dresden was questioned on both strategic and moral grounds. In the end, it was condemned by the man who had precipitated it.

The prime minister's personal intervention to initiate the terror bombing of Dresden is inconsistent with his earlier condemnation of frightfulness. You might say that shooting civilians who are attending a meeting, as was the case at Amitsar, is different from creating a firestorm with their houses. The difference could not be the innocence of the victims, the threat to the military forces posed by the victims, or the belief of a wider impact on civilian morale. The difference is between colonial policing and world war. Yet, that difference is less compelling when you recall the allied military superiority at the time of the bombing and the anticipation of victory. In comparing the two events, what comes to mind is what came to Churchill's mind with that earlier massacre of civilians: "and then was seen what we believe to be the most frightful of all spectacles, the strength of civilization without its mercy."[37]

Audience Pressures

For some time, Churchill had worried about the political consequences of bombing operations.[38] Bombing policy was subject to parliamentary scrutiny. In the House of Lords, almost exactly one year before the bombing of Dresden, the Bishop of Chichester, George Bell, and the former Archbishop of Canterbury, Lord Lang, had spoken against the undeclared policy of bombing civilians. The Bishop of Chichester began with his anti-Nazi credentials and made clear that his opposition to bombing civilians was not a criticism of the men in the bombers who bravely carried out their orders. He referred to international law, including the draft rules of the 1922 Washington Conference on the Limitation of Armaments, which had prohibited terror bombing, and the Hague Conventions and quoted the French jurist Henry Bonfils: "If it is permissible to drive inhabitants to desire peace by making them suffer, why not admit pillage, burning, torture, murder, violation?" He noted that the Nazis had pioneered the bombing of towns but observed that he preferred not to compete in barbarity with barbarians. He conceded that destroying war industry and transport was a legitimate aim and that civilian deaths were inevitable in the process but argued for a balance between the cost in civilian lives and the objectives. The purpose should not be to "obliterate a whole town." He described the practice of bombing through clouds and characterized it as indiscriminate. He warned of impending attacks on old cities and their "historic and beautiful things."[39] Presciently, he named Dresden as a possible target one year before it was destroyed.

Lord Lang of Lambeth specifically drew attention to the undeclared nature of the policy of bombing civilians. He said that "apparently deliberate attempts to destroy whole cities" breached policy and that "either the hitherto declared policy is to be changed or this new policy is to be definitely adopted. That I think would give rise to a good deal of criticism which has hitherto been quite silent."[40] He wanted plain English and an honest account from the government.

After Dresden, on March 6, 1945, the Labour member of Parliament for Ipswich, Richard Stokes, asked "whether at this period of the war indiscriminate bombing of large centers of population, full of refugees, is wise?" He read the *Manchester Guardian* newspaper's account of Dresden to the House of Commons: "Even an attempt at identification of the victims is hopeless. . . . The raging fires which spread irresistibly in the narrow streets killed a great many from sheer lack of oxygen." He noted that the Associated Press report about the terror bombing was available in America but had been suppressed in Britain. It was "objected to by some people and at 11.30 on the same night it was suppressed from publication in this country." Stokes then asked "Is terror bombing—perhaps the Minister will answer me—now part of our policy? . . . Why is it that the British people are the only people who may not know what is done in their name? I think we shall live to rue the day we have done this . . . it will stand for all time as a blot upon our escutcheon."[41] Once the backlash to Dresden began, Churchill tried to remove this blot.

The Techniques: Denial and Delegation

In November 1944, Winston Churchill was asked about a British bombing survey to assess the effects of the bombing campaign. He dismissed it as a "sterile task."[42] The prime minister did not want to know.

Sir Arthur Harris did not consider civilian deaths bad news. The nation was at war. All wars caused civilian deaths. His stock response was that Britain's World War I blockade of Germany had caused 800,000 deaths, far more than Bomber Command. He was straightforward about what was being done and thought others should be, too. As Tami Biddle says, "Harris's continuing obstinacy on this issue was derived in part from his utter unwillingness to engage in pretence about the nature of Bomber Command's wartime work."[43] He was willing to face the consequences of area bombing for civilians. He was disappointed that political leaders were not. He criticized the secretary of state for air, Sir Archibald Sinclair, for his failure to speak in plain English:

> In the House of Commons he should have been far more forthright than he was. It was, for instance, a long time before he described the kind of bombing we were doing. I personally thought that this was asking for trouble; there was nothing to be ashamed of, except in the sense that everybody might be ashamed of the sort of thing that has to be done in every war, as of war itself.[44]

Harris, like the religious leaders, wanted an honest account of what Bomber Command was doing.

Instead, the government relied on denial. When the Bishop of Chichester raised the issue in the House of Lords in 1944, the government response came from the secretary of state for dominion affairs, Viscount Cranborne. He assured the House that "the Royal Air Force has never indulged in pure terror raids" and said that "we have never concentrated upon sleepy country towns and villages. That would not only have been unnecessarily brutal; it would have been utterly futile from our point of view."[45] Small towns had been considered and dismissed, although not on the grounds of the brutality of bombing them. In the House of Commons, the joint under secretary for air staff, Commander Brabner, responded to Richard Stokes after Dresden by claiming to concentrate on war targets; the secretary of state for air added his authority to the denial that they were deliberately killing women and children.[46] Stokes, no doubt, expected this reply, as he had heard it before. In March 1943, in a reply to Stokes, the secretary of state had informed the House of Commons that "the targets of Bomber Command are always military, but night bombing of military objectives necessarily involves bombing the area in which they are situated."[47] In December, the persistent Stokes asked, "Does not my right honourable friend admit by his answer that the Government are now resorting to indiscriminate bombing, including residential areas?" Sinclair replied that "the honourable gentleman is incorrigible. I have mentioned a series of vitally important military objectives."[48] What he did not mention was the policy calculation that 99 percent of bombs aimed at cities would miss the military target and hit civilians and thereby be 100 percent useful.

The secretary of state did not inform the public that "one of the objects of area bombing was the reduction of civilian and especially industrial morale by the bombing of housing and public utilities and . . . of the populations themselves. He usually, and, on public occasions, invariably, suggested that Bomber Command was aiming at military or industrial installations as, of course, it sometimes was."[49] In October 1943, the secretary of state explained to the chief of Air Staff, Sir Charles Portal, that his main concern was to protect the air crews, not the government, from criticism. Harris had told Sinclair that his crews "had begun to think that they were being asked to do something of which the Air Ministry was ashamed."[50] Sinclair did not respond directly to the question of whether the Air Ministry was ashamed. The reason, Sinclair said, that he "should find great difficulty in approving any such deviation from our present publicity line" was external audience pressure and his concern about the effect this pressure would have on the crews. He had said to Harris that "I did not suppose that he received letters, as I do, from leaders of various schools of opinion, including the Archbishop of Canterbury, the Moderator of the Church of Scotland and other leaders of Churches." The effect of these leaders' views on the crews was more important than "another which Sir Arthur Harris had raised, namely, that the Bomber Command crews might form the impression that they were being asked to perform deeds which the Air Ministry was ashamed to admit."[51] Sinclair's words to Portal were as follows:

I always emphasise that our objectives are the centres of war power and that the damage to built-up areas, though inevitable and huge, is incidental. If we were to abandon this line and to adopt as the principal measure of our success the number of men, women, and children killed and the number of houses burnt out rather than the number of factories damaged or destroyed, we should provoke the leaders of religious and humanitarian opinion to protest. I pointed out to the Commander in Chief [Harris] that public protest about our bombing policy from such men . . . might, indeed, trouble the minds and consciences of his crews . . . there must be no departure from our present line without consultation with me.[52]

So it was denial, but a "white" denial, if you like. The goal was not, according to the politician, to enable the government to evade accountability to Parliament and to the public for making bombing policy. It was not to refuse the ethical burden. It was, he explained to the top RAF officer, to protect those who carried out the policy. The source of denial, white or otherwise, is to be found in London and not in a more remote location such as High Wycombe, the headquarters of Bomber Command.

Denial was a collective responsibility for Churchill's coalition government. On May 27, 1943, Clement Attlee, the deputy prime minister, gave his support to bombing policy. Stokes asked, "Is the right honourable gentleman aware that there is an ever-growing volume of opinion in this country which considers the indiscriminate bombing of civilian centers both morally wrong and strategic lunacy?"[53] Attlee replied, "There is no indiscriminate bombing. As has been repeatedly stated in this House the bombing is of those targets which are most effective from the military point of view."[54] A loyal backbencher wanted to stop Stokes's contributions and asked whether there was "any way of preventing statements like this being made in the House?" Another member suggested the "Gestapo."[55] Stokes's questioning of the government's policy continued.

When the newspapers described it as terror bombing,[56] when awkward questions were asked in Parliament, and in America, part of the response was that the bombing was a response to a request by the Soviet Union. Specifically, there was a written request from General Antonov of the Red Army to bomb Berlin and Leipzig, in East Germany.[57] Oil, communications, and support of ground operations were also in the targeting mix. The Soviet memo referred to Berlin and Leipzig as centers of communications, and some officials advocated targeting these alternative sites. Nevertheless, Harris was an extremely forceful champion of area bombing, and he was backed by a powerful patron, until blame management moved to the delegation stage.

On March 28, 1945, Churchill let the blame fall. He wrote to the chief of Air Staff, saying,

> it seems to me that the moment has come when the question of bombing of German cities simply for the sake of increasing the terror, though under other pretexts, should be reviewed. . . . The destruction of Dresden remains a serious query against the conduct of Allied bombing. . . . The Foreign Secretary has spoken to me on this subject and I feel the need for more precise concentration upon military objectives, such as oil and communications . . . rather than on mere acts of terror and wanton destruction, however impressive.[58]

There are a variety of points in Churchill's memorandum that are of interest. First, in it, Churchill changes his position. He credits the foreign secretary, Anthony Eden, with helping to effect this change, perhaps intending to imply to his internal audience that his shift in position was not opportunistic. The foreign secretary had no principled opposition to bombing civilians; in 1942, Eden advocated bombing cities for the psychological effect, "even though those towns contain only targets of secondary importance."[59] Churchill concedes that it was civilian morale in Germany that was the target, although the bombing was done under other "pretexts." Finally, the words "wanton destruction" anticipate the London Agreement of August 8, 1945, which provided for the Charter of the International Military Tribunal for the Prosecution and Punishment of the Major War Criminals of the European Axis. The Charter established the principle of leaders' individual responsibility for war crimes. It described war crimes as "violations of the laws or customs of war. Such violations include, but not be limited to, murder, ill-treatment . . . wanton destruction of cities, towns, or villages, or devastation not justified by military necessity."[60]

Frederick Taylor describes Churchill's memorandum as "a thunderbolt" in Whitehall and says that "to speak, even in a secret memorandum of bombing simply for the sake of increasing the terror . . . when the public stance of the government had always been to deny any such policy, broke all the rules of discretion."[61] Taylor's analysis of Churchill's switch is that criticism in the House of Commons and from neutral countries abroad— the involvement of the foreign secretary—had influenced the prime minister (the Swedish press, fed by Nazi propaganda, had the number of dead at Dresden at 200,000). Taylor argues that the switch may have "showed a certain instinctual politician's feeling for subliminal changes in the country's mood. Possibly he sensed that, from being war-weary and vengeful, the British people had become—though still eager to see an end to the war—concerned about the things that were being done in their name to gain the final victory."[62] It may be that Churchill now perceived an audience that expected better of him. Having urged the bombing in the first place, Churchill switched to dropping and denigrating this strategy.

His international allies were not the restraining influence. They either participated in the bombing or approved it as a means of aiding the Red Army's campaign. It would cause chaos and a refugee crisis and harm German communications. After the bombing of Dresden and after Churchill was alerted to the controversial nature of the bombing and perhaps even cued to recall his own "British" position on frightfulness, adopted decades earlier after the slaughter of Indian civilians, Churchill had choices. He could have backed his man and stuck with the strategy. He could have acknowledged that he had ordered the bombing but that he had been wrong to do so. Or he could have let the blame fall and distanced himself from loyal Arthur Harris. That is what he chose to do, although not without generating some resistance among his own officials.

Churchill's use of the word "terror" in his memorandum echoed previous uses in the press and House. Sir Charles Portal persuaded Churchill to withdraw this memorandum. He substituted one that dropped mention of terror and pretexts and that argued the case for changing strategy on the basis of national interest, rather than moral indignation. His revised memorandum was sent to the chiefs of staff on April 1, 1945:

> It seems to me that the moment has come when the question of the so called "area bombing" of German cities should be reviewed from the point of view of our own interests. If we come into control of an entirely ruined land, there will be a shortage of accommodation for ourselves and our Allies. . . . We must see to it that our attacks do not do more harm to ourselves in the long run than they do to the enemy's immediate war effort. Pray let me have your views.[63]

Portal's intervention modified the judgmental language. It lightened the moral burden for that controversial operation that Churchill had originally deeded his air staff. Two weeks later, the order was given to Bomber Command that the primary objective was supporting the ground troops.[64]

The public perception of prior performance can create a reservoir of goodwill for the management of blame. Churchill's reservoir was quite full.

It was notably so for his choices in 1940.[65] His actions during that critical period show his confidence in his own sense of rectitude and his ability as a leader to resist pressure from all around. When asked which year he would most like to relive, Churchill replied, "1940 every time."[66] On May 27, 1940, the American ambassador, Joseph Kennedy, informed his president that the situation was very grave. He mentioned cabinet divisions and said that "Churchill, Attlee, and others will want to fight to the death but there will be other members who realize that physical destruction of men and property in England will not be a proper offset to a loss of pride . . . the English people . . . really do not realize how bad it is."[67] Among the "other members" was the foreign secretary, Lord Halifax. Belgium surrendered to Germany that day. The Dutch had surrendered two weeks before. Denmark and Norway had been invaded. France's collapse was imminent. Italy was about to enter the war; the Soviet Union and America were not. Meanwhile, President Roosevelt had approached the Canadian prime minister on May 24 requesting that he pressure Churchill to take the Royal Navy out of the action. He wanted it at anchor on the other side of the Atlantic. The president anticipated that Hitler's surrender terms would include the fleet.[68] Without the fleet, Britain could not fight.

Churchill, two weeks into his term as prime minister, resisted this disastrous tide of events. He was deaf to pleas from home and abroad to negotiate. He defied the German threat, ignored American advice, outmaneuvered Halifax in the War Cabinet, and rejected French enticement to get Britain on the "slippery slope" of negotiation. He said: "Nations which go down fighting rise again, but those which surrender tamely are finished."[69] Colonel Villelume, a French officer who accompanied Prime Minister Reynaud to London on May 26, described Halifax as "understanding," but Churchill, "prisoner of his habit of blustering, was absolutely negative."[70] Wherever he found his personal resolve, Churchill won the argument and instructed the cabinet and senior officials that in public they should display confidence in the military outcome.[71]

It is surely a complex task for biographers to weigh the decisions, successful or unsuccessful, that make up a leader's term. They might take guidance from Lord Alanbrooke's assessment of Churchill: "Without him England was lost for a certainty, with him England has been on the verge of disaster time and again. . . . Never have I admired and despised a man simultaneously to the same extent."[72] In the aftermath of the bombing of Dresden in February 1945, with newspaper accounts and parliamentary questions about the terrible slaughter, Prime Minister Winston Churchill switched from advocating to condemning the terror bombing of German cities. The official history of the strategic air offensive ascribes the prime minister's choice to the "singular effectiveness of the attacks and to the widespread publicity which they immediately attracted."[73] He was concerned about accountability for a large number of civilian deaths.

Consequences

The most immediate consequence of Churchill's switch in position was an end to the targeting of cities by Bomber Command. To Harris's dismay, there was not an honest account of British bombing strategy. Politicians were never forthcoming about the destruction of German cities. And, after Dresden, the prime minister let blame for the raid fall on Harris.

Churchill lost the election in the summer of 1945. But analysis suggests that this loss came about not because of questions about Churchill's war leadership or damage to his reputation after Dresden. The reason was the association of the Conservative Party with the economic depression of the 1930s and changes in the electorate. There had not been an election since 1935, and a new generation of voters had been socialized and mobilized by the Labour Party: "the gratitude of Labour voters towards Churchill as a war leader simply did not extend to the point of voting for his party. In sum, Churchill was apparently beaten not by ungrateful converts but by insensitive demography."[74] Churchill returned as prime minister in 1951.

Arthur Harris was left out of the victory parade in Berlin. Bomber Command was left out of Churchill's victory-in-Europe speech. Harris "was astonished and appalled that in the prime minister's long litany of courage and victory . . . Bomber Command's great four-year-long battle over the skies of Germany was not directly mentioned."[75] Bomber Command did not get its own campaign medal. Harris notified the Secretary of State and Portal that "I must tell you as dispassionately as possible that if my Command are to have the Defence Medal and no 'campaign' medal . . . then I too will have the Defence Medal and no other—nothing else whatever, neither decoration, award, rank, preferment or appointment, if any such is contemplated or intended."[76] After the war, Harris left his native land for South Africa, unwept, largely unhonored and unsung. Fighter Command, not Bomber Command, got the attention. In 1946, Churchill commented on a paper on the bombing campaign by Harris. Churchill's "most private & confidential" letter to Harris's assistant warned that "our friend should be very careful in all that he writes not to admit that we ever did anything not justified by the circumstances and the actions of enemy in the measures we took to bomb Germany." He continued, "I am not quite clear about Dresden. It may be we were asked to do this as part of some large military combination, but I am afraid the civilian losses there were unduly heavy."[77] Harris's name does not appear in the index of Churchill's concluding volume on the Second World War.[78] Churchill's narrative, which could not be described as a "warts-and-all" approach,[79] describes Dresden as a center of communications and mentions his post-Dresden memorandum. It does not mention his pre-Dresden memorandum precipitating the destruction of that city.

Historians try to put matters straight. Webster and Frankland are explicit that "neither the Air Staff nor Sir Arthur Harris can justly be accused of waging war in a different moral sense from that approved by the Government."[80] Of Harris's responsibility Richard Overy wrote: "After the war he carried the blame for launching a campaign of indiscriminate terror-bombing . . . in pursuit of a strategic chimera, the critical fracturing of morale. Neither of these accusations carries conviction. The strategy of area bombing was already in place months before Harris took command."[81] Harris made the same point in his memoirs, which reveal a measure of reputational and personal accountability and a loss of peace of mind about the policy.

Harris was unequivocal in his admiration for Churchill, forceful in his defense of Bomber Command and of his own role, and mostly stoical about his selection as fall guy:

> There is a widespread impression, which has often got into print, that I not only invented the policy of area bombing but also insisted on carrying it out in the face of the natural reluctance to kill women and children that was felt by everyone else. The facts are otherwise. Such decisions of policy are not in my case made by Commanders-in-Chief in the field but by the Ministries, by the Chiefs of Staff Committee, and by the War Cabinet. . . . But whenever anyone wishes to blackguard me, as the *Economist* and the *Daily Worker* have done . . . they accuse me of being not only the executor of the bombing policy but also its author.[82]

The distinction between "executor" and "author" is significant. It is an important component of the fall guy's natural first line of defense— that he was following orders. But the policy influence of "executor" and "author," or agent and principal in our terms, is not so neatly separated. Harris's close relationship with the Prime Minister gave him "co-authorship." Harris is correct to claim that the Prime Minister and his cabinet ministers had supported the policy and had "backed their man" until the aftermath of Dresden. And, as he said of that specific episode: "Here I will only say that the attack on Dresden was at the time considered a military necessity by much more important people than myself."[83] It was a graceful exit under the circumstances.

Harris was true to his beliefs about what was necessary to win the war with Germany. He would not use pretexts, while others deviated because of new information about the benefits of targeting oil or because of the audience reminders and the political costs of killing civilians. If he had an audience, it was composed of his Bomber Command crews. They suffered disproportionately in the war effort. Out of every hundred men who served in the bombers, Biddle reports that only twenty-four escaped death, injury, or capture.[84] Bomber Command lost fifty-five thousand dead during the course of the war. In 1943, just 17 percent of crews completed thirty missions.[85] Harris, who had fought in World War I and in Iraq in the 1920s, was intensely loyal to these men.

Churchill had a wider audience. Parliament and the press reminded him of it. And, amorphous though it was, Churchill had an idea of what the "British people" would put up with. He seemed to have this conception when he spoke for the government over Amritsar, condemning terrorism and the killing of civilians in order to teach people a lesson. He said that "such ideas are absolutely foreign to the British way of doing things."[86] When it became the British way of doing things in the war, it was press and parliamentary pressure that eventually awoke Churchill to the heavy liability of frightfulness. It serves to illustrate that even the strongest of political leaders are not wholly independent and self-sufficient in terms of their rectitude. A leader's democratic conscience can become more active when he is aware of the "national theatre of his actions."[87] Listening to the audience, Churchill repudiated terror bombing. It was left to historians to provide an honest account. He let a subordinate bear the costs and left a blot on his escutcheon.

%// 6 %//

Londonderry

There are two things you can get from aiding the civil power, and two things only—brickbats and blame.[1]

The story goes that the Irish Taoiseach, or Prime Minister, Bertie Ahern, on a visit to the office of the British foreign secretary in 1997, was unhappy to see a portrait of the "murdering bastard" Oliver Cromwell, the seventeenth-century perpetrator of a brutal slaughter in Ireland. Apparently, Foreign Secretary Robin Cook had it taken down.[2] Ahern's preoccupation with the portrait shows that the fallout from atrocities in Ireland has a long half-life. We should not be surprised, then, to learn that the management of the blame for the British Army's 1972 shootings of civilians in Londonderry has taken almost four decades.

Cromwell is remembered in Ireland for the events of September 11, 1649. His forces took the fortified city of Drogheda, north of Dublin. The Royalist commander, actually an Englishman, Sir Arthur Aston, would not surrender. Cromwell's artillery made a breach in the fortifications, and, after a failed attempt, he led his men through. In the fighting that followed, he gave no quarter. Between two and four thousand people were killed. Cromwell reported his victory in a letter to the Speaker of the Parliament of England, William Lenthal. He describes the assault against both "horse and foot, and we only foot" that drove the defenders back. Cromwell's men "getting up to them, were ordered by me to put them all to the sword. And indeed, being in the heat of action, I forbade them to spare any that were in arms in the town, and, I think, that night they put to the sword about 2,000 men."[3] Some who surrendered the following day were spared but sent to Barbados.

In the letter, Cromwell mentions the "heat of action" as an excuse, but he knows it is inadequate; later in the letter, he offers justifications for his

order, which otherwise is a matter of "remorse and regret." The justifications are reprisal for earlier massacres of Protestants and the benefit of a
fearsome reputation "to prevent the effusion of blood for the future." Neither is convincing. Of the earlier massacres, "there can have been few—if
any—at Drogheda who had taken part in them; certainly not the officers,
certainly not the English soldiers."[4] If terror were an acceptable strategic
efficiency, Cromwell would have used it elsewhere. Beyond his excuse and
justifications, he submits an unvarnished account of what transpired and
admits he ordered the slaughter. He had an alternative. Cromwell might
have chosen the option of vain command in the manner of Shakespeare's
Henry V before the walls of Harfleur. He resisted the temptation to let
blame fall.

Neither did he evade responsibility for his deeds in England. He signed
the death warrant for King Charles I. The king's execution cost Cromwell political support; Cromwell's biographer, Antonia Fraser, says that
accounts from that time suggest that there was little public support for
the action and that Cromwell was well aware of that.[5] Counterfactually, a
more Machiavellian and blame-sensitive leader would have had Charles
I meet with an accident or succumb to illness. Plots existed to poison
the king. Alternatively, the king could have been killed while attempt-
ing to escape. Cromwell rejected such tactics. In fact, he took measures
to protect the king.[6] Despite the political costs of the public execution,
Cromwell took responsibility for it. After the event, the poet John Milton tried to restore public support by writing an extended justification for
the tragic choice Cromwell had made.[7] The year of the execution, 1649,
was a bad year for Cromwell, as well as for his opponents. But he did not
evade his responsibility, in January, for the execution of the king or, in
September of that year, for the slaughter in Ireland. Oliver Cromwell was
a responsibility-taking murdering bastard.

In the seventeenth century, Catholic Ireland was a security concern for
English governments in their struggle with the major Catholic European
powers, France and Spain. Alliance between the Irish and these powers posed a danger, and, apart from the land itself, this security threat
explains England's continuing interest in establishing a sizable and domi-
nant Protestant community in Ireland. Demands for "home rule" and
independence grew in Ireland during the late nineteenth and early twentieth centuries. With the passage of time, Irish Protestants, mostly in the
North, changed from a strategic asset into a political liability for Britain;
they feared anything that endangered their privileged position and union

with Britain. For them, home rule was "Rome rule." They were a hard-line, status quo–seeking constituency. Any British government had to handle them with care.

In 1914, before the outbreak of World War I, Prime Minister Herbert Asquith's Liberal government introduced the Third Home Rule Bill, which provoked an extreme reaction among Protestant Unionists in Ireland. The year before, in 1913, Sir Edward Carson had organized a pro-Union militia, the Ulster Volunteer Force, some ninety thousand strong. The British government's options were limited by the opposition of its own officers, who threatened resignation rather than accept deployment against the Protestants in the North. The Conservative Party, which was out of power, identified with the Protestant cause; the political scientist Paul Arthur says of this period, which saw the formation of a militia and the officers' threats, that "a surprising feature of these events was total Conservative acquiescence in this semi-constitutional activity."[8] World War I, however, intervened. The Ulster Volunteer Force volunteered to fight for Britain and fought at the Battle of the Somme. That same year, 1916, republicans in Dublin took up arms in the Easter Rising, but the Rising was brutally suppressed and the survivors hanged. Germany, rather than the Catholic superpowers, was now the larger threat. After the war, violence again erupted in Ireland, resulting in the partitioning of Ireland into the Irish Free State and Protestant-led Northern Ireland, which remained part of the United Kingdom and which retained a substantial Catholic minority.

British troops were sent to Northern Ireland in 1969. The immediate context was the civil rights movement, which opposed the continued Protestant ascendancy. Prime Minister Harold Wilson's Labour government sent the troops to support the civil power. The troops were welcomed by the minority Catholic community as an alternative to the Protestant-dominated police force, the Royal Ulster Constabulary. But relations deteriorated. There was pressure from the Protestant community not to tolerate any threats to the rule of law coming from the Catholic minority. In 1970, the United Kingdom elected a Conservative government, which increased the level of repression in Northern Ireland. In August 1971, internment was introduced as the army rounded up and detained individuals without trial. The security forces subjected the detainees to hooding and other cruel and degrading techniques, further worsening relations between the government and the minority community.

Bloody Sunday

There are archives of information about what took place within a half-hour on a Sunday afternoon in 1972 in Londonderry. Two tribunals of inquiry have contributed to what we know of the event.[9] They address the mystery of how not one or two but twenty experienced soldiers from an elite regiment of the British Army, using high-velocity weapons, expended 108 bullets to shoot dead that day thirteen unarmed British citizens (another died later but of an illness unrelated to his wound, according to the latest inquiry) and wound fourteen others.

Prime Minister Edward Heath was at the prime minister's weekend residence, Chequers. A sailor in his spare time, he was with the crew of his boat when the news came through in the late afternoon. Soldiers of the 1st Battalion, the Parachute Regiment (1 Para), had opened fire. They had been deployed to stop a civil rights march organized by the Northern Ireland Civil Rights Association (NICRA). The army equated this group with the Irish Republican Army (the IRA, with both Official and Provisional wings), although it had broad support from the Catholic community.[10] The march was part of a campaign against internment and took place in defiance of a ban on marches. It was to have speeches by, among others, the Member of Parliament (MP) for Mid-Ulster, Bernadette Devlin, and the octogenarian Lord Fenner Brockway. It followed a march a week earlier that had seen violent confrontations between protestors and the soldiers of the Parachute Regiment.

The army decided to stop the January 30 march in the Bogside and Creggan area of Londonderry. The marchers would not be allowed to proceed to the Guildhall, in the city center. The army's decision "to put civilians at risk," in the words of two *Sunday Times* journalists, Peter Pringle and Philip Jacobson, ignored the advice of Chief Superintendent Frank Lagan of the Royal Ulster Constabulary. The chief superintendent told army commanders that the decision made "intense violence" likely.[11] They were undeterred.

When the marchers arrived at the army barriers, some began throwing bottles, bricks, and stones. Soldiers in the surrounding buildings occupied countersniper positions. The expectation was that the IRA would use the march and the ensuing rioting to draw in the soldiers. By this action, the IRA would set up opportunities for shooting soldiers. At 3:55 p.m., two soldiers, positioned in a building, shot and wounded Damian

Donaghey, age fifteen; bullet fragments hit John Johnston, age fifty-nine. At some point after this first shooting, a shot fired by an Official IRA gunman hit a church drainpipe near some soldiers. While other army units had a more passive role and the water cannon had some effect in dispersing the rioters, shortly after 4 p.m the Parachute Regiment went through the barriers and into the streets as a snatch squad to arrest rioters. Armored vehicles also went in at this point. Of the troops going after the rioters, a lieutenant, who had arrived in one of the armored vehicles, was the first to begin firing.[12] His three shots hit a building. More lethal fire by his soldiers followed.

The soldiers of 1 Para were deployed in platoons. Members of the lieutenant's platoon, Mortar Platoon, shot civilians in Rossville Flats car park. They killed Jackie Duddy. He was running away. Six others were wounded in this area. The lieutenant who had opened the firing then likely shot and wounded Michael Bridge.[13] Soldiers of another platoon, Anti-Tank Platoon, shot and mortally wounded Michael Kelly at a range of about eighty yards on Rossville Street. Five others—Hugh Gilmour, William Nash, John Young, Michael McDaid, and Kevin McElhinney—were shot and killed near this location. Alexander Nash, William's father, was shot and wounded while trying to help his dying boy. Members of Anti-Tank Platoon then went into Glenfada Park North and continued firing. They killed Jim Wray and William McKinney and wounded four others. Gerard McKinney and Gerald Donaghey were mortally wounded nearby, as were Bernard McGuigan and Patrick Doherty. According to the Saville Inquiry Report, none of the shooting was considered to be the result of accidental firing or the unintentional discharging of rifles.[14] It was a little more than ten minutes since the soldiers had gone through the barriers. Arrests followed the shooting.

As at Amritsar, days before this confrontation, there had been violence and killing directed against British authorities. It was an illegal assembly. A prior warning had been issued. The army was acting in support of the civil power. Civilians were shot dead. Afterwards, the commander at the scene reported a triumph, not a disaster. And then there was outrage. Unlike the protesters assembled at Amritsar, some of the Londonderry crowd were throwing bottles and stones, and three or four shots were fired back at the soldiers—not by any of the civilians who were killed or wounded. And, while a general was on the scene on Bloody Sunday, he left it to those lower in rank to give the orders. There was no equivalent to General Dyer putting his responsibility to the fore.

Following the shooting, Lord Chief Justice Lord Widgery's tribunal investigated the event. Then, in 1998, a second inquiry was authorized in the context of the Good Friday Agreement, which as part of a political solution to the conflict set up a new elected assembly in Northern Ireland and improved inter-governmental communication between Dublin and London. Prime Minister Tony Blair agreed to the second inquiry as a result of pressure from the families of victims and in the effort to improve cooperation from the Irish government and from the Catholic community in Northern Ireland. The second inquiry had a panel of three judges, including an Australian and a Canadian judge, and was chaired by Lord Saville. The Widgery Inquiry was noted for its speed, the Saville Inquiry for its lack of it. But the benefit of time allowed the Saville Inquiry to produce accounts of what happened from a large number of witnesses, from the prime minister of the day to the individual soldiers, from bystanders to the media. It aimed to establish the truth in the light of new evidence. The aim was not to accuse or punish individuals but to establish an accurate description of what happened, which is itself an essential element of accountability. The testimony and evidence Saville gathered contributed to that. Those soldiers who had not previously been identified retained their anonymity. On setting up the inquiry, Prime Minister Blair repeated the statement by his predecessor, John Major, that those shot should be considered innocent of handling guns or bombs. The Saville Inquiry verified their innocence. One victim, Gerald Donaghey, probably had nail bombs in his pockets according the Saville Inquiry report, but was not shot because of those nail bombs. In addition to the great wealth of testimony and documentary evidence that it accumulated, that verification of innocence was its major accomplishment.

Motives

Churchill, with his Amritsar tests, would have asked whether the crowd was attacking, whether it was armed, and whether more force was used than was necessary to secure compliance with the law. He would have wanted assurance that the officer in charge had confined himself to a well-defined objective and had not violated his general prohibition: "I mean a prohibition against what is called frightfulness. What I mean by frightfulness is the inflicting of great slaughter or massacre upon a particular crowd of people, with the intention of terrorising not merely the rest of the crowd, but the whole district or the whole country." He might have asked why the fiercest of British regiments, the Parachute Regiment, was chosen to police a civil rights march? And why did politicians go along with this choice?[15] Were "frightfulness" and "lesson-teaching" at work on Bloody Sunday?

Individually, the soldiers might have had a variety of motives. They might have fired in self-defense, out of panic, or in ill-disciplined revenge and enjoyment of the violence. Three police and two soldiers had been shot and killed the previous week. Nine months before Bloody Sunday, three Scottish soldiers, including two brothers, seventeen and eighteen years of age, who were off duty and out drinking were lured to their deaths. Their roadside killing shocked the country.

The Bloody Sunday soldiers claimed self-defense. They said they had come under fire from gunmen and that they had responded to attacks from nail, petrol, and acid bomb throwers. As a consequence, they were within their orders to return fire. No evidence that the victims were armed was found, with the exception of what was later discovered in Gerald Dona-ghey's pockets.[16] One shot was fired at the soldiers early on, and perhaps three were fired from a hand gun later. Bishop Daly, who went to the aid of Jackie Duddy, shot while fleeing the soldiers, reported seeing a man fir-ing two or three shots at the soldiers.[17] No soldier was hit. Years later, in an interview with the BBC in 2007, General Sir Mike Jackson, a captain in the Parachute Regiment at the time, conceded that innocent people were shot that day.[18] His role in giving the army's version of what happened became an issue for the Saville Inquiry because, on the night of the massacre, he had written up a "shot list" of the victims, using notes provided by his supe-rior, Major Loden. This list was typed and titled "Gun battle." On Loden's and Jackson's list, there were no innocents; all the dead had guns or bombs. This list was used to brief politicians and the media.

One of the older victims was Patrick Doherty. He was thirty-two and the father of six children. The autopsy states:

> The bullet had entered the right buttock and penetrated the right iliosacral joint, entering the abdominal cavity. It had then lacerated the aorta and the inferior vena cava, the two main blood vessels in the abdomen, and torn the colon and the bowel attachments. Then it had lacerated the diaphragm and entered the left chest cavity, lac-erating the lower outer part of the left lung before fracturing the 8th and 9th left ribs and leaving the body through the left side of the chest, well below and somewhat in front of the armpit.[19]

In other words, he was shot in his buttocks while crawling. He was seeking safety, not attacking. A photographer who was directly behind the Parachute Regiment as it went in spoke of his shock at seeing the soldiers fire into the crowd.[20] A BBC radio journalist, David Capper, reported seeing soldiers open fire as they got out of their vehicles and said he had seen no evidence of the soldiers coming under fire; he reported that one soldier had said to him, "'It is all fucking go here, mate', this can be heard on the recording."[21] The one soldier willing to speak out after the event testified that, in his view, some soldiers enjoyed the shooting.[22]

On the morning after, the *Times* observed that either ill discipline or an ill-conceived operation had led to the shooting.[23] Lord Widgery's inquiry largely ruled out ill discipline. Ill discipline requires correction, but there was no punishment of officers or men. Thirty years later, Prime Minister Heath was asked about punishment; specifically, he was asked about Patrick Doherty and why Soldier (Lance Corporal) F (who allegedly killed him) was never prosecuted for murder. He replied that it was not his responsibility.[24] It was no one's responsibility. Military commanders at the time were satisfied that the force was not ill disciplined. If discipline did not break down and if the claim of self-defense was undone by the fact of unarmed victims, then there was an ill-conceived operation. What evidence is there for such an ill-conceived operation? What was the aim of the operation?

Immediately after Bloody Sunday, political leaders had to deal with this question. The Labour MP Merlyn Rees told the House of Commons that he had received a "telegram from a very eminent Catholic . . . Can assure you Army shooting was planned. Indiscriminate. Designed to teach Bogside a lesson."[25] The home secretary, Reginald Maudling, said, "Let me dispose of this rumour straight away. There was never for a moment a suggestion that the time had come to teach the people of Bogside a lesson."[26] But, for the lawyers of the relatives at the Saville Inquiry, the rumor could not be disposed of in this way. What evidence is there to support the assertion that the shooting was planned? The question gets to the motives of military and political leaders. It gets at why they might have put the soldiers of this elite battalion in this position. It gets to their failure to restrain the soldiers once the shooting started or to punish them once it had ended.

An indicator of the significance the authorities placed on the civil rights march was the presence on the streets of Londonderry of the top general in charge of day-to-day operations in Northern Ireland. He was

General Robert Ford, commander of land forces. Ford regarded the march as a critical test for the reestablishment of law and order in the province. If his forces were successful at maintaining order, it would demonstrate to Protestants in the North that the British authorities were willing to use the force required to restore law and order and provide an opportunity for political progress for the province as a whole.

There are both testimony and documentary evidence that suggest the existence of a plan to shoot the leading rioters and that political leaders, careful to use "political language" rather than Sir Arthur Harris's plain English, weighed the costs of taking "harsh steps," using "firmer measures," or "inconveniencing the civilian population." Beyond this evidence, the idea of such a plan does help explain some of the puzzles raised by Bloody Sunday. It helps explain how the victims could have been wrongly identified as carrying bombs or guns. It helps explain how not one or two but twenty well-trained soldiers could have convinced themselves that they could shoot civilians in car parks, housing estates and on city streets in the United Kingdom without fear of consequences. It helps explain why 1 Para suffered no casualties. It helps explain the subsequent preparation and submission of an inaccurate account of the event by the soldiers. It helps explain why officers were willing to help them prepare this account. It helps explain why political leaders were willing to accept and repeat the account, despite the seriousness of the event and the international outrage that they had to deal with. It helps explain why no soldier or officer was punished for the events on Bloody Sunday. It helps explain the inadequacies of the initial tribunal of inquiry.

If it helps with these puzzles, there are reasons to doubt that the shooting was planned. While it has emerged that a general in Northern Ireland put the idea of shooting "hooligans" on paper, those who deny that there was a plan point to the lack of a record of how it was communicated to the soldiers and dispute the notion that military and political leaders in a democracy could think that it was acceptable to kill unarmed civilians, even if they were participating in a riot.

General Ford had been appointed to his post in Northern Ireland six months before Bloody Sunday. His superior was General Officer Commanding (GOC) Lieutenant General Sir Harry Tuzo. Late in 1971, Ford assessed the security situation and recommended that the security forces offer a more aggressive response. He thought that some of his officers, notably Brigadier Pat MacLellan, lacked initiative.[27] He was concerned about Londonderry and, in particular, about the activities of the Derry

Young Hooligans (DYH), or "yobbos," who rioted on a daily basis and threatened a shopping precinct. The shop owners' organization had met with Ford and complained about the situation, although the owners later denied that they had requested a shoot-to-kill policy. A 1985 account by Desmond Hamill describes the pressure on Ford from the Northern Ireland government and the locals: "Ford had been told in no uncertain terms that the Army was failing to protect the local shopkeepers. So it was decided that the climate of opinion would support the view that the Young Derry Hooligans should be taught a lesson."[28] From the information that was available to Hamill, the lesson was to be in the form of a mass arrest of the hooligans, but harsher methods were under consideration.

In early January 1972—in other words, a few weeks before Bloody Sunday—General Ford wrote a memorandum, marked "personal and confidential," to GOC (General Tuzo)]. It was titled "The Situation in Londonderry as at 7th January 1972." Within the memo, Ford explained how shooting "selected ring leaders" of a group of young rioters was the only effective way to fulfill his duty.

> The Londonderry situation is further complicated by one additional ingredient . . . the Derry Young Hooligans (DYH). Gangs of tough, teen-aged youths permanently unemployed, have developed sophisticated tactics of brick and stone throwing, destruction and arson . . . the Army in Londonderry is for the moment virtually incapable. . . . Attempts to close with the DYH bring the troops into the killing zones of the snipers. As I understand it, the commander of the body of troops called out to restore law and order has a duty to use minimum force but he also has a duty to restore law and order. We have fulfilled the first duty but are failing in the second. I am coming to the conclusion that the minimum force necessary to achieve a restoration of law and order is to shoot selected ring leaders amongst the DYH, after clear warnings have been issued. I believe we would be justified in using 7.62mm but in view of the devastating effects of this weapon and the danger of rounds killing more than the person aimed at, I believe we must consider issuing rifles adapted to fire RV .22 inch ammunition . . . to enable ring leaders to be engaged with this less lethal ammunition. Thirty of these weapons have been sent to 8 Brigade this weekend for zeroing and familiarization training. They, of course, will not be used operationally without authorisa-

tion. . . . If this course is implemented, as I believe it may have to be, we would have to accept the possibility that .22 rounds may be lethal. . . . I am convinced that our duty to restore law and order requires us to consider this step. . . . We have also to face the possibility of a NICRA march. . . . I have issued a warning order to 1 Kings Own Border . . . and 1 Para. . . . It is the opinion of the senior commanders in Londonderry, that if the march takes place, however good the intentions of NICRA may be, the DYH backed up by the gunmen will undoubtedly take over control at an early stage. . . . I have issued very firm directions to the Brigade Commander that he is to take all possible steps within his capability to inhibit and deter the operations of the bombers.[29]

This is a rare document. On the basis of what we know from other conflicts, if you have a plan to victimize civilians, you do not write it down.[30] While the Saville Report said Ford should have known that shooting hooligans was a "wholly unacceptable form of riot control," it asserted that "we are sure that the suggestion to shoot selected ringleaders was not put into effect on Bloody Sunday," stating that "there is nothing to indicate that authorization for this method of controlling rioters . . . was even considered by General Tuzo or politicians."[31] The Saville team said that "there is also nothing to suggest that any of those shot on Bloody Sunday were given warnings or shot because they were or were believed to be the ringleaders of hooligans, nor that the soldiers who fired used .22 bullets."[32] Saville accepted General Ford's defense of his memorandum before the Inquiry. The Inquiry placed a relatively high level of confidence in the points about warning, authorization and types of bullets used.

Regarding warnings, there was a telegram from the prime minister's press officer (Mr. Maitland at No. 10), sent on the Friday before Bloody Sunday, suggesting that the Northern Ireland government issue a statement that "all responsible citizens in Londonderry keep off the street" and prepare public opinion for violence.[33] Such actions could be regarded as a warning. The issue of authorization speaks to the reliability of Ford's memory. When he appeared before the Inquiry in November 2002, Ford said he had "no recollection of dictating this personal and confidential memo; I therefore, of course, have no recollection of signing and dating it either; nor have I any recollection as to whether it ever went to General Tuzo or not—I, of course, accept that this is my dictation."[34] But his recollection of the event did extend to the claim in his written statement to the Saville Inquiry that "there was no question of implementing any such policy without proper authorisation. By proper authorisation I mean the Ministry of Defence and ultimately the Cabinet."[35] Without knowing the habits of command, one might perhaps read the memorandum's reference to authorization as his authorizing the use of the rifles by 8 Brigade. It is correct that there is no documentary evidence that politicians approved this memo. There is, however, other evidence that shooting hooligans was discussed at the highest levels.

The day after the shooting, Ford's and Tuzo's military superior implied that the shooting of hooligans was acceptable, not unacceptable. The chief of staff, Lord Carver, remarked to ministers in London that the only shooting had been directed at hooligans.[36] According to Carver, the firing was directed, not ill disciplined, and he implies that hooligans, presumably casually identified under the circumstances, were an acceptable target for lethal force, consistent with Ford's memo. The Saville Tribunal's point about the bullets seems a minor one. Earlier in the memo, Ford says that using the more lethal rounds "would be justified." The rifles for killing only "the person aimed at" had been adapted, although they were not ready for use on the day of the march.

In his memo, Ford describes the shooting of unarmed "ringleaders" of the teenage youths after issuing a warning. He mentions the army unit involved and the civil rights march. He notes progress on adapting the rifles and anticipates many of the actual victims—teenage boys. Of those killed on Bloody Sunday, all were males, six were seventeen, one was nineteen, one was twenty, one twenty-two, one twenty-six, one thirty-two, one thirty-five, and one forty-one. The first one shot was a fifteen-year-old rioter. He survived. The age and sex of the victims—young and male—are consistent with Carver's remark about the only shooting being directed at hooligans. Ford's memo finishes by drawing attention to the impending march, the seriousness with which Ford regards the situation, his certainty about the presence of hooligans and gunmen, and the very hard line that he expects from his officers.

In earlier assessments, Ford had identified Londonderry as the outstanding security issue and indicated, in his notes for his meeting with Home Secretary Reginald Maudling on December 14, 1971, that "the position is good with the one exception of Derry and here a major decision will have to be taken shortly."[37] There was testimony at the Saville Inquiry about the use of a similar tactic of shooting ringleaders in Aden and Cyprus, where some soldiers and officers from 1 Para served.[38]

Ford believed that stopping the march was essential for the future security of Northern Ireland.[39] Although he felt that so much was riding on the march, on the actual day he shifted responsibility for the operation to his subordinates. At the march, he chose to be an "observer." He exhorted the soldiers of the Parachute Regiment when they went through the barriers and then testified that he "went away from the scene" when he heard firing.[40] During the operation, Ford claimed that he had no way of directly communicating with the Parachute Regiment and did not want to interfere with ongoing radio communications, despite the shooting. At the end of the operation, he congratulated 1 Para. There is a transcript of a conversation between two army officers about how it had "gone badly wrong" and the numbers of "stiffs" being cleared away after the march. They describe Ford as "lapping it up," congratulating the Parachute Regiment and saying that the army has been too passive and that "this is what should happen."[41] It is a conversation consistent with Ford's memo. When asked about it, Ford responded that the officers' words were "highly emotional and exaggerated."[42] While the age and sex of the victims on Bloody Sunday generally fit with Ford's memo and with Lord Carver's remark about the shooting being directed only at hooligans, the number actually killed and wounded in the operation would seem to exceed a target defined as "selected ring leaders."

When questioned about his plan, Ford replied, "I do not see how there ever could have been one, because how was this covert plan, which you would like to suggest I had in mind, going to be passed to the troops who would be concerned?" Eilis McDermott, a lawyer representing Patrick Doherty's family at the Saville Inquiry, suggests that "it was passed at the last minute."[43] One soldier has suggested that that is what happened. In 1975, Soldier 027 stated that, on the eve of Bloody Sunday, members of his platoon were briefed by a lieutenant. This officer notified them of the operation in Londonderry and said, "Let us teach these buggers a lesson, we want some kills tomorrow."[44] Lawyers for the other soldiers questioned the motives and credibility of the informer. The Saville team accepted their view that the informer's testimony was unreliable. But, the day after the shooting, the *Times* quoted an army officer who denied that the shooting was indiscriminate; he noted that those hit were about the same ages, pointing out that if the shooting had been indiscriminate, women and children also would have been shot.[45] Again, the claim that was volunteered to the press is that the fire was directed, and directed against the young hooligans. If the shooting was not indiscriminate, there was no need for disciplinary action against the soldiers. General Ford said that action against Soldier F for the killing of Patrick Doherty was not his responsibility. Eilis McDermott said "there would be no need to discipline Soldier F or any other soldier . . . if they had been doing exactly what they were supposed to do."[46] The general could not be drawn to comment.

Lieutenant Colonel Derek Wilford, who led the soldiers on the day, later made comments that point to "frightfulness." He ruled out ill discipline and vain command. He claimed that his troops "had behaved magnificently," saying that the death toll would have been far higher if they had been out of control. He said (and later retracted) that "it smacked of it's time we taught these people a lesson . . . and er that's what it smacked of."[47] Wilford's subordinate officers made similar remarks. A year or so after Bloody Sunday, one was quoted in a book saying the time had come "to teach these young thugs and particularly those who had become known as the Derry Young Hooligans, a lesson."[48] Wilford remembers, at the end of the operation, being bemused by General Ford's asking him what he was going to do, because "he [Ford] was the two star general and I was a lieutenant colonel."[49] But Ford had delegated responsibility for the operation.

The week before Bloody Sunday, other British soldiers had warned publicly against the use of the Parachute Regiment. In a front-page *Guardian* article on January 25, 1972, Simon Hoggart reported that senior officers thought the Parachute Regiment too "brutal." Some regiments had informally requested not to have to work with 1 Para. These soldiers were thought ill suited to police cities. Ford defended his choice of regiment. The regiment was available but also was tough and had an intimidating reputation, which had been inculcated by Brigadier Frank Kitson.[50] Kitson was a veteran of British insurgency operations, including the campaign against the Mau Mau rebellion in Kenya. After Bloody Sunday, Ford took responsibility for the decision to use 1 Para. The politicians went along with that account, although, as we shall see, there is evidence that ministers knew and approved of the decision prior to the march. The newspaper coverage prior to the shooting drew politicians' attention to the importance of the decision on the choice of troops.

Ford said that his memorandum about shooting ringleaders went no higher than General Tuzo. Tuzo is reported to have said, at a conference on the Wednesday before Bloody Sunday, that "it will shortly be necessary to warn the Catholic population of Londonderry of the dangers of continuing to support the Provisional IRA."[51] Colonel Henry Dalzell-

Payne, who worked for the director of military operations in the Ministry of Defense, authored a paper that argued for "not ruling out" shooting to disperse crowds. Presciently, he said, "inevitably it would not be the gunmen who would be killed but 'innocent members of the crowd.' This would be a harsh and final step."[52] The Saville Report dismisses a relationship between this document and Ford's memo. It claims that Dalzell-Payne "was not recommending a policy of disperse or we fire and his paper was not confined, as was that of General Ford, to the problem of hooliganism in Londonderry."[53] Again, the report seems distracted by minor differences and loses sight of the moment when the army planners crossed the Rubicon—when they decided that shooting at unarmed crowds within the United Kingdom was a measure to be considered.

Dalzell-Payne's MoD paper may not mention Londonderry, but it does concern crowd control in Northern Ireland in January 1972. The paper says that shooting is the "only additional measure for the physical control of crowds" that "must be rejected except in extremis" but that it "cannot be ruled out. We must await the outcome of the events planned for the weekend 29/30 Jan, 72, see what effect our firmer measures have."[54] Whether or not confined to Londonderry, shooting into crowds was clearly under consideration by the Ministry of Defense and by commanders in Northern Ireland in the days prior to the march. There was recognition that innocent people might suffer. What is striking is that there were, in January 1972, two senior British officers willing to examine the circumstances under which it is permissible to fire into crowds, even when the lives of soldiers are not in danger. They were willing to document their arguments.

Peter Pringle and Philip Jacobson, of the *Sunday Times*, investigated the event. They wrote that the unarmed men and boys were "killed as part of a deliberate plan, conceived at the highest level of military command and sanctioned by the British government, to put innocent civilians at risk by authorizing the use of lethal force during an illegal civil rights march."[55] If a plan to shoot hooligans was implemented on Bloody Sunday, we would have to accept that either the extraordinary political expense of such lessons escaped serious consideration or it was considered but failed to deter decision makers.

The military leaders, like General Dyer before them, may have discounted the severity of the political storm that they were heading into. By his own account, Lord Carver discounted it. In his memoirs, he says that "my first reaction was gravely to underestimate the furore it would all arouse."[56] If he did, his subordinates probably did, as well. For the politi-cians, there is evidence that the Conservative government did consider the political costs of harsh measures. Government officials indicated that they were willing to accept political penalties in order to bring an end to the conflict. Leading up to the shooting, the British government and the army made a series of decisions that undid the goodwill that had greeted the army's arrival in 1969. Rod Thornton, drawing parallels with the 2003 invasion of Iraq, describes how the army mismanaged things and alien-ated the Catholic minority. With the advent of a Conservative govern-ment in June 1970, ministers put fewer constraints on the army as it car-ried out its duties: "the Conservatives were more inclined to let the Army do as it desired."[57] The repressive measures included internment, "deep interrogation," and the use of cruel and degrading treatment of detainees, if not actual torture; this was ratcheted up to shooting on Bloody Sunday. Come Monday, the claim to have delegated responsibility to the army was politically useful. But there was not a clean separation between the gov-ernment and the army on the management of events in Northern Ireland.

At a January 27 meeting of the cabinet committee with responsibil-ity for Northern Ireland, Heath summed up by saying that civil rights marches posed difficulties for the army and that "incidents of confron-tation between the army and the civil population were inevitable."[58] The expected costs and benefits attached to the choice of alternative lev-els of repression in Northern Ireland were discussed explicitly by the prime minister and his colleagues. They might have expected relatively low mainland political costs from the geographically concentrated use of repression at that time, given the murderous tactics of the Provisional IRA. The major British political parties generally refrained from seeking political advantage from the situation in Northern Ireland. The British electorate was not likely to be outraged over the treatment of anyone who could be connected to the IRA. In this context, by October 1971, Prime Minister Heath "believed that the first priority should be the defeat of the gunmen using military means, and that in achieving this we should have to accept whatever political penalties were inevitable."[59] By penalties the prime minister stated that he meant loss of votes. That same month, the Heath government established the strategic goal of ending the con-flict as quickly as possible. It lifted all the normal restraints on the army with regard to the means necessary to achieve this goal. The government requested "an assessment of what measures the Army would propose if they were instructed that the primary objective was to bring terrorism in Northern Ireland to an end at the earliest possible moment, without regard to the inconveniences caused to the civilian population and what forces they would require to carry these measures out."[60] The measures that had already "inconvenienced" the civilian population included internment, harsh interrogation techniques, and the use of rubber bullets. There was little else left in the way of measures, other than Ford's memorandum on using real bullets.

A hard line was welcomed by leaders of the Protestant community. The willingness of the Conservative government to accept measures proposed by the army without regard to inconveniences to civilians, the declared priority to end the conflict, and the pressure from the Protestant community suggested that there would be fewer constraints on the future use of force.

Other democratic leaders have been willing to kill civilians. The political scientist Alexander Downes has analyzed civilian victims in wars for the period 1816–2003. He shows that, while killing civilians is antithetical to democratic norms and is often considered a poor strategic move because it hardens resistance, democracies do target civilians in war. They do so for two major reasons: because they are out of options and desperate to finish a costly war or because they wish to change the demography of a territory and drive out an unwanted or suspect population. The explanation is that of "strategic necessity," where leaders have limited other options in trying to terminate a costly conflict.[61] Ford and others made precisely this type of argument: all other alternatives to restore law and order had been tried.

While the government was encouraging the army to ratchet up repressive measures and was willing to give the army latitude, there is evidence that, at the highest levels, it remained interested and informed about events and tactics in Northern Ireland. It had not shifted responsibility. The committee of the cabinet that dealt with Northern Ireland (cabinet committee GEN 47) met frequently during this period—eighteen times between October 1971 and January 27, 1972. The prime minister chaired the meetings. Furthermore, ministers had indicated to their military commanders a tolerance for tougher action.

The lord chancellor, Lord Hailsham, expressed the view that anyone who resisted the armed forces was an enemy of the queen and could be shot by the army. According to the lord chancellor, soldiers could take this step whether or not they were being shot at.[62] Lord Hailsham's comment, lifting all normal restraints, suggested desperation. Heath addressed Hailsham's contribution to Northern Ireland policy in his oral testimony to the Saville Inquiry: "So at the time people just said, 'well, that was Quinton [Quintin Hogg, later Lord Hailsham],' and we got on with it and certainly as a government, of which I was Prime Minister, we took no notice at all."[63] Even if one ignores Lord Hailsham, there is evidence that the government in London anticipated violence on Bloody Sunday.

Two days before the march, there was the telegram from the prime minister's press officer to the Northern Ireland authorities suggesting that they warn the public of the likelihood of violence at the march and "prepare public opinion here and in Northern Ireland for violent scenes on TV following the march."[64] Despite Heath's denials, which the Saville team accepted,[65] there is other evidence that he had been advised of the likelihood of shooting prior to the march. An assistant to Lord Carver was confident that the prime minister, in addition to the secretary of state for defense, was told by the chief of staff of the "substantial risk of a shooting war" and that measures were taken prior to the march to ensure that the secretary was informed immediately of events.[66] Military commanders may have come up with the desperate options, but the evidence suggests that they were not willing to keep them to themselves.

At the Saville Inquiry, former prime minister Heath was asked by one of the lawyers of the victims' families:

MANSFIELD: Was this disclosed to the British public, that the Chief of the General Staff has said that the only shooting into crowds was directed against hooligans; was that disclosed?

HEATH: That I cannot say. Mansfield: Well, it was not. It is not even in the typed note . . . of this meeting . . . I want to ask you just once more, why it is you do not say to the Chief of General Staff, "That is unacceptable and outside the Yellow Card," which, you say, almost the Bible for military operations?

HEATH (PAUSE): No. Mansfield: Do you have any explanation as to why you do not ask him a single question? Heath: I do not understand the question appearing there because it is not in my memory at all, but I said, "Disclose all this in today's Parliamentary statement," and that should have covered everything.[67]

That day, when Carver made his remark about shooting only hooligans, Simon Winchester, in the *Guardian*, compared Bloody Sunday to Sharpeville, a notorious massacre of civilians in apartheid South Africa in the 1960s, raising doubt that the Londonderry shooting was justified.[68]

Heath was the politician left with managing the blame, faced with this sort of publicity, and dealing with visceral international outrage. At the same time, as Mansfield's line of questioning suggests, this Oxford man and former soldier was not demanding explanations about how his army had created such a disaster and why its commanders seemed to think that directing fire at hooligans was acceptable.

Years after Bloody Sunday but before the effort to deliver accountability re-opened in the form of the Saville Inquiry, remarks made by the former prime minister invite renewed speculation about the motivation for shooting. The occasion was the Chinese government's decision to open fire in Tiananmen Square in 1989. Heath first visited China in 1974 and was a frequent visitor over the years. He developed an admiration for Mao and for Deng Xiaoping. He compared Mao to "Churchill, Adenauer and Tito" and praised Deng for transforming China.[69] In 1987, he returned to China and, as an accomplished musician, was invited to conduct the China Philharmonic Orchestra. After Tiananmen, Heath's "first, unguarded reaction was to claim that the Chinese Government had the right to take police action on its own territory and to suggest that the incident was, in essentials, no different from Bloody Sunday."[70] He clarified later in the House of Commons that he did not condone the massacre.[71] Oddly, Heath returned to the theme eight years later. He repeated the comparison that he had drawn between the two events. In February 1997, on Deng's death, a television interviewer said to Heath that Deng "killed rather a lot of people in Tiananmen Square, didn't he?" Heath replied:

> Well, of course this is just like the British. It is the only thing which you can bring up, and we are the only country that does still bring it up. There was a crisis in Tiananmen Square after a month in which the civil authorities had been defied and they took action about it. Very well, we can criticise it in exactly the same way as people criticise Bloody Sunday in Northern Ireland, but that isn't by any means the whole story, and why can't we also look at the rest of his achievements?[72]

His biographer says that "Heath's remarks suggest an alarming readiness to condone the activities of a brutally repressive regime."[73] Equally alarming is Heath's unprompted readiness, on separate occasions, years apart, to put the action in Northern Ireland in the same category as the action taken by the Chinese government against those who defied civil authority.

So how do we summarize the evidence for a strategic motive for shooting? The army had been encouraged to consider what forces it would need. It decided on the fiercest troops available. It was invited by the government to consider tougher measures and to disregard "inconveniences to the civilian population." Military planning memos, the profiles of the victims, the information from the soldiers involved (from the unreliable Soldier 027 to Colonel Wilford and up to Lord Carver), information from journalists for the mainstream press, and the reactions of politicians after the event suggest frightfulness as a motive. These streams of evidence are consistent if not dispositive. While 1 Para was congratulated by its commanders after the event, there are no witnesses except for the unreliable soldier and no specific documentary evidence to prove that the soldiers of 1 Para were authorized or encouraged to shoot on January 30, 1972.

Audience Pressures

In the House of Commons, Gerry Fitt, MP for Belfast West, described the anti-British sentiment in Ireland after Bloody Sunday as comparable to that during the 1916 Easter Rising.[74] The British embassy in Dublin was set on fire. It shook the British ambassador, a veteran of postings in Cairo and elsewhere, who had never experienced such anti-British sentiment.[75] On the Sunday evening, Heath received a concerned phone call from the Irish prime minister. The government had a clear incentive to discover what had gone wrong and to punish those responsible.

Protestant politicians reacted differently. Days after Bloody Sunday, the prime minister of Northern Ireland, Brian Faulkner, met with Heath and cabinet ministers in London. He said that the operation had produced "a new solidarity" and might at some stage be seen to have "cleared the air."[76] Prior to Bloody Sunday, Faulkner had advocated internment. As Home Secretary Reginald Maudling explained: "I think if we hadn't introduced internment there was a danger of a Protestant backlash . . . if people did not think the British government were doing all they could to deal with violence, they might take the law into their own hands."[77] Other Conservatives were very aware of the expectations and demands of this audience. William Whitelaw, appointed secretary of state for Northern Ireland in March 1972, described the situation: "One had to move very carefully. The place was in an uproar when I went there . . . if you didn't keep at least enough of the Protestant community believing that you meant to deal with the I.R.A. they would have, in their turn, went [*sic*] berserk."[78] But, while there may have been some solidarity with the Protestant community, there was intense pressure to account for the shooting.

Techniques of Evasion

General Ford and Colonel Wilford were interviewed on television immediately following the shooting. Even at this early moment, Wilford was asked about the use of "excessive force" and whether he was worried about the action. He claimed that his men had come under fire and had been petrol-bombed and attacked with acid.[79] General Ford said that the soldiers of the Parachute Regiment had been attacked "not only by the hooligans but also by . . . half a dozen nail bombers and then seven gunmen opened up on them from on top of the flats."[80] The number of armed attackers mentioned exactly matched the number of dead in this account. The following day, in a press briefing by Colonel Dalzell-Payne, the location of the attackers was adjusted to the "lower floors and car parks." A lawyer cross-examining Ford at the Widgery tribunal pointed out that, by then, it was known that those shot had all been shot on the ground and "the Army changed their version."[81] Meanwhile, other officers wrongly told the press that some of the dead and injured were on an army wanted list.[82] No evidence was ever presented to substantiate these claims. No "wanted list" was produced.

After both Ford and Wilford spoke to the press on the Sunday evening, two of their officers compiled the "shot list." Major Ted Loden drew up the notes for the list of fifteen engagements detailing the dead and wounded. He said it was based on platoon commanders' reports and on interviews with the soldiers conducted in the back of an army vehicle. When asked later, only one soldier remembered an interview with Major Loden.[83] On the Sunday night, Captain (later General)Mike Jackson, adjutant of 1 Para, wrote up and amended the list of engagements from Loden's notes. Jackson's list itemized the casualties: "1 Nail bomber shot . . . 2 Petrol Bomber shot . . . 3 Bomber . . . shot . . . Gunman with pistol . . . shot . . . 5 Nail bomber . . . shot 6 Nail bomber . . . shot . . . 14 Gunman, rifle (at barricade), shot."[84] It was difficult to reconcile this list with those shot. Loden was unable to help the inquiry with the puzzle of how the soldiers, none of whom admitted firing accidentally or mistaking their targets, could then have hit the unarmed civilians.

Captain Jackson's contribution was revealed by the discovery of a hand-written copy of the list at the Ministry of Defense and the denial by Major Loden that the copy was his hand-writing. The shot list was "for higher command, setting out the facts as they were then understood to be, by the senior officers of the battalion involved," and, when he was recalled before the inquiry to explain, Jackson, by then a general, said that he had "sat down in the small hours of the night to write a fair copy for submission to higher authority."[85] He was asked about how the list helped explain who was actually killed on Bloody Sunday: "The point is, General, the ones who were killed were not bombers and were not firing weapons. That has been accepted on behalf of the Army; do you follow?" Jackson responded that he knew that. Mansfield continued: "The whole point of the list . . . was in order to justify publicly why people had been shot so they were described as 'nail bombers' 'pistol firers' 'carrying rifles' and so on. . . . Every single one of them, General." Jackson said, "I hear what you are telling me, but this is surely a matter for the tribunal."[86] Jackson stated that while he could not explain errors in the list, it was not a cover-up.[87] The Saville Report concluded that individual soldiers submitted false accounts to justify their shooting.[88] Officers were not faulted for passing on those falsehoods. The home secretary and the minister of state for defense relied on this list in giving an account of the event to the House of Commons.

On the Monday after the shootings, Home Secretary Reginald Maudling stated in the House of Commons that "the Army returned the fire directed at them with aimed shots and inflicted a number of casualties on those who were attacking them with firearms and with bombs," which prompted, Bernadette Devlin, MP for Mid-Ulster, to ask, "Is it in order for the Minister to lie to this House?"[89] Devlin had been one of the leaders of the march; when the shooting began, she had lain face down in the road.

On Tuesday, Lord Balniel, the minister of state for defense, described disciplined and controlled firing in self-defense. He said the soldiers "came under fire from gunmen, nail bombers and petrol bombers, some in the flats and some at ground level. Between 4:17 and 4:35 p.m., a number of these men were engaged. Some gunmen and bombers were certainly hit and some almost certainly killed . . . soldiers fired aimed shots at men identified as gunmen or bombers." He denounced "a deliberate propaganda campaign to vilify the regiment" and stated that the "soldiers fired in self-defence or in defence of comrades, I reject entirely that they fired indiscriminately and into a peaceful and innocent crowd, I reject utterly the slurs made on the Parachute Regiment."[90] The shock caused by the shooting invited historical parallels. In their book, Pringle and Jacobson go back to the Peterloo massacre of 1819 to find a comparable example in the United Kingdom (the other cases they mention include Amritsar and Sharpeville).[91] About the same number had been killed by the army as were killed at Peterloo. All the same, Heath and his ministers made no effort, as far as one can tell, to verify the reliability of the information prepared by the officers of the Parachute Regiment and that they then submitted to the House.

Heath had recognized very quickly that simply asserting self-defense would not be sufficient. On January 31, the government appointed the Lord Chief Justice, Lord Widgery, to conduct an inquiry. Heath decided Widgery would inquire alone. The lord chancellor, Lord Hailsham, was challenged in the House of Lords about the composition of the inquiry at the time—and in strong terms: "I do not think the Government have yet realised . . . the immense change in opinion that has taken place in Ireland as a result of what happened on Sunday. . . . I am very much afraid that, so long as an Englishman is in charge of the Tribunal, there will be a lack of co-operation and this will be tragic."[92] Lord Hailsham responded that it was "unthinkable" that the British government or British troops would kill indiscriminately; "wild" charges had been made against the soldiers, and he was sorry that anyone doubted the impartiality of English judges. Under terms of the 1921 Tribunals of Inquiry (Evidence Act), he conceded, it was unusual for a judge to sit alone, but he put that down to the special circumstances. He described the need for a skillful judge who could protect the witnesses.[93] The Lord Chief Justice had been appointed by Hailsham the year before. It later came to light that Heath had briefed the Lord Chief Justice about his inquiry, telling him that there was a propaganda war as well as a military war going on in Northern Ireland.[94] Further doubt about the inquiry's purpose is evident in the inquiry secretary's note that Widgery would "pile up the case against the deceased."[95] So how did he go about his task?

Lord Widgery heard 114 witnesses. He found that "the soldiers fired in the belief that they were entitled to do so by their orders."[96] He did note that he "heard a great deal of evidence from civilians, including pressmen, who were in the crowd in the courtyard, almost all to the effect that the troops did not come under attack but opened fire without provocation."[97] He did not hear from the soldier who broke ranks with the other members of 1 Para. In statements to the Royal Military Police and to a lawyer for the Widgery inquiry, this soldier had said that there was no justification for the shooting. He was not asked to appear at the Widgery tribunal. In 2002, he was in the Northern Ireland Office witness protection program.[98] Another soldier, Soldier S, later retracted some claims about nail bombers and gunmen that he had made to the Widgery tribunal and to the Royal Military Police (RMP). He said that the military police might have had some responsibility for the inaccuracies. He said that "those statements were made when I was an 18-year-old soldier on the day of Bloody Sunday. . . . I am conceding to the fact that those statements are inaccurate. . . . I mean, that was made to the RMPs, which— making a statement to the RMP . . . can be quite a frightening affair."[99] Evidence was not heard from all journalists. On the evening of the massacre, two journalists had been sent to Derry by the editor of the *Sunday Times*, Harold Evans. They wrote an article suggesting that the shooting might have been planned. Evans says he was told by Lord Widgery that he would be charged with contempt if the paper published the article.[100]

Widgery reported that no firearms were recovered from the dead, that no soldiers were shot, and that there were eye witnesses who said the victims had not been armed. Yet he decided in favor of the army's evidence. He was sure that the soldiers had been fired at first. He said he had come to his conclusion as a result of "many days of listening to evidence and watching the demeanour of witnesses. . . . It does not mean that witnesses who spoke in the opposite sense were not doing their best to be truthful. On the contrary I was much impressed by the care with which many of them, particularly the newspaper reporters, television men and photographers, gave evidence."[101] He says that "in the relevant half hour as many rounds were fired at the troops as were fired by them. The soldiers escaped injury by reason of their superior field-craft and training."[102] He rules out panic: "They were far too steady for that." He concedes that "in the circumstances mistakes were made and some innocent civilians hit."[103] He concludes that "at one end of the scale some soldiers showed a high degree of responsibility; at the other, notably in Glenfada Park, firing bordered on the reckless. These distinctions reflect differences in the character and temperament of the soldiers concerned."[104] Glenfada Park is the likely location of the soldier who shot Patrick Doherty, as well as Bernard McGuigan, who had gone to Doherty's aid with his arms above his head or carrying a handkerchief. He was shot in the back of his head. Widgery ruled out panic, admitted mistakes, and accepted the army's denials of the allegations made against them. The soldiers were found to be acting within their orders given the claims that they were coming under fire and targeting those with firearms.

Consequences

Neither military nor political leaders submitted an accurate account of the afternoon's events. No one has been punished, either for the shooting or for the cover-up. No one lost his liberty or his job. The first inquiry blamed the dead. Widgery explained Bloody Sunday as self-defense. His interpretation was treated with skepticism, yet, as the sociologist Stanley Cohen says: "The point is not to persuade audiences to agree with the account—that is, to support the action—but to make it sound credible and reasonable."[105] And events moved. Just three weeks after Bloody Sunday, the Provisional IRA seized the moral low ground by exploding a car bomb at an army barracks in Aldershot that killed five women kitchen staff, a gardener, and a priest.

The second inquiry blamed the soldiers of 1 Para. Saville explained Bloody Sunday as ill discipline. As with Widgery's findings, awkward facts remain. If the shootings were caused by ill discipline, not just one or two but twenty soldiers had to have lost control during the operation and fired unjustifiably. As the report states, "none of those who were killed or injured by Army gunfire in the five sectors was posing a threat of causing death or serious injury; and in our view none of them was shot in error by a soldier who was aiming at anyone posing such a threat."[106] An officer led this major breach of discipline. Some elements of the report's interpretation are difficult to reconcile. It suggests both that the officer's firing led other soldiers to think mistakenly that they were under attack and that they then shot individuals who were not attacking them. The officer then is thought to have shot Michael Bridge. That shooting is ascribed to the officer's possible state of panic. Widgery was very clear the soldiers did not panic. The colonel in charge had said the soldiers were under control. Senior officers were present, yet no officer witnessed or intervened to correct such a breach of discipline. The general went away from the unjustified firing after having refused to take control when offered it by his subordinate. Despite such catastrophic incompetence within an elite regiment, no soldier was punished. The Saville Report did not tidy up the loose ends. Its clearest achievement was to overturn Widgery's burial of the blame with the dead. Saville exhumed the innocent. That may explain why the report was well received on its release.

On the report's release, in June 2010, Prime Minister David Cameron made a statement to the House of Commons. He said that "what happened

on Bloody Sunday was both unjustified and unjustifiable. It was wrong."
He explained that "you do not defend the British Army by defending the
indefensible. We do not honour all those who have served with distinction in keeping the peace and upholding the rule of law in Northern Ireland by hiding from the truth." And he apologized: "Some members of
our Armed Forces acted wrongly. The Government is ultimately responsible for the conduct of the Armed Forces. And for that, on behalf of the
Government—and indeed our country—I am deeply sorry."[107] The prime
minister's statement, like the report, was well received. He accepted the
truth that unarmed civilians had been shot and accepted some notional
responsibility for the government, while pointing to those who were in
the wrong. With notional responsibility, one owns up to the responsibilities of occupying a high office but not to being at fault or to having acted
wrongly oneself. The prime minister was sorry for the wrong done to the
victims.

In contrast, the government of the day was sorry for insults to the soldiers: "I am sorry that the hon. Member should choose this occasion to
cast a slur on the Regiment's reputation."[108]

Ministers denied responsibility for the killings. The Saville Report
accepted that denial. The grounds for holding ministers responsible are
incompetence or complicity. Ministers' competence in supervising, investigating, and correcting this ill-disciplined regiment was not questioned,
and the report ruled out complicity. The report states that "any action
involving the use or likely use of unwarranted lethal force . . . would have
been entirely counterproductive to the plans for a peaceful settlement; and
was neither contemplated nor foreseen by the United Kingdom Government."[109] The suggestion is that, because the consequences of the action
were so negative, it was not a contemplated action. Reasoning from consequence back to cause is not persuasive. We can agree with Saville that
it would be a better world if the policies contemplated by the British government were never counterproductive. But governments miscalculate,
particularly when it comes to the use of force. It is very difficult to manage
the application of force and to anticipate the consequences of that action.
With the use of repression, democratic governments do get it wrong.
The British, American, or Israeli government may plan to destroy enemy
morale, enhance national security, or bring an end to terrorist violence
by implementing harsh measures against civilians and detainees. But the
measures, such as the introduction of internment or harsh techniques of
interrogation, may spark more violence or terrorism, not less, as intended.

The Saville Report described Bloody Sunday as a "catastrophe for the people of Northern Ireland." [110] If it was caused by widespread ill discipline and had policy consequences said to reach the scale of a "catastrophe," then there would be some expectation that it ought to invoke the doctrine of ministerial responsibility. The Inquiry heard testimony from ministers, but the report did not hold individual ministers responsible. The report examines the responsibility of senior officers individually but not ministers. It did not assess whether, for example, alerted by army officers in press accounts to the dangers of deploying the Parachute Regiment that Sunday, ministers were diligent or negligent in not intervening or questioning the choice. We have to go to Israel for an application of this doctrine to unjustified killings. As the next chapter describes, the Israeli Kahan Commission inquiry did apply what it called this "English" doctrine to the atrocity in Beirut. While the consequences of the application may have been disappointingly "English" as well, at least the doctrine was considered in a systematic way by the Israeli inquiry. The Kahan inquiry was willing to hold ministers "indirectly responsible" for not exercising good supervision. [111]

There is evidence that ministers approved the arrest operation prior to Bloody Sunday. Secretary of State for Defense Lord Carrington said he knew of the use of 1 Para only after the event. He was asked about this claim at the Saville Inquiry: "You told me a moment ago that you were not aware that the 1st Battalion of the Parachute Regiment was to be or had been used until after the event. Should we take it from that that so far as you recall, GEN 47, the members of GEN 47 other than yourself were not aware either?" Carrington responded: "No, if I did not know, they certainly would not." [112] Like Carrington, Heath simply denied any knowledge of ministerial involvement or responsibility for decisions relating to the operation. [113] Others gave testimony that seems to conflict with the denials offered by Heath and Carrington. Minister of State Lord Balniel informed the House of Commons on February 1, 1972, that, on the Thursday before Bloody Sunday, the "arrest operation was discussed by the Joint Security Council after decisions had been taken by Ministers here." [114] A junior minister, Sir Geoffrey Johnson-Smith, stated that "I think I would have been aware of the decision to use the Parachute Regiment that is on Bloody Sunday to assist in handling the civil rights march, as this was, at the time, au courant." But, when asked about this statement at the Saville Inquiry, he contradicted himself: "I think my first awareness of it was after the event." [115] He had said in April 1972 that the "general concept of the plan was discussed by . . . ministers at Westminster including the Secretary of State."[116] Lord Carrington himself had given a newspaper interview in April 1972 in which, noting that no officers or men would be punished, he said "that the secret plan approved by ministers in London and Army chiefs for dealing with the illegal civil rights march had included provision for a possible arrest operation by the Parachute Regiment. . . . The arrest operation would have gone perfectly all right if the IRA had not fired on our soldiers."[117] At his appearance before the Saville Inquiry, Carrington relied on a simple denial. He said: "I certainly did not say that."[118] A Ministry of Defense document prepared after the Widgery report was issued stated that "ministers approved the general concept of the operation."[119] A telegram from Heath's press secretary to a government official in Belfast on January 27 read "this morning ministers discussed the public relations aspects of the coming weekend's marches and particularly Sunday's in Londonderry," and a January 28 telegram said "ministers would like . . . a statement be issued by the Northern Ireland government before Sunday's march" warning that (A) citizens should not march, "(B) the security forces will use minimum force, (C) the security forces will take the measures which the tactical situation requires, (D) they will do everything possible to minimize inconvenience to peaceful citizens."[120] Despite this level of involvement, and despite the policy catastrophe, no minister took responsibility.

The Saville Report exonerates ministers of involvement of having a plan for or prior awareness of the possibility of a "shooting war."[121] Yet, the shooting was, at the least, "an immense administrative disaster," in Enoch Powell's phrase. At the time, it was compared to the momentous events at Peterloo, Sharpeville, and Amritsar. Yet, after the shooting, there were no political consequences for this policy disaster. There were no obvious reputation costs or damage to future careers. The home secretary went in the summer of 1972, but over a corruption scandal, not Bloody Sunday. Heath narrowly lost the election in February 1974 (although he won the most votes), but on economic issues. His defense secretary, Carrington, went on to serve in the Thatcher government, resigning over the Argentine invasion of the Falkland Islands, and then served as Secretary General of NATO.

Of the soldiers, Ford received a knighthood and further appointments. MacLellan rose to major general and became a Commander of the British Empire. Wilford received the Order of the British Empire six months after Bloody Sunday, although looking back in disappointment he felt that the killings ended his career. His adjutant, Captain Jackson, became head of the British army.

No soldier was disciplined for what had happened. Soldier F, who is alleged to have killed Patrick Doherty, was asked, "As far as you were concerned and obviously as far as your chain of command was concerned, they never expressed any disapproval to you, at any stage, in relation to your activities on Bloody Sunday?" He replied, "That is correct."[122]

The Saville Report assessed and exonerated senior officers. It did not fault Ford's decision to deploy 1 Para, as "he neither knew nor had reason to know at any stage that his decision would or was likely to result in soldiers firing unjustifiably on that day."[123] Nor did it fault his refusal to take control, despite how badly wrong things were going. The report noted that Ford cheered on the Paras, "for which we do not criticise him, he correctly in our view did not seek to interfere with or to influence what then happened," which "were matters for Brigadier MacLellan."[124] The only officer faulted by Saville is Colonel Wilford, who sent "his soldiers in vehicles into the Bogside." In doing so, he "failed to obey the order that Brigadier MacLellan gave" and "created a situation in which soldiers chased people down Rossville Street."[125] Ironically, on visiting Wilford after the event, Brigadier Frank Kitson faulted him for not chasing them far enough. According to General Mike Jackson, who had overheard a conversation between Kitson and Wilford, Kitson supported Wilford's actions but thought he should have retaken the whole area. In Jackson's view, Kitson "had a point. . . . There was no doubt that we could have gone on to retake the 'no-go area,' though this would almost certainly have resulted in more deaths."[126] These comments suggest that the officers on the ground were unaware that Bloody Sunday represented the "breach of discipline that the Saville Report observed.[127] They saw strategic benefits.

Saville exonerated Major Loden and Captain Jackson of having participated in a cover-up. The lawyers for the families pointed to these officers' list as "material from which it may be inferred that some members of the Parachute Regiment decided at an early stage to provide a bogus account of what happened."[128] Saville noted that the list was used to brief the media and the House of Commons and that, despite Loden's claims, "most of the soldiers told us they could not recall being interviewed by Major Loden . . . and the one who did, Private H, said he could not remember the details." Nevertheless, the Saville team members said that they "accept Captain Jackson's evidence . . . find nothing sinister" and "are satisfied that Major Loden prepared his list in good faith and not for the purpose of deliberate deception or cover-up."[129] All responsibility for what happened on the day fell at or near (except for disobedient Colonel

Wilford) the bottom of the chain of command, according to Saville. The responsibility for the killing rested with the soldiers. The responsibility for the false account of Bloody Sunday given to the victims' families and to the public, submitted to Parliament, and offered to the Lord Chief Justice rested with the soldiers.

The Saville Report ruled out an *operational misjudgment* or strategic motive for the use of lethal force. It concluded that ill discipline—albeit unbeknownst to the officers who were in charge on the day in question— was the explanation for Bloody Sunday: "our overall conclusion is that there was a serious and widespread loss of fire discipline among the soldiers of Support Company."[130] So blame for the shooting and the cover-up rest at the bottom of the chain of command.

Long after Bloody Sunday, Wilford admitted that he felt that he and his soldiers were left with the blame.[131] The only sanctions, however, were self-imposed. He said that Bloody Sunday ended his first marriage after even his wife had difficulty believing him. She questioned whether civilians were deliberately targeted He said that "I could see I was going to be the scapegoat. They all walked away and left me to carry the can."[132] Sorry for themselves, later some of the soldiers may have felt sorry for their victims. Twenty-five years after the event, a Welsh soldier telephoned, anonymously, the daughters of one of the victims seeking forgiveness. Soldier S denied that he made the phone calls but said that did not mean he was not sorry.[133] The phone calls were traced to a public phone, and the daughters, who had heard Soldier S at the inquiry, recognized his voice. So the story of Bloody Sunday may end with some "remorse and regret," in Cromwell's words. But there was no murdering bastard to take responsibility.

7

Beirut

The killing of seven hundred or more Palestinians in the Sabra and Shatila refugee camps in West Beirut took thirty-six hours. According to the Israeli inquiry that followed, the killings were done by members of an Israeli-allied Lebanese Christian militia. These militiamen were let into the camps on the night of Thursday, September 16, 1982, by the Israeli Defense Force (IDF). In the early morning of Saturday, September 18, they were ordered out. After initial doubt over which Christian militia was involved, attention focused on the role and responsibility of Israeli leaders. These leaders included present and future prime ministers. Individually no strangers to controversy, had they now come together to make Israel party to a pogrom?

The Christian militia had its own motivation for killing Palestinians. Less clear is why the Israeli leaders gave it the opportunity and the means to do the killing and why they did not bother to stop it. Was it an accumulation of errors or calculated passivity? Although the reporting and the Israeli inquiry provided a detailed account of what happened, we may never know for sure. The killing was organizationally removed from the IDF. In the investigations after the massacre, there were no defectors from the close-knit Israeli leadership group. The militia commander never informed. He died violently, in 2001.

A key issue is how information passed up the chain from agents to principals. The conventional complaint that supports a principal's claim of *can't control* is a lack of knowledge of the agent's activities. In this case, the lack of knowledge was self-inflicted. Individual IDF soldiers quickly pulled the alarm on the massacre, but there was no response from above. The transmission of reports of atrocity was interrupted at the rank of general hours after the start of the operation on Thursday evening. With unresponsive superiors, IDF soldiers leaked outside; they informed journalists, who contacted ministers. The reports got to the cabinet minister level at least by late Friday morning. But the

Israeli leaders refrained from ordering the militia out of the camps until Saturday morning.

When news reports revealed the massacre to the Israeli public and to the world, the democratic leaders of Israel did not respond in a principled way. They denied and delegated responsibility. After the initial denials failed to convince the world, Israeli leaders claimed to be deeply shocked by their agents' activities. Their excuse was a simple agency problem: they discovered that the private goals of the militia were at variance, to an extraordinary degree, with their own. The criminal intention and actions of the militia had been hidden from them. This seems a barely plausible excuse in light of the evidence of earlier massacres by this group and the information flowing to the Israelis as the killing happened. The government's opponents in the Israeli parliament, the Knesset, did not believe it at the time. Even Israel's commission of inquiry seemed to struggle to accept it. Yet, it was enough to maintain the presumption of political innocence. The Israeli cabinet survived the storm of outrage. It lost a minister—but he went in dismay at the activities of his colleagues and their support of the militia.

In the days following the atrocity, an account of what had happened was pieced together and reported in the Israeli and foreign press. The pressures of domestic and international outrage saw to the appointment of the commission of inquiry. Importantly, pressure came from members of the Israeli armed forces, themselves outraged at the massacre. As Hume says, that group has to be led by opinion. The inquiry delivered a detailed report of the event. We will see how accountability was delivered after we describe the event, likely motives, and the techniques of evasion.

To Cedared Lebanon

The Holocaust—and the awareness of what happened to Jews without a nation to secure—explains the priority Israel gives to national security But there is division over how security is best achieved. In Israel, decision making on national security has been a struggle between activists and moderates that stretches back to the country's beginnings. It has been a struggle between those who are willing to use violent strategies to defeat enemies, to let loose irregulars, settlers, and special units, and to lie for the good of the state and those who are reluctant or who refuse to do so. Israel's first prime minister, David Ben-Gurion, "believed that under certain circumstances, it was permissible to lie for the good of the state. But Moshe Sharett [the second Israeli prime minister] was astounded by his behaviour."[1] One Israeli scholar shows how this difference between activists and moderates influences their sensitivity to external audiences. Contrasting Israel's first two prime ministers, he says that "Ben-Gurion espoused a hawkish and activist approach to the Arab-Israeli conflict, while minimizing the prominence of external constraints. . . . Sharett represented a . . . more restrained line . . . attributing great importance to foreign powers, the United Nations and international public opinion."[2] At the core of their belief system, activists fear that not meeting violence with violence will be seen as weakness, leaving their own forces and people more vulnerable.[3] Moderates see no end to reprisal and retribution.

In the early 1980s, activists were ascendant. Prime Minister Menachem Begin's Likud Party held onto office in the June 1981 election. Support from three small religious parties gave Begin's new government a majority of one. Yitzhak Shamir continued at the foreign ministry, while Begin moved Ariel Sharon from agriculture to defense. Around him, he had assembled a small group committed to the use of force and deception in pursuit of national security. The group extended to the Israeli ambassador to the United States, Moshe Arens, and the chief of staff of the IDF, Rafael Eitan; according to Israeli journalists, it formed an "ideologically high-pitched quintet."[4] Prior to his move to defense, Sharon was involved in the Israeli government's June 1981 decision to bomb Iraq's nuclear plant.[5] That bombing clearly signaled to the Israeli electorate Likud's willingness to resort to military action. Although the United Nations Security Council passed a resolution condemning the action, it was received well at home. It may have given Begin and Likud a 4 percent boost in the opinion polls prior to polling day.[6] The electorate also knew of the Israeli government's close alliance with the Lebanese Christians and their Lebanese Forces or Christian Phalange militia. In the run-up to the 1981 election, the Israeli air force shot down two Syrian helicopters that were attacking the Christians. Begin's commitment to protect this militia from the Syrians became an election issue.[7] A consequence of these events was that the electorate could make an informed vote about Likud's choice of allies and its readiness to use force.

About a year after the election, on June 6 1982, Israel invaded Lebanon. The idea was to take the fight to the Palestine Liberation Organization (PLO). The trigger was the shooting of the Israeli ambassador in London three days earlier. Begin knew that the London gunman was not from the

PLO; he was from Abu Nidal's Iraqi-sponsored group. The prime minister did not share this information with his cabinet.[8]

The immediate invasion aim was the establishment of a twenty-five-mile northern buffer zone to prevent the PLO shelling and rocketing Galilee. But the IDF did not stop until it reached Beirut, an objective long on the mind of the defense minister.[9] In January 1982, Sharon had secretly visited Beirut and discussed with Phalangist commanders their contributions to an Israeli invasion and the areas around Beirut to be targeted.[10] Once in Beirut, Israeli leaders secured the withdrawal of PLO forces from Lebanon on September 1, 1982. They claimed that some two thousand "terrorists" remained in the refugee camps in West Beirut. Rather than use the IDF, Sharon chose the Phalange (Lebanese Forces) militia to go into the camps to "clean" them out. He made this choice despite the assassination of Bashir Gemayel, the leader of the Phalange and the president-elect of Lebanon. The day after the assassination, Sharon visited the Gemayel family to pay condolences. The day after that, the Phalange moved through IDF lines into the camps.

At 6 p.m. on Thursday, September 16, 1982, about 150 members of an intelligence unit of the Phalange militia entered the refugee camps.[11] In the fading evening light, the IDF lit the militia's way with flares. Tineke Uluf, a nurse in the camp, later suggested that the camp was as bright as a football stadium during a night game.[12] Early reports mentioned that Major Haddad's Army of Free Lebanon, a Christian force based in South Lebanon, participated in the operation, but these reports were found to be incorrect. Both the Phalange and Haddad's militia wore uniforms with a cedar tree emblem. One question raised by journalists was why, with Sharon's estimate that there were two thousand PLO fighters in the camps, the Israelis sent such a small unit against them?

At 7 p.m., Lieutenant Elul of the IDF was at the IDF forward command post. This post was about two hundred meters from the Shatila camp. The Israeli soldier was beside the Phalange communications equipment and the militia commander, Elie Hobeika. He overheard a Phalange officer ask Hobeika what was to be done to fifty women and children. The reply was, "This is the last time you're going to ask me a question like that, you know exactly what to do," accompanied by "raucous laughter" from the Phalange group at the command post.[13] Elul understood the reply to mean the killing of the women and children. He informed Brigadier General Amos Yaron. Yaron's testimony to the commission was that he understood Elul to be referring to forty-five dead terrorists, not to women and children.

The commission accepted the lieutenant's version.[14] Two hours into the thirty-six-hour operation, a Phalange officer told Israeli officers at the command post that approximately 300 (later changing his account to 120) people had been killed in the camps, including civilians.[15] At some point that night, after the killing of two militiamen, Hobeika asked the Israelis for better lighting. An Israeli officer was reported to have refused at first, as the Phalange had killed three hundred people. But he did provide more light.[16]

General Yaron held a briefing on the Thursday night that was recorded. An IDF intelligence officer began to describe the situation in the camps: "There are no terrorists there, in the camp . . . they have amassed women, children and apparently also old people . . . I also heard [from the Phalangists' liaison officer G] . . . 'do what your heart tells you, because everything comes from God.'" Yaron interrupted, "Nothing, no, no. I went to see him up top and they have no problems at all . . . . It will not, will not harm them." [17] The commission interpreted this interruption as an attempt to "play down the importance of the matter and to cut off the clarification of the issue."[18] It faulted the general for not acting on the various reports of the killing of women and children within the first two hours of the operation, for failing to convey the information to his superiors, for allowing the Phalange to send in reinforcements on Friday, and for not instituting any supervision of the Phalange in the camps.[19] Yaron was not the only senior Israeli commander found negligent. According to the commission, for the thirty-six-hour period that the militia operated in the camps, all the senior Israeli commanders involved with events in Beirut experienced problems fulfilling their duties.

On that same Thursday night, a cable on the killing of civilians was sent to IDF headquarters. The cable was distributed to twenty to thirty senior officers, including the chief of staff.[20] Even the pro-Likud newspapers later reported that ministers and generals knew of the massacre hours after it started but that they took no action until Saturday morning.[21] Sharon later claimed to have learned of the killing only on Friday evening. Meanwhile, earlier, at 7:30 p.m. on Thursday, the cabinet met in Jerusalem.

At that meeting, Sharon and Chief of Staff Eitan informed Prime Minister Begin and the cabinet that the militia was in the Palestinian refugees' camps in Beirut. Eitan spoke to the consequences of Bashir Gemayel's assassination. First, he said that it was possible that the Phalange leadership would disintegrate. He then said, "I can already see in their eyes what they are waiting for . . . now they have just one thing left to do, and that is revenge; and it will be terrible." His words prepared the cabinet for what happened. The plea was Henry V's before Harfleur. It was "vain command" over agents with "conscience as wide as hell." Eitan predicted a loss of control of the agents. The chief of staff continued, fatalistically, on the topic of revenge: "During Bashir's funeral Amin Jemayel, the brother, said 'revenge'; that is already enough. This is a war that no one will be able to stop."[22] It was phony fatalism. He and Sharon had set the fates of those in the camps in motion. If Eitan knew the unstoppable power of the private motivations of the Phalange, then why had he and Sharon let them into the camps? The director of military intelligence, who had opposed using the Phalange, left the meeting shortly after it started, with permission of the defense minister. Just one cabinet minister, Deputy Prime Minister David Levy, voiced alarm. He thought of the blame: "When I hear that the Phalangists are already entering a certain neighbourhood—and I know what the meaning of revenge is for them, what kind of slaughter. Then no one will believe we went in to create order there. . . . I think that we are liable here to get into a situation in which we will be blamed, and our explanations will not stand up."[23] No one at the meeting reacted to his remarks. Here was a moment, already too late for many civilians in the camps, when a more risk-averse prime minister might have asserted control. Begin chose not to.

Overnight, a note was left on a table in the IDF's Northern Command post in Beirut. It said that the Phalange had gone in and "butchered."[24] At the 8 a.m. Friday staff meeting at that post, there was no discussion of the reports of the killing of women and children. Later on Friday morning, Brigadier General Yaron told his superior, Major General Amir Drori, that he had a "bad feeling" and that the Phalangists were doing "an unclean mopping-up."[25] Drori ordered Yaron not to withdraw the militia but to stop them where they were. Drori phoned the chief of staff, saying the Phalangists might have "gone too far."[26] Reports of a massacre were accumulating.

That morning, IDF soldiers in a tank unit saw five women and children killed by the militia. The soldiers reported this killing. The battalion commander was reported to have said, "We know, it's not to our liking, and don't interfere."[27] Also that morning, an IDF captain told Lieutenant Colonel Reuven Gai, of the National Security Unit, that three hundred people had been killed in the camps. Gai phoned the personal aide to the minister of defense, Avi Dudai, and informed him of the reported killing.

Dudai later denied receiving the report.[28] Meanwhile, the Israeli journalist Ze'ev Schiff was phoned by an IDF source in the general staff in Tel Aviv and told that there was a "slaughter in the camps." Information on the massacre had now traveled from Beirut to Tel Aviv. It was not acted upon, but someone did try to get a response. One way around a block in the flow of information was to leak outside. With this information, the journalist, who later refused to disclose his source's name to the Kahan Commission, met with Minister of Communication Mordichai Zippori. Zippori contacted the foreign minister, Yitzhak Shamir, and told him of the "slaughter" by Phalangists. Shamir later testified to the commission that he could not remember mention of slaughter. He said that he thought the conversation was about IDF losses.[29] Schiff's information got no further than Shamir.

On Friday afternoon, the chief of staff arrived in Beirut and met with his generals. According to him, Drori and Yaron told him nothing about the slaughter. He then met with the Phalangists at 4 p.m. He approved of how the militia had conducted the operation, approved the provision of a tractor with the IDF marking removed, and told militia commanders they would have to leave by 5 a.m. Saturday as a result of "American pressure."[30] It turned out that the Phalange had enough tractors and did not use the Israeli one. The tractors were used to get rid of bodies.[31] The Phalangists finally left the camps at 8 a.m. on Saturday, having been ordered out by Yaron.

The Kahan Commission, which investigated what happened at the refugee camps, accepted an Israeli intelligence estimate of between seven hundred and eight hundred victims, but noted that Palestinian leaders numbered the victims in the thousands.[32] In its investigation, the commission documented a close relationship and repeated meetings between the militia leaders and Israeli leaders and commanders prior to the atrocity. It noted the Phalange's reputation as the perpetrator of earlier massacres of Druze and Palestinian noncombatants and its fresh desire for revenge. The commission and press reports established that some of Israel's top commanders and individual ministers knew of the massacre as it was happening and that participants in the Thursday evening cabinet discussion anticipated a slaughter. The challenge is to understand why, knowing what they knew, these politicians and commanders chose the Phalange and then why they stood by while the militia killed civilians.

Motives

The militia sought revenge. Massacre and reprisal were features of the Lebanese conflict. The Phalange's motives should be considered in that context, shaped by the immediacy of their leader's violent death. Chief of Staff Eitan suggested after the massacre that the Phalange commanders had simply lost control of their men, that the Phalange itself had an agency problem.[33] The reported exchanges between militia men in the camps and Phalange commanders show otherwise. From the evidence presented in the Kahan account, the commanders were in control and ordered the slaughter in language that everyone understood. Yet, if the Phalange militia members and their commanders shared private and revenge-inspired motivations for going into the refugee camps, why would the Israelis risk keeping such company?

Were the Israelis unaware of the risks? Did they know what motivated their allies? Although after the massacre Begin and Sharon expressed shock at the behavior of the Phalange, it seems safe to assume that they knew their ally at least as well as they knew their enemy. They had risked their own forces and had invested hundreds of millions of dollars in the alliance with the Christians. The chief of staff at the Thursday cabinet meeting was in no doubt of their murderous agenda. Yet, in the Israeli parliament, the Knesset, four days after the massacre, the Israeli leaders' excuse was that it had been beyond their imagination that the Phalange could behave in such a way. Such behavior belonged to an unfamiliar "world of dark instincts."[34] They made this claim even though that very specter had been raised in the cabinet discussion on Thursday, September 16, and despite the fact that it was a matter of public discussion and international diplomacy in the summer of 1982 that the militia posed a threat of atrocity to West Beirut. Prior to the massacre, the Christian militia's agenda was known to the news-reading public and to the U.S. envoy, Philip Habib. He had extracted a pledge from Phalange leaders that they would not enter West Beirut. An August 11 1982, article in the *Washington Post* described the fear of the Phalange among Beirut's Moslem population.[35] If the Israeli leaders were not reading American newspapers, their intelligence service had warned the prime minister and the defense minister of the chance of a massacre.[36] According to an Israel television report, the Israeli military knew the motives of its allies. IDF officers had known that one of the Phalange commanders had been involved in an earlier massacre of Palestinians at Tel Zaatar refugee camp in 1976, which had followed a massacre of Christians by Palestinians in January 1976 in the city of Damour. Another Phalange officer had warned IDF officers that militia members intended to kill.[37] On an individual level, Sharon knew the Phalange leaders from before the invasion. When he paid his respects to the Gemayel family on September 15, *Time* alleged, Sharon discussed the family's need for revenge (Sharon subsequently sued *Time* for libel).[38] The evidence of this discussion was allegedly detailed in a classified part of the Kahan Commission of Inquiry report, which was not released. At the trial, Sharon did not answer questions about the Phalange leader, Elie Hobeika. His aides, who accompanied him on the visit to the Gemayel family, did not testify. At the time, Israeli opposition politicians, the newspapers, and large sections of the public greeted with disbelief Sharon's claims that he could not have imagined that the Phalange could behave this way. The BBC reporter who broke the news of the massacre later put it this way: "In the late summer of 1982, there was nobody who did not know that the Lebanese Christian Maronites, as represented by the Phalangist party and its military wing, the Lebanese Forces, regarded the Palestinians as vermin to be exterminated. We all knew it and the Phalangists made no secret of it, even to Israeli officers."[39] Assuming that Israeli politicians and commanders were aware of the risks of an atrocity, who among them would have been willing to take the decision?

Despite its importance, it was a decision taken by Sharon without Begin's knowledge. The Kahan Commission is clear: "We may certainly wonder that the participation of the Phalangists in the entry to West Beirut and their being given the task of mopping up the camps seemed so unimportant that the Defense Minister did not inform the Prime Minister of it and did not get his assent for the decision."[40] What equipped Sharon to take this risk?

Individually, Sharon and his fellow activists Begin and Shamir could not be described as risk averse. They each had had their individual experience of dangerous operations, irregular units, and killing civilians. As a soldier, Sharon had led Unit 101, an out-of-uniform formation within the IDF that carried out a reprisal raid on the Jordanian border village of Qibya in October 1953, killing sixty-nine men, women, and children. In response to international criticism, Prime Minister Ben-Gurion denied IDF involvement in the attack and blamed it on settlers. Cabinet minister Moshe Sharett objected to the lie and said he would have been even more vociferous in his opposition if he had known the scale of the killing.[41] A friend wrote to Sharett describing Qibya as "this Dir [sic] Yassin under the auspices of our government, under its full responsibility, and executed by the IDF."[42] Deir Yassin was an Arab village near Jerusalem that was the site of a massacre in April 1948. Fighters from two irregular armed groups, the Irgun Zvai Leumi (IZL) and Avraham Stern's Lohamei Herut Israel (LHI), both of which fought against the Arabs and against the British during the Mandate, attacked the Arab village and killed civilians. Begin belonged to the Irgun, though he was not at Deir Yassin.[43] His foreign minister, Yitzhak Shamir, had been a member of the LHI. This group murdered the UN representative Count Bernadotte in September 1948.

Each of these actions had brought passing storms of protest. Looking back from their elevated status in 1982, these activists could see that the political damage had been limited. They had not been blown off career course. Now, together, in each other's company and running the country, they were no less willing to take the risks of a military operation, whether it was bombing a nuclear reactor in a foreign country or using groups with a reputation for committing war crimes. In Beirut, as commentators pointed out, Sharon may have discounted the risk. After all, he was delegating the action to a Lebanese group in a conflict zone where previous massacres and reprisals had not generated high levels of outrage. Like Lord Carver after Londonderry, he may have been surprised by the subsequent furor.

The use of a special or irregular unit was in keeping with past Israeli policy. It was not an innovative piece of decision making. Indeed, the innovation could be traced to the Mandate and a British officer who had set up "special night squads" to conduct violent reprisal raids on Arab villages. Leading units of British and Jewish soldiers, Captain Orde Wingate, later famed for his guerrilla operations against the Japanese, had conducted cross-border operations in the effort to suppress Arab insurgency in the late 1930s. Wingate's Jewish sympathies troubled his commanders, and he was sent home in 1939. But his use of special units and his improvised aggression may have left a mark. Some leading Israeli soldiers served with Wingate.[44] Furthermore, the relationship with the Lebanese Christians was itself a feature of Israeli strategic thinking that went back to the 1950s.

In 1955, a plan to invade Lebanon with militia participation was drawn up by General Moshe Dayan and Prime Minister David Ben-Gurion. Foreign Minister Sharett's view was "we'll get bogged down in a mad adventure that will only bring us disgrace."[45] But, in a secret meeting in 1978 and in later communications, Prime Minister Begin committed to aiding the Phalange. The preceding Labor government of Yitzhak Rabin had also allied with and armed the Christians.[46] Yet, there was some disagreement over the alliance. The two Israeli intelligence services had different views; the IDF's Military Intelligence tended to stress the dangers and costs of the relationship with the militia, whereas the Institute for Intelligence and Special Assignments (Mossad) saw the advantages. Mossad was responsible for managing the relationship with the Phalange and its commanders.[47] So Sharon's choice of the Phalange was not uninformed. Nor was it a new departure in Israeli defense policy. Using the militia would avoid IDF casualties.[48] That was a motive he offered.

Beyond the immediate gratification of revenge and reprisal, going into the camps offered longer term benefits for the Phalange. Their Lebanese dreamland was one with a different demography. The Palestinians might leave much as they had arrived—in fear. In 1948, Lebanon had offered Palestinians a refuge from massacre.[49] Oddly, in the cabinet discussion of the Beirut massacre, Begin recalled an earlier massacre. He remembered Deir Yassin, in April 1948, and used it to point out that he had not let blame fall on his men then. He would not let blame fall on Sharon for those killed in the refugee camps.[50] In Begin's memoirs, he described Deir Yassin as a formative event for the State of Israel. According to the journalist Anne Karpf, he said that Deir Yassin contributed decisively to the Israeli victory in the conflict, but this reference was later removed.[51] In the 1948 conflict, the "atrocity factor," or "calculated massacres," as the British commander of Jordan's Arab Legion called them, sparked an exodus from their towns and villages by hundreds of thousands of Palestinians. The Israeli historian Benny Morris says "it is possible to say that at least 55 per cent of the total of the exodus was caused by our [Haganah/IDF] operations and by their influence."[52] (Haganah was the Jewish defense force that operated during the Mandate.) The "atrocity factor" was "reinforced periodically during the months of fighting by other Jewish massacres."[53] These operations were conducted at a distance from policymakers. Importantly, the highly controversial expulsion of the Arabs could not be linked to the top leaders and to formal policy. It was not first discussed in cabinet meetings: "No expulsion policy was ever enunciated and Ben-Gurion always refrained from issuing clear or written expulsion orders; he preferred that his generals 'understand' what he wanted . . . while there was no 'expulsion policy', the July offensives were characterised by far more expulsions and, indeed, brutality than the first half of the war."[54] Echoing this earlier period, there is evidence that the Phalange wanted to expel the Palestinians from Lebanon using similar methods.

The sociologist James Ron examined the evidence for an exodus agenda. He provided a detailed comparative analysis of Israel's actions in Lebanon in 1982 and Serbia's in Bosnia ten years later, assessing their tacit plans and their use of militias.[55] There is evidence from the Kahan Commission report that Israeli intelligence officers were aware of the chance that the Phalange would commit a massacre, given an opportunity. Two months before the massacre, Mossad officials had met with Bashir Gemayel and heard that "the intention of this Phalangist leader was to eliminate the Palestinian problem in Lebanon when he came to power—even if that meant resorting to aberrant methods against the Palestinians in Lebanon. . . . Similar remarks were heard from other Phalangist leaders."[56] In addition, there were intelligence reports of "liquidations of Palestinians carried out by the intelligence unit of Elie Hobeika."[57] Hobeika's reasons for revenge were personal; he had lost his fiancée and family members in the Palestinian massacre at Damour.[58] Yet, the Israelis allowed this man and his unit to go into the refugee camps on the Thursday.

Although the Kahan Commission report contains information on the Phalange's intention of eliminating the Palestinian problem by aberrant methods, it did not pursue this line of inquiry. Others raised the issue at the time. The military correspondent for the Israeli newspaper *Haaretz*, Ze'ev Schiff, referred to a plan to massacre the Palestinians on September 28, 1982. An atrocity might provoke Palestinians to flee Lebanon for the safety of Syria.[59] The journalist and author Jonathan Randal says: "The operation served both Israeli and Lebanese Forces purposes. As the Israeli Army monthly Skira Hodechith was to note blandly by way of confirmation, the Lebanese Forces hoped to provoke 'the general exodus of the Palestinian population, first from Beirut, then from all over Lebanon.'"[60] In their book, the Israeli journalists Ze'ev Schiff and Ehud Ya'ari point out that destruction of the camps and deportation of Palestinians "was an objective that Bashir had proposed well before the war. Now Sharon was coaxing his senior officials to set their minds to the task."[61] Schiff and Ya'ari quote Sharon, at a July 11, 1982, Ministry of Defense meeting, saying, "It's in our interest to have [the Palestinians] move on elsewhere. The Lebanese will take care of that . . . to my mind, we mustn't leave a single terrorist neighbourhood standing."[62] As these authors suggest, Sharon tended to refer to the refugee camps as terrorist camps. This reference undermined the protected status of the civilians in these camps. Sharon returned to this theme in a meeting with Bashir Gemayel on September 12, 1982. At that point, he envisaged the Lebanese Army going into the camps with the Phalange militia, as well, but the Lebanese prime minister refused to allow the Lebanese Army to participate in the operation.[63] Bashir Gemayel spoke of replacing the camps with an "enormous zoo" and transporting the refugees to the Syrian border.[64] In short, there is evidence of an exodus agenda and an "atrocity factor" in Israel's actions, a record of past "understandings" that would put distance between Israeli leaders and atrocities, and evidence that Israeli officials had knowledge of the Christian militia's "aberrant methods."

The Kahan Commission dealt with the issue of the complicity of Israeli political and military leaders by simply declaring that there was no complicity: "We assert that in having the Phalangists enter the camps, no intention existed on the part of anyone who acted on behalf of Israel to harm the non-combatant population, and that the events that followed did not have the concurrence or assent of anyone from the political or civilian echelon."[65] Allowing the killing to continue was not evidence of "assent." In the wake of the massacre, some within the government were reported to hold Sharon responsible "for suppressing the information and allowing the killing to continue."[66] In contrast, the commission's view was that the killing was allowed to go on as a result of incompetence. The defense minister was faulted for the "blunders" of not foreseeing that a massacre was likely and not taking measures to reduce the danger of massacre. The commission noted that the choice to send in the militia was made "without consideration of the danger . . . [of] massacres and pogroms . . . when the reports began to arrive about the actions of the Phalangists . . . no proper heed was taken . . . no energetic and immediate actions were taken to restrain the Phalangists and put a stop to their actions."[67] Israel's indirect responsibility reflected the parallel incompetence of the military and of political leaders, according to the commission. For the commission, it was a *can't control* problem caused by the selfish motivations of the Phalange, compounded by incompetent monitoring and supervision by the Israeli leaders.

Not all accepted the commission's argument. A *New York Times* reporter in Beirut during the massacre, Thomas Friedman, later said "the Israelis knew just what they were doing when they let the Phalangists into those camps."[68] Prime Minister Begin seemed particularly indifferent to what his Christian allies did. He showed no interest in the activities of the Phalange and no interest in the warning offered by the deputy prime minister concerning their desire to slaughter, as the commission pointed out.[69] At the cabinet meeting following the massacre, Begin, apparently unmoved by what had happened in the territory his forces controlled, was reported to have said, "Goyim kill goyim, and they immediately come to hang the Jews."[70]

Audience Pressures

When the militia left, Red Cross representatives and journalists entered the camps. According to the commission, "a considerable number of the killed had not been cut down in combat but had been murdered, and that no few acts of barbarism had also been perpetrated. These sights shocked those who witnessed them; the reports were circulated by the media and spread throughout the world."[71] Pressure for accountability came from the international community, domestic public opinion, and, most significant, from among those serving in the IDF and the government. There were resignations by the energy minister, Yitzhak Berman, and the director of the Government Press Office, Zev Chafets (dissatisfied "with the way the Government has handled the massacre issue and because of the damage it has done to Israel's reputation"), among others.[72] It was IDF dissent that "finally roused the press to confront Sharon."[73] Army officers demonstrated outside the Defense Ministry. The brigadier general commanding the staff college resigned. Others threatened resignation and accused Sharon of lying.[74] Some one thousand soldiers petitioned the Ministry of Defense not to be ordered to Lebanon.[75] The government was losing agent confidence. Normally progovernment newspapers called for Sharon's resignation. The largest circulation newspaper, Yediot Ahronot, stated that "Government ministers and senior commanders already knew during the hours of Thursday night and Friday morning that a terrible massacre was taking place . . . and despite the fact that they knew this for sure, they did not lift a finger . . . until Saturday."[76] Crowds of demonstrators estimated at 400,000 strong chanted for Begin's resignation. In the Knesset, members heckled Sharon with shouts of lies and calls for his resignation and with the question "Who sent the murderers?"[77] Abroad, American Jews questioned the direction of Begin's government. The U.S. president was reported to have had enough. The magazine Newsweek, on October

4, 1982, declared Israel's special relationship with America in danger as a result of the massacre. It reported a dramatic decline in support for Israel, with some 70 percent of Americans viewing Israel as partially or very much responsible for the massacre.[78] How did Israeli leaders manage the pressure?

Techniques of Evasion: "The Hands of the IDF Are Clean."

All involved with the massacre denied responsibility. The Phalange's radio station "broadcast an emphatic denial that its forces had anything to do with the carnage in the camps."[79] On Saturday afternoon, the IDF spokesman's office denied knowledge of the massacre.[80] Israeli officials made the further claim that they had been stopped from creating order in West Beirut by U.S. and Lebanese politicians. The *Washington Post* was scathing about this excuse in its editorial the next morning.[81] The Foreign Ministry condemned the massacre and falsely claimed that the IDF had had to fight the Phalangists to drive them out.[82] The Kahan Commission noted the Israeli evasions and the Foreign Ministry and IDF communi-qués that stated or suggested that the IDF had not known that the militia was going into the camps or had not coordinated the operation.[83] Begin wrote a defiant letter to Senator Alan Cranston, a Democrat from California, who had publicly criticized Begin and Sharon over the massacre. Begin's letter, which was released by the Israeli embassy, presented the international response to the massacre as the latest in a well-known pattern of false accusations in Jewish history.[84] At the Sunday cabinet meeting, Eitan and Sharon said that "the Phalange command had simply lost control of its men," and they assured ministers that as soon as they knew what was happening, "they had intervened to drive the Phalangists out."[85] The cabinet released a communiqué regretting the harm to civilians done by a "Lebanese unit which had entered a refugee camp at a place distant from an I.D.F. position . . . immediately after learning about what had happened in the Shatila camp, the I.D.F. had put a stop to the murder of innocent civilians and had forced the Lebanese unit to leave the camp." It stated that any accusations that the IDF was responsible for the massacre was "a blood libel against the Jewish state and its Government." It claimed that there were two thousand terrorists in West Beirut, denied any blame, and stated that "no one will preach to us ethics and respect for human life."[86] The Israeli government bought advertising space for this statement in American newspapers. From denying that they had let the Phalange into the camps, Israeli leaders retreated to an emphasis on the presence of "terrorists" among the victims, delegation, and the Phalange's profoundly shocking display of goal variance. They were to add an ill-considered *tu quoque* swipe at their parliamentary opposition.

Begin addressed the Knesset on September 22. He mentioned blood libel and denied that the IDF was to blame.[87] He said there would be no resignations. He informed parliament that the only way to get rid of his government was through a vote of confidence or elections and warned the opposition that "just as you failed in the vote on the destruction of the nuclear reactor . . . so too you will fail in this incitement campaign."[88] When Sharon spoke to the Knesset, he asserted that "the hands of the IDF are clean. We have ethically used our weapons in this case. . . . It should be remembered that the Phalange is not the IDF. Its units and members are not subordinate to us and do not have to report to us."[89] He denied that he had command and denied knowledge of what they were doing: "we did not clearly know what was happening . . . since the Phalange rather than the IDF soldiers were inside the camps." Then he went on the offensive. He said, "I would like to ask you MK Shimon Peres: Another affair took place . . . when you were the Defence Minister. The affair in Tel Zaatar . . . . Did you not feel pangs of conscience? Where were the IDF officers on the day of the massacre at Tel Zaatar?"[90] This ploy was not successful. It suggested that there was previous IDF experience with the Phalange in the earlier massacre and served to annoy IDF commanders, as well as the opposition.

In an interview broadcast on Israeli television on September 24, 1982, Sharon again offered the familiar plea of the principal: he did not know what his agents would do when they got into the camps. The interviewer suggested that if he had "stood up before the nation and announced openly and publicly what had happened, the disaster that had occurred . . . would not an outburst of anger, a wave of hatred in the world, all the terrible deterioration we have been witness to during the week have been prevented?" Sharon replied that "we knew only later the size of the shock. We were also shocked. But actually we only knew later."[91] Sharon floated the idea that he might have made an error, stemming from his lack of knowledge of the Phalange, in delegating. He said to the Knesset that "we delegated to them . . . . We agreed to the entry of the Phalange to avoid risking our soldiers . . . even in our worst dreams, we did not conceive that the Phalangists would do the worst. . . . You may say that this was a miscalculation and a mistake in assessing the situation."[92] For a moment it seemed as though he might take some measure of responsibility. He then went on to say that the opposition had been prodding him to make the Phalange do something to liberate Lebanon, that the opposition had begun the relationship with the Phalange, and that the Middle East is a bad neighborhood (a well-worn justification used in the Gaza blockade action in 2010). At this stage, he would not even accept responsibility for an error. But Sharon's line of argument did anticipate the version of his responsibility adopted by the inquiry.

Facing continuing disbelief, threats of resignation from IDF officers and from ministers, and a massive public protest and after initially rejecting calls for an inquiry, Begin asked Supreme Court Justice Yitzhak Kahan to do an "administrative" investigation. But the prime minister had let time go by. He was losing control of the management of the blame. He faced international, domestic, and internal pressure for an impartial investigation. Heath, remember, appointed Widgery the day after the Londonderry massacre. In the Israeli case, the chief justice did not respond to Begin's initial request because there were formal requests for a more powerful and independent commission of inquiry. Ministers in Begin's coalition government threatened to resign and bring down the government if the prime minister did not agree to a judicial commission with a panel that could hear sworn testimony. Begin conceded. A three-person commission was set up, headed by Kahan, that also included fellow justice Aharon Barak and Major General Yona Efrat. It was a fact-finding inquiry, not a criminal court. Most sessions were held in private for reasons of national security. Like the Widgery tribunal of inquiry, there was no direct reporting and public comments during the investigation.[93] So the government had some time to continue to try to manage the blame.

Consequences

The massacre raised two key issues for Israel: the decision to send the Phalange into the camps and the lack of response to reports of atrocity. The Kahan Commission delivered its report on February 8, 1983. It cited the "English" doctrine of ministerial responsibility and considered the actions of both political and military leaders.[94] According to the commission, the decision to use the militia was justifiable if it was done to save IDF lives and if proper measures had been taken to safeguard the civilians.[95] This finding does not fit easily with the material presented in the commission's report, which detailed the militia's poor combat morality, their rage, and the likely control problems. The commission report itself cited "experienced intelligence officers" who said that if "the Phalangists had an opportunity to massacre Palestinians, they would take advantage of it."[96] The information suggested that the Christian militia was simply too dangerous to use. But, to the commission, it implied a need to take appropriate measures to monitor and supervise its use.

Once the militia was in the camps, officials had failed to respond to reports of atrocity. Individually, the commission faulted ministers and commanders for indifference, insensitivity, and incompetence. It did not accept the claim that the slaughter was unforeseeable. The prime minister was blamed for his indifference. After he was told of the entry of the Phalangists, the prime minister "showed absolutely no interest in their actions in the camps. . . . The Prime Minister's lack of involvement in the entire matter casts on him a certain degree of responsibility."[97] The commission faulted the defense minister for not informing the prime minister and for negligence in not putting supervisory measures in place. It noted his close relationship with the Phalange commanders and suggested that "no prophetic powers were required" to anticipate what the Phalange would do. In choosing to use the militia, Sharon should have given a "clear and explicit order barring harm to civilians." The report concluded that he made a "grave mistake" and that his "blunders constitute the non-fulfilment of a duty."[98] The foreign minister's mistake was not acting on the message of slaughter delivered by his cabinet colleague Zippori. Of the politicians, the severest criticism was reserved for the defense minister. Sharon was the only minister asked by the commission to "draw the appropriate personal conclusions . . . with regard to the manner in which he discharged the duties of his office."[99]

Chief of Staff Eitan was faulted for not anticipating the danger of massacre, for not taking measures to monitor the Phalange, for not raising the issue of slaughter with the Phalangists in his meeting with them on Friday, and then not ordering them out. His going along with the Phalange was attributed to his "fear of offending their honor." The commission also faulted him for ordering that a tractor be given to the Phalange for their operations. His conduct amounted to "a breach and dereliction of duty."[100] Other senior officers were criticized for allowing in Phalange reinforcements on Friday and not monitoring what they were doing. In discussing the role of Major General Drori, the commission noted that the militia's request for tractors signaled that something was wrong and his "refraining from any action regarding the danger facing the civilian population from the Phalangist forces" amounted to a breach of duty.[101] General Yaron's error in reacting to the information he received was evaluated similarly.[102] The serial negligence of the military commanders in the chain of command combined with the politicians' indifference and blunders together constituted what the commission saw as Israel's indirect responsibility.

The chief of staff was due to complete his service in two months, so the commission did not recommend further sanction against him. There was to be no sanction for Major General Drori. Brigadier General Yaron was barred from serving as a field commander for three years. The director of military intelligence, Yehoshua Saguy, received the harshest treatment from the commission. The commission recommended that he not continue in office and faulted him for, among other things, not responding to the report he had received on Friday morning that three hundred people had been killed. In contrast to Mossad officers and unlike Sharon, he had always been concerned about the use of the Phalange and had not wanted anything to do with the operation in Beirut. In August, he had warned the defense minister that "the Phalange will find a way to . . . settle old scores . . . every paper in the world will be there to cover the extermination. . . . How can we operate without being tainted?"[103] He knew that Sharon had backed Mossad's approach, not his. He testified to the commission that once he knew the militia was in the camps, despite his opposition, he felt there was little more he could do. In the commission's assessment, the fact that the director felt he would not be listened to by his superiors was not a justification for doing nothing.[104] Knowing that his superiors wanted to use the Phalange, he seemed to be saying that it was pointless to pass information of Phalange killing to them; nobody would pay attention. What his attitude and his behavior implied about the intentions of his superiors is not addressed by the commission. So there is some irony, as well as tragedy, to this story. Of the military men, the man who opposed using the Phalange received the most severe of the commission's recommended punishments. In contrast, the report found no serious fault with the head of Mossad.

The victims thought that Begin should have been punished and considered the report a whitewash.[105] The activists thought it harsh. Their earlier experience with storms of outrage did not prepare them for the recommendation that Sharon should resign. So what legal, political, reputational, and personal penalties followed the massacre in Beirut?

Even if one thinks the commission's interpretation of unintentional negligence is a safe one, the consequences were light. As the BBC reporter who originally broke the news of the massacre put it, "it was either criminal negligence on the part of Israeli commanders . . . or deadly connivance."[106] There were no legal proceedings in Israel. If the killing was the result of the Phalange's betrayal of the mission that the Israeli leaders had given them, as the defense minister protested, then Israel had an obligation to punish its militia agents. But lines of accountability were less clear than if the militia were part of the IDF; instead, they were based and operated in Lebanon. No Phalangist was held to account. According to Major General Drori, the militiamen were puzzled about why the Israelis were upset with them.[107] Hobeika remained in his post. His associates claimed that he was in Finland at the time of massacre.[108] Two decades on, a Belgian court started war crimes proceedings against Ariel Sharon, by then Israel's prime minister. Hobeika said that he would testify in Belgium. Two days after that announcement, he was killed by a car bomb.[109] According to the journalist Robert Fisk, Hobeika would have provided evidence that he believed pointed directly to Sharon's responsibility for the massacre.[110] Belgium later retreated from its universal competence to try war crimes.

Of the military men, Thomas Friedman, who won the Pulitzer Prize for his coverage of the massacre, said "Rafael Eitan . . . who had lied to dozens of world newsmen when asked if Israel had sent the Phalangists in, was allowed to finish his tour of duty with dignity and was then elected to the Israeli parliament. Brigadier General Yaron . . . was then promoted to major general. . . . An investigation which results in such 'punishments' is not an investigation that can be taken seriously."[111] The director of military intelligence did resign from his post, but the army kept him on with an assignment to "unspecified duties."[112] He was elected to the Knesset in 1988.

The political consequences have been described as follows:

In 1982, Menachem Begin's government was hounded from power after an Israeli judicial committee concluded that Begin and Ariel Sharon, his defense minister, bore indirect responsibility for the Sabra and Shatila massacres. These cases can hardly be said to be victors' justice. Rather, they suggest that a country's norms can be so sincerely held that it will put its *own* soldiers and leaders on trial even in times of national upheaval.[113]

Israeli institutions did provide some compensation for their leaders' opportunistic efforts to evade blame. Important questions were raised in parliament. The Commission of Inquiry provided an account of what had happened in the camps and was willing to assess leaders' responsibilities and found members of the government indirectly responsible. But the government did not lose power in 1982. It did not lose a vote of confidence or an election.

In 1983, Sharon did lose his department after the Commission of Inquiry's report was released. But he did not lose his seat in the cabinet. Prior to the inquiry, Sharon had made a promise that "I do believe in ministerial responsibility and I will certainly respect any decision of any committee that is set up."[114] But ministerial responsibility operates in Israel much as it does in Britain. It is consistent with Finer's analysis of that doctrine and his observation about reappointment. After a period of indecision, Sharon was removed from Defense, yet continued in the cabinet as minister without portfolio.[115] His fellow activist, Arens, then replaced him at Defense. Sharon's assessment was "there was a reshuffle of portfolios, and that's the end of the problem. I am still in the cabinet. Begin did not fire me."[116] As far as he was concerned, he had not been removed from government office.

Nor was Begin removed from office. He continued as prime minister and left that office at a time of his choosing. He submitted his resignation in September 1983 citing health and personal reasons after the death of his wife.[117] The Israeli journalists Schiff and Ya'ari say, "aides say that just before announcing his intention to retire in midterm, the prime minister had been engrossed in reading minutes of the General Staff meetings held in May and June 1982."[118] According to the historian Martin Gilbert, Begin's health and mood were affected by criticism of the war: "with continuing criticism of that war and following his wife's death, Begin fell into a sharp decline. On leaving office, he became a virtual recluse."[119] Begin's foreign minister, Yitzhak Shamir, who was also criticized in the inquiry, became prime minister. Ariel Sharon continued to hold office in Begin's and Shamir's governments.

Schiff and Ya'ari's assessment is as follows: "And when it was all over and the terrible truth had come out, almost everyone scrambled to pass the blame as far as it would go rather than ask themselves what went wrong."[120] At the top, there was some form of self-imposed personal accountability, at least from the accounts of the change in Begin's mood. He is reported to have had anxiety related to the invasion and the management of the blame for the massacre. When the commission delivered its report, Begin confessed to a sleepless night worrying about what to do with Sharon.[121] As for Sharon, his clean hands claim suggested that remorse was not on his mind. He was litigious not sleepless. He brought a libel suit against *Time* in the United States over its claim that he had discussed the need for revenge with the Gemayels. The jury considered the reporting defamatory but not intentionally so.[122] If continuing one's political career is an indication, the reputations of the activists survived the outrage. By that measure, the management of the blame was a success. Despite the intense pressure from some officials and soldiers, the domestic and international media, and the large public demonstration, Israeli public opinion remained broadly supportive. During the initial outrage over the massacre, the percentage of Israelis satisfied with Begin's performance did decline, but from 82 percent to 72 percent. Although there was intense criticism from some in the media and the IDF, he retained broad public support for his leadership. Even Sharon retained a surprisingly strong 64 percent favorable rating in the polls.[123] As already noted, both Shamir and Sharon went on to serve as prime minister. The excuse the activists offered—that they couldn't have imagined the Phalange doing what they did—seems barely plausible. But they stuck to it, and they stuck together, and that provided sufficient insulation from the democratic institutions and processes of accountability.

8

Baghdad

In 2004, the U.S. secretary of defense, Donald Rumsfeld, faced questions about the treatment of captured Iraqis. Secretary Rumsfeld was due to testify before a U.S. Senate committee about his management of what went on at Baghdad Central Correctional Facility, Abu Ghraib. It was a news story that shocked Americans and dominated headlines around the world. One might spare a thought, as no doubt the secretary did, for the loss of American lives, for what was at stake in the new kind of warfare, for the responsibility of putting young soldiers in such a difficult place, and for the critical need for "actionable intelligence." Public self-recrimination might seem an indulgence at such a time. A Princeton University graduate, a Navy pilot, a former congressman, a member of President Nixon's administration, and a two-time defense secretary, Rumsfeld had had a lifetime's preparation for high-stakes political moments. But he was at the mercy of events and needed answers.

The secretary denied any connection between government policies and the abuse of prisoners at Abu Ghraib. He pointed to control problems, to deviant agents, and to the pictures from the prison. One of those photographed showed a high school graduate and former employee of a chicken-processing plant, Specialist Lynndie England. Unhelpfully, she had claimed that the abuses had been ordered, that useful information had resulted, and that she and her fellow soldiers had not realized that they were doing anything they were not supposed to do.[1] Prior to the scandal, in December 2003, she had confided in her divorce lawyer that officers were aware of what she and her fellow soldiers were doing.[2] At her court-martial, the court did not allow testimony from an army officer about patterns of abuse. The court's view was that what happened elsewhere did not reduce her culpability.[3] Secretary Rumsfeld agreed that that was where the blame for the abuse should fall.

The Events at Abu Ghraib

General Antonio Taguba was the first to investigate the abuses at the prison at Abu Ghraib, committed in the last three months of 2003. His internal report found that there was systematic, intentional, and illegal abuse of detainees by the military police, by military intelligence officials, and by private contractors. The soldiers and contractors committed "numerous incidents of sadistic, blatant and wanton criminal abuses," including: "punching, slapping, and kicking . . . forcing naked male detainees to wear women's underwear . . . arranging naked male detainees in a pile and jumping on them . . . writing 'I am a Rapest'[sic] on the leg of a detainee alleged to have forcibly raped a fifteen-year old fellow detainee and then photographing him naked . . . placing a dog chain . . . around a naked detainee's neck and having a female Soldier pose for a picture . . . using military working dogs (without muzzles) to intimidate and frighten detainees and in at least one case of biting and severely injuring a detainee." Beyond this, the Taguba Report found credible evidence of other acts, including "threatening detainees with a charged 9mm pistol . . . threatening male detainees with rape . . . sodomizing a detainee with a chemical light and perhaps a broomstick."[4]

One difficulty with explaining what went on at Abu Ghraib as individually initiated rather than state-initiated violations was that the Taguba Report, like Lynndie England, linked the abuse to interrogation practices. Ill-treating detainees was expected to produce information on the Iraqi insurgency. The report stated that U.S. interrogators "actively requested that MP guards set physical and mental conditions for favorable interrogation of witnesses."[5] Sergeant Javal Davis said that military intelligence personnel complimented one of those convicted of abuse, Corporal Charles Graner: "Good job, they're breaking down real fast. They answer every question. They're giving out good information . . . and keep up the good work. Stuff like that."[6] The report noted that the relevant units of the 800th Military Police brigade had little training in Geneva Convention requirements and that the commander, Brigadier General Janis Karpinski, did not maintain discipline.[7] The Taguba Report commended three U.S. personnel for refusing to participate in and for reporting the abuse: William J. Kimbro, a U.S. Navy dog handler, refused to participate in the abuse; Joseph Darby, MP, provided evidence of abuse to the authorities; and Lieutenant David O. Sutton intervened to stop the abuse.[8] At Abu

Ghraib, it was some of those at the bottom of the chain of command who demanded monitoring and supervision, whereas those at the top did not respond to the reports, for example, of the International Committee of the Red Cross. Dissenting opinions about the legality of the abuse within the Department of Defense and other agencies were ignored by political and military leaders.

The abuse of detainees by U.S. forces began before and continued after the scandal at Abu Ghraib broke. One 2006 study found 330 cases of abuse committed by U.S. security forces or civilian contractors in Iraq or Afghanistan and at Guantanamo. These cases implicated about six hundred individuals.[9] The abuse included the sorts of things described by the detainee at Abu Ghraib but extended to murder.

Before Abu Ghraib was a worldwide scandal, there were authoritative news reports of abuse by U.S. security forces. For example, in December 2002, on the front page of the *Washington Post*, Dana Priest and Barton Gellman described the abuse done to detainees in Afghanistan. They itemized sleep deprivation, hooding, forced stress positions, the use of female interrogators, beatings, secret detention centers, and the rendition of detainees to the custody of governments that practice torture. One official suggested that it was likely that human rights were violated in the process.[10] The *Post* reporters documented statements by national security officials justifying violence against detainees. They had the story a year and a half before Abu Ghraib, but they lacked the pictures. Only because of the outrage that followed the release of the Abu Ghraib photos did political and military leaders face serious pressure for accountability.

The evidence of abuse from Abu Ghraib implicated individuals and policymakers. It fitted a wider pattern of abuse and was consistent with a strategic narrative emphasizing the use of violence and humiliation to extract information.

Motives

The abusers at Abu Ghraib said they acted within the approved procedures for the treatment of detainees. The relaxed way they went about their duties suggests that they did not anticipate correction or punishment. At the same time, they appeared to get private enjoyment from what they were doing; later, Lynndie England said that she had to be coaxed to smile for the camera. If the evidence for the participants' willingness is not incontrovertible, it was good enough for the court-martial to establish that the individual agents had a selfish motive for the violations.

An agent's selfishness does not preclude a leader's complicity. The leader may want the violation for strategic reasons, whether or not the agent gets private gratification from it. He may order the agent to carry out a violation that the agent wants to do. Alternatively, he may know the agent's inclinations and establish a "permissive environment," a term used by one of the inquiries into Abu Ghraib, as long as the violations are perceived to offer strategic benefits. The *won't control* leader refuses to control the agent acting on a selfish motive.

In occupied Europe during World War II, there were both agents who committed violations for policy or strategic reasons and agents who did so for personal and sadistic reasons. Presumably, the Nazis sought the strategic goals of intimidating the local population or extracting information, and the motivation of individual agents was not likely to be a concern. Yet, ultimately, as the group at Abu Ghraib found out, having personal motives can make a vast difference to the agents. For Danish citizens who collaborated with the Nazis, their individual motives were relevant to their punishment: "Those who mistreated or killed individuals for personal motives or pique were less likely to get the death penalty than those who did so to serve German interests."[11] In Denmark, treason was more serious than perversion. In Italy, it was the other way around. "Bestial insensibility" received punishment, rather than torture "for intimidatory purposes" such as "electric torture on the genitals applied through a field telephone."[12] America's view, with its hard line on "bad apples" and perversion, was nearer to that of Italy than to that of Denmark.

The important point is that the bestial goals of the agents may align with, rather than conflict with, the declared or undeclared goals of policymakers. President George W. Bush and his senior officials, for reasons of national security, approved the use of techniques that Lynndie England and her unit appeared to enjoy. The administration authorized these measures in order to deal with a security threat to America. For the Bush administration, fighting its worldwide war against terror, obtaining intelligence was a strategic priority. Al Qaeda had demonstrated its willingness to use any means to attack innumerable civilian and military targets. The scale of the insurgency in Iraq made the gathering of intelligence information of vital importance. The administration specifically linked the harsher treatment of detainees to its strategic goal of obtaining that intelligence.

The administration prepared the political context for taking these repressive measures. It had to explain to the public the need to relax conventional standards and the rule of law. Marking the new political context, on February 7, 2002, President Bush declared that the Geneva Convention did not apply to all detainees. His officials claimed that, under the Convention against Torture, the United States was allowed to utilize all but the most extreme measures on detainees. The Iraq conflict was supposed to be covered by the Geneva Convention, yet that conflict was defined as part of the war on Al Qaeda. Despite its public declarations, the administration developed a policy of using the interrogation techniques tested in Afghanistan and at Guantanamo on the detainees it held in Iraq.

To secure the cooperation of its agents, the administration also prepared the legal context. It had to eliminate the legal risks for abusers and assure military and security personnel that their actions would carry no penalty. To get the agents to cooperate, they lined up supporting opinions from government lawyers for the range of harsh techniques to be employed. In 2002, Assistant Attorney General Jay Bybee approved the CIA's use of a variety of techniques on Abu Zubaydah, a high-ranking member of Al Qaeda. The techniques ranged from the mild "attention grasp" of the detainee's collar, to exploiting fears, as with the "insects placed in confinement box" technique, to waterboarding. Bybee's memo was specific. Interrogators should not, for example, inform Zubaydah that the insect was in the box and should not "lead him to believe that any insect is present which has a sting that could produce severe pain or suffering or even cause his death."[13] The CIA's request to use these techniques drew on the experience of the Survival, Evasion, Resistance, Escape (SERE) training for U.S. personnel, which exposed trainees to unlawful techniques that had been used against captured Americans in other wars.

The lawyer for the CIA's Counterterrorist Center, Jonathan Fredman, briefed Guantanamo staff on October 2, 2002: "Severe physical pain [is] described as anything causing permanent damage to major organs or body parts. Mental torture [is] described as anything leading to permanent, profound damage to the senses or personality. . . . It is basically subject to perception. If the detainee dies you're doing it wrong." Fredman advised against videotaping interrogations, as "even totally legal techniques look ugly." At the same meeting, the Guantanamo judge advocate, Diane Beaver, suggested that the Guantanamo staff "curb harsh operations while the [International Committee of the Red Cross] is around." Fredman informed the staff that "when the ICRC has made a big deal about certain detainees, the DoD [Department of Defense] has moved them away. . . . Upon questioning from the ICRC . . . the DoD's response has repeatedly been that the detainee merited no status under the Geneva Convention."[14] In short, the agents' Machiavellian legal brief was to be cruel and use discretion. The advice seemed to be do not get caught with a body, a visual record, or by the external monitors.

The Department of Defense developed three categories of increasingly severe but "legally available" interrogation techniques to use on detainees at Guantanamo.[15] These techniques included category one techniques such as direct questioning and yelling; category two techniques such as isolation, forced stress positions, use of phobias such as fear of dogs, and forced grooming; and category three techniques that required approval by the Commanding General, such as the use of scenarios to make the detainee believe death or severe pain was likely for himself or his family and simulated drowning. The secretary trimmed the list of techniques for use at Guantanamo, as initially advised by the General Counsel of the Department of Defense in a memo of November 27, 2002.[16] The secretary later revised his blanket approval of the four-hour standing stress position, stating that he would review written requests for additional techniques.

Rumsfeld set up a Detainee Interrogation Working Group. On January 24, 2003, this group recommended the use of the "deprivation of clothing to put detainees in shameful, uncomfortable situations, food deprivation, sensory overload . . . controlled fear through the use of muzzled, trained, military working dogs."[17] In February 2003, the administration ruled these techniques legal for use at Guantanamo and in Afghanistan. (The use of dogs was part of the standard operating procedure used by conventional forces and the Special Mission Unit Task Force in Afghanistan.)[18] The Department of Defense simply transferred the techniques to Iraq. The Special Mission Unit (SMU) Task Force in Iraq, set up in February 2003, just before the invasion, "obtained a copy of the interrogation SOP [standard operating procedure] in use by the SMU personnel in Afghanistan, changed the letterhead, and adopted the SOP verbatim."[19] The administration made a public distinction between Afghanistan and Iraq with regard to the applicability of the Geneva Conventions. From the top of the chain of command to the guards, interrogators, and detainees, this became a distinction without much difference.

In March 2003, the legal counsel for the Department of Justice, John Yoo, restated the 2002 position of his office that torture meant pain at "organ failure" levels and that general criminal statutes, including prohibitions on torture, did not apply to military personnel during armed conflict.[20] The Yoo memo was withdrawn in June 2004, after Abu Ghraib. An August 2003 memorandum from General Ricardo Sanchez's Iraq headquarters stated that "the gloves are coming off regarding these detainees" and that a military intelligence officer "has made it clear that we want these individuals broken."[21] ("Gloves off" was the euphemism of the day. A CIA official at the September 26, 2001, hearing of the House and Senate intelligence committees talked about the gloves coming off after 9/11.)[22] The August 2003 memorandum sought suggestions for possible interrogation techniques. Among the suggestions submitted, Thomas Ricks recounts, was the 4th Infantry Division's advocacy of "low-voltage electrocution."[23] Electrocution is fixed in our memory of Abu Ghraib by the image of the hooded man, standing on a box with wires dangling, in fear of electrocution if he fell off. The Senate Committee report concluded that Sanchez's policies and the confusion about authorization of military working dogs and stress positions "were a direct cause of detainee abuse in Iraq."[24] Surprised by the sudden ferocity of the insurgency in the summer of 2003, Sanchez placed a high priority on obtaining human intelligence.

A team of interrogators who had served at the Bagram Airfield detention unit in Afghanistan were transferred to Abu Ghraib in the summer of 2003. Two men had died while in custody at the airfield. Reports stated that one had been tied by his arms to the ceiling and the other had been beaten.[25] After arriving at Abu Ghraib, a member of the team submitted a proposal to use techniques used in Afghanistan and authorized by the defense secretary.[26]

Major General Geoffrey Miller visited detention facilities in Iraq from August 31 to September 10, 2003.[27] About a month before the abuse captured in the photos, he told personnel at one facility that they were "running a country club" and that they need to "GTMO-ize their facility."[28] Miller and his team from Guantanamo visited Abu Ghraib over a period of three days. One member of Miller's team described his conversation with the head of intelligence at Abu Ghraib, Colonel Thomas M. Pappas, who said, "I mean you use stress positions, dogs, nakedness . . . the concept of the conversation was as you develop these techniques, talk to the interrogators."[29] This account suggests that there was a degree of improvisation and that "development" of technique was encouraged.

Colonel Pappas talked about dogs with Major General Miller. Miller said they were effective in "setting conditions for interrogations." Pappas says that during his visit Miller met the interrogators and suggested that they be more aggressive without being precise about the method to be employed.[30] Officers at Abu Ghraib said Miller had advised them that Arabs were scared of dogs and that dogs had a "tremendous affect." A month or so after Miller's visit, the dogs and their handlers arrived, and "abusing detainees with dogs started almost immediately."[31] This senior commander's visit linked Iraq to central policy.

The CIA had its own rules at Abu Ghraib. It contributed to the repertoire of techniques used within the prison's walls. The Jones/Fay Report on Abu Ghraib, a report ordered by Lieutenant General Ricardo Sanchez to investigate the abuse and the involvement of members of the Military Intelligence Brigade at the prison and released in August 2004, claimed that the CIA's techniques and methods contaminated the atmosphere and Sanchez's own soldiers' behavior.[32] It was helpful to Sanchez to shift some of the responsibility to agents outside his control. Yet, however blame was to be distributed across agencies, it was clear, at least to a Senate committee, that it did not belong to those at the bottom alone. In November 2008, as President Bush was preparing to move out of the White House, the U.S. Senate Committee on Armed Services finished its report on the treatment of detainees. It concluded:

The abuse of detainees at Abu Ghraib in late 2003 was not simply the result of a few soldiers acting on their own. Interrogation techniques such as stripping detainees of their clothes, placing them in stress positions, and using military working dogs to intimidate them appeared in Iraq only after they had been approved for use in Afghanistan and at GTMO. Secretary of Defense Donald Rumsfeld's December 2, 2002 authorization of aggressive interrogation techniques and subsequent interrogation policies and plans approved by senior military and civilian officials conveyed the message that physical pressures and degradation were appropriate treatment for detainees in U.S. military custody.[33]

In other words, what happened at Abu Ghraib was not a simple agency problem.

Audience Pressures

The 2002 *Washington Post* article by Dana Priest and Barton Gellman on abuse in Afghanistan raised the "plain English" issue and the democratic accountability for the abuse. The article questioned whether the government was being clear about what policies it was pursuing and whether the public would care. The reporters noted that, despite public statements against torture, U.S. officials were justifying the violent treatment of prisoners and that they had confidence it would have public support.[34] The confidence seemed justified.

Neither the electorate nor Congress restrained the Bush administration. The electorate had an opportunity to do so in 2004 and did not take it. Despite the headline-dominating interruption of Abu Ghraib in the midst of the election campaign, there were other issues being contested. In November, George Bush won reelection. Members of Congress did not sense sufficient concern among their constituents to move them to push for restraint. When Bush officials started talking about methods of interrogation and gloves coming off, Priest said that "there was nobody I could find in Congress who said, well, wait a minute. Maybe you should not do that." Speaking to an audience at the New York University School of Law in September 2004, she said that administration officials asked members of the U.S. Congress "do we have the go-ahead—never, never using the word torture—to use extraordinary interrogation techniques. They not only got a free hand, but many members of Congress who were on those oversight committees said yes, and make sure that you are pressing as hard as you can. And the gloves are off."[35] This journalist concluded that accountability was most likely to be delivered by the legal system: "If there is one way that the chain of command at DoD will ever be revealed, it is through, I believe, the discovery method, through the defense of the troops at Abu Ghraib, who have been charged with committing crimes."[36] She made this remark to an audience of lawyers before the Abu Ghraib courts-martial.

Dana Priest said to her law school audience that "it is hard to believe that we are sitting here talking about torture . . . it is [a] very strange, topsy-turvy time for me, as an American and as a journalist."[37] The grip on values of political leaders, like that of the rest of us, is unlikely to depend solely on internalization or strength of character. To paraphrase George Eliot, our behavior is influenced strongly by what we think others expect of us. In this sense, our "rectitude" depends on our audience. We are lucky if we get an audience that demands our best. Why did the president's domestic audience not demand his best? Americans are schooled in self-evident truths about all humanity deserving protection from abuse and having rights to life, liberty, and the pursuit of happiness. What suddenly loosened their adherence to basic American values and principles?

The administration's decision to take its gloves off was defended by some distinguished public intellectuals and opinion leaders. The *Newsweek* writer Jonathan Alter considered, in November 2001, what sorts of measures might be effective. He was in favor of rendition and could live with the hypocrisy of getting others to do unpleasant things for you.[38] Mark Bowden, in a long article in the *Atlantic Monthly* in October 2003, argued for the use of coercive measures to extract information from important detainees. Alan Dershowitz, professor of law at Harvard University, with his ticking-time-bomb scenarios, was the most consistent public advocate of torture.

It is a compelling argument. Imagine having to balance an individual's discomfort against a nuclear or biological threat to a community. Beyond the immediate importance of safeguarding the community, we have freedom thanks to the community that we hope to save, for our freedom is dependent on the infrastructure of laws and enforcement capabilities that exists within that community and, more informally, on patterns of interactions and beliefs that have developed within it. The legal infrastructure and the cultural support for freedom would not exist without it. Preservation of the community is a condition for our future enjoyment of individual freedom; circumstances that pose a serious threat to the community may justify resort to the torture of an individual, either here or abroad. By adding judicial approval to the application of torture, we avoid being barbarians.

Those on the other side point out that, legally, torture is against international law. Prudentially, if we torture, we make it easier for the enemy to do it to us if the situation is reversed in the future. Practically, the information extracted by torture is of poor quality. Politically, the effect of the use of torture on public support in minority or occupied communities is devastating. Morally, this infectious practice spreads out to lesser threats and corrupts the individuals, institutions, and professions that deliver torture. The political philosopher Steven Lukes argues that torture cannot be "rendered liberal-democratically accountable."[39] Under extreme and imminent threat, perhaps we can rely on individual officials who are willing to take it on themselves to violate the prohibition against torture. When challenged on this point, Lukes asserts the strictest position on prohibition.[40] One way to view the practical and political issues related to torture is as a trade-off between information and motivation: the information gained has to be balanced against the motivation the abuse supplies to the opposition. Whatever the winning position, the debate itself brings torture into the realm of available policy options.

In the 2004 election campaign, the Democratic Party provided little leadership to the American public on this issue. Between April and October 2004, the campaign of the Democratic presidential candidate, John Kerry, produced more than seventy advertisements. These advertisements focused primarily on domestic issues and the candidate's credentials. Kerry campaigned on the high costs of health care in America, Republican tax incentives for exporting jobs, and the personal attributes that suited him for the job (combat veteran, tough prosecutor, man of faith, husband, father, hunter, and pilot). When Iraq received attention, it was for the costs of the war in American lives and dollars, the need to build international alliances, and the administration's shifting reasons for the war. The advertisements did not assess the cost in values abandoned of the redefinition of torture and the treatment of detainees at Abu Ghraib and elsewhere.[41] The point is not that a defense of decent treatment would have changed the course and outcome of the election. Although Abu Ghraib occurred during the campaign, if the Democrats had made the abuse a campaign issue, Republicans would likely have responded by accusing the Democrats of not "supporting our troops." It might have worsened the Democrats' position with the electorate. The point is that, notwithstanding the conventional assumption about accountability in democracies, the process of democratic competition in America did not hold Bush and his senior officials to account for their radically new policy of repression.

The lack of leadership on this issue may help explain why American public opinion is not as strongly opposed to torture as is public opinion in other long-term democracies. In the summer of 2006, the BBC commissioned a twenty-five-country survey on torture. The survey items captured the debate. Respondents were asked about a ticking time-bomb scenario involving the use of torture and an alternative absolutist prohibition on torture: "Terrorists pose such an extreme threat that governments should now be allowed to use some degree of torture if it may gain information that saves innocent lives" or "Clear rules against torture should be maintained because any use of torture is immoral and will weaken international human rights standards against torture."[42] The best audience in the sense of adherence to human rights standards was in Italy;

81 percent of Italians were against torture, and just 14 percent were willing to allow it. In France, Australia, Canada, Germany, and the United Kingdom, 70 percent or more were against torture. The percentage in the United States who were opposed to torture was 58 percent, a smaller percentage than in other long-term established democracies and closer to the percentage in Ukraine (54 percent), Philippines (56 percent), and Iraq (55 percent). In Professor Dershowitz's homeland, 36 percent endorsed his view that torture could be justified. Torture found the most support in Israel, India, and Russia. In Israel, 43 percent agreed to some degree of torture. It is likely that public opinion, like politicians and intellectuals, adjusts its grip on principled ideas according to the level and proximity of fear in a roughly rational way. India, Russia, and Israel have had long experience with terrorist attacks and have suffered substantial fatalities, and the United States has had one devastating attack. Perhaps predictably enough, in demographic terms, the least demanding audience were young men. Overall, people who were under thirty-five and male were more likely to favor torture than were people in other demographic groups. Religious differences were significant only in Israel. Muslims in that country, perhaps considering themselves the most likely victims, were less likely to favor torture than were members of other faiths.[43]

The attitudes of American soldiers and marines toward torture are similar to those of the general public. A survey conducted by the Mental Health Advisory Team between August and October 2006 assessed the mental health of American forces. One component of the survey was devoted to "battlefield ethics." It included two items on torture. The Advisory Team found that 41 percent of soldiers and 44 percent of marines thought "torture should be allowed if it will save the life of a soldier/marine." These percentages fell to 39 percent and 36 percent when the item in question was "Torture should be allowed in order to gather important info about insurgents."[44] When asked whether they had committed abuse, 7 percent of marines and 4 percent of soldiers admitted to kicking or hitting noncombatants when it "was not necessary." Some 38 percent of marines and 47 percent of soldiers agreed that noncombatants should be treated with dignity and respect. It is difficult to know quite what to make of these data. The differences across units are interesting. They are in the direction expected, given the Marines' exposure to combat and reputation for aggression. Given a very bloody insurgency and a civil war where different elements of the community were wantonly killing noncombatants, one might have expected fewer soldiers to value dignity and respect.

There were lawyers and others within the internal audience of government officials who did not want to give their agents a license to torture. They sounded the alarm. But the leadership ignored them. In November 2002, Major Sam McCahon questioned the "utility and legality of applying certain techniques" and recommended that his personnel in the Criminal Investigation Task Force (CITF) "not participate in or even observe the use of aggressive techniques." He alluded to Machiavelli and registered his opposition: "I cannot advocate any action, interrogation or otherwise, that is predicated upon the principle that all is well if the ends justify the means and others are not aware of how we conduct our business."[45] He had the support of the commander of the CITF, Colonel Britt Mallow. Mallow e-mailed the commander at Guantanamo, Major General Miller, expressing his opposition to the use of many of the techniques in question and voicing concern about the legal and ethical issues that military personnel would face. Miller's response was to say that he would not share the results of the interrogations with Mallow's unit.[46] Agents of the Federal Bureau of Investigation registered their opposition in 2002. One agent noted that "I concur that we can't control what the military is doing, but we need to stand well clear of it and get as much information as possible to D'Amuro [Pat D'Amuro, FBI assistant director], Gebhart [*sic*; Brian Gebhardt, FBI deputy director], and Mueller [Robert Mueller, FBI director] as soon as possible." It proved difficult to get the attention of superiors. Robert Mueller, claimed he did not know of the problems his agents had with Department of Defense interrogation techniques until May 2004.[47] In December 2002, the Navy general counsel, Alberto Mora, advised the Department of Defense general counsel, Jim Haynes, that some of the techniques could amount to torture.[48] In January 2003, in another meeting with Haynes, Mora said that the techniques "could threaten Secretary Rumsfeld's tenure and could even damage the presidency."[49] The secretary did modify the approval process for the techniques some days later. Meanwhile, Major General Miller told dissenters that "you have got to put on the same jersey if you want to be on the team."[50] Jersey on and gloves off was the General's uniform.

Evading Accountability

For Secretary Rumsfeld, the time for that rare thing, instantaneous courage, Napoleon's two-in-the-morning courage, came when he found out that the CBS television program *60 Minutes* intended to broadcast pictures of American soldiers, including female soldiers, abusing Iraqi prisoners at what had been Saddam Hussein's place of torture. He could have released the pictures ahead of CBS, admitting responsibility for sanctioning degrading treatment and torture by any other name and offering the justification of the grave threat facing America and its troops. He could have taken a substantial share of the load for Abu Ghraib.

Instead, the secretary denied that the treatment of detainees in the pictures was linked to administration policy. Rumsfeld commissioned inquiries to support his claims. But his first step was to try to reestablish control of the agenda and to stop the display of the pictures. CBS went along with a delay.

Then, hearing that the photos would be released through other sources, namely by Seymour Hersh and *The New Yorker* magazine, CBS aired the story. It put Rumsfeld in front of hostile senators who questioned him about the way the information had become public and left him denying he had tried to suppress the news of the scandal.[51] A Republican senator from Maine, Susan Collins, offered advice to the secretary: "It would have been far better if you . . . had come forward and told the world about these pictures and of your personal determination . . . to set matters right and to hold those responsible accountable."[52] Now exposed, the administration moved to point to the worse horrors of the Saddam Hussein regime. Yet, this comparison did not divert attention. A one-man-one-party dictatorship is an embarrassing benchmark for a liberal democracy.

Then, more imaginatively, the administration saw the positive side to exposure. It could deny the denial phase. This step involved the claim that the United States was a democracy and that accountability is a feature of democracy. On May 10, 2004, the president released a statement. He began by informing Secretary Rumsfeld that he was doing a "superb job." He told Rumsfeld that he was "a strong Secretary of Defense and our nation owes you a debt of gratitude." He thus lifted blame from his secretary. Then the president prepared the way for dropping it on those at the bottom. He continued: "Because America is committed to the equality and dignity of all people, there will be a full accounting for the cruel and disgraceful abuse of Iraqi detainees. . . . One basic difference between democracies and dictatorships is that free countries confront such abuses openly and directly."[53] A few days earlier, the president had arranged interviews on Arab television stations. He offered a similar theme about openness and accountability as a feature of democracy and acknowledged that democracies make mistakes. Then he explained that "in a democracy . . . those mistakes will be investigated and people will be brought to justice. We're an open society." He contrasted this approach with Saddam Hussein's approach: "His trained torturers were never brought to justice under his regime. There were no investigations about mistreatment of people. There will be investigations. People will be brought to justice."[54] To bring the people at the bottom to justice, administration officials required evidence of differences between the administration's goals and those of its agents. It needed private motivations for the abuses. The investigation had to show that those who had committed the abuses were selfishly motivated, and beyond the principal's control.

In his statement to the Senate Armed Services Committee, Rumsfeld observed that "these events occurred on my watch. As Secretary of Defense, I am accountable for them and I take full responsibility."[55] His "full responsibility" offered no protection to those at the bottom. Leaders may concede that the office they occupy carries a burden. It is not an acknowledgment that their own actions or policies or lack of action and responsiveness to reports of wrongdoing have led to the policy disaster.

An example of this notional responsibility taking is to be found in President Richard Nixon's speech on the Watergate burglary in April 1973:

> I will not place the blame on subordinates—on people whose zeal exceeded their judgment and who may have done wrong in a cause they deeply believed to be right.
>
> In any organization, the man at the top must bear the responsibility. That responsibility, therefore, belongs here, in this office. I accept it. And I pledge to you tonight, from this office, that I will do everything in my power to ensure that the guilty are brought to justice and that such abuses are purged from our political processes in the years to come, long after I have left this office.
>
> Some people, quite properly appalled at the abuses that occurred, will say that Watergate demonstrates the bankruptcy of the American political system. I believe precisely the opposite is true. Watergate represented a series of illegal acts and bad judgments by a number of individuals. It was the system that has brought the facts to light and that will bring those guilty to justice—a system that in this case has included a determined grand jury, honest prosecutors, a courageous judge, John Sirica, and a vigorous free press.[56]

Nixon took responsibility as "the man at the top," while promising to find those who were truly to blame. And he voiced a strong appreciation for all the features of an open society.

Secretary Rumsfeld noted that he was in charge of a million people who were working around the clock in distant places. Consequently, he encountered some information and monitoring problems: "Needless to say, if you are in Washington, D.C., you can't know what's going on on the midnight shift in one of those many prisons around the world."[57] He said he himself was just learning about the abuses, which were a "terrible thing to have happened. . . . We keep learning more all the time. . . . It's a bit of a discovery process."[58] It is a reasonable position for a principal to take. All organizations have simple agency problems, and the larger and more dispersed the organization, the greater the challenge. Beyond pointing to this general principal-agent problem, he claimed that there was also a clear distinction between the abuse and interrogations. He had said earlier that the abuse was not related to interrogations. As the *New York Times* pointed out, he later had to retract his characterization of the finding of the army's own investigations. He "misspoke."[59] He was left trying to make a clear distinction between the instructions issued by his department and the abuses implemented by his agents.

It was necessary to deny that the abuses were ordered. Rumsfeld repeatedly made this denial: "And when one looks at the abuses and the cruelty, the idea that you would have regulations that would permit or condone or encourage that type of thing is just not comprehensible."[60] Senator Hillary Clinton had pointed out the denial phase and observed that we had learned what had happened only from leaks. In response, Secretary Rumsfeld said: "I can't conceive of anyone looking at the pictures and suggesting that anyone could have recommended, condoned, permitted, encouraged, subtly, directly, in any way, that those things take place."[61] The question he raises is how would one expect to visualize the use of the approved techniques.

One of the pictures from Abu Ghraib shows Lynndie England setting the conditions for interrogation. From her perspective, she was implementing policy. She was looking down at a male detainee, prone, naked and at the end of a tether. Her presence as a female was approved. The prone stress position was approved. Nakedness was approved by Rumsfeld in December 2002 and recommended as an effective technique by his Detainee Interrogation Working Group in its January 24, 2003 memo. It was a technique recommended for shaming and humiliating detainees, as was the use of dogs and dog accessories.[62] Both dogs and nudity exploited perceived Arab cultural fears and dispositions. A very senior officer, Major General Miller, had carried this message personally from Guantanamo to Abu Ghraib six weeks before the picture was taken. The picture is conceivably a faithful representation of the techniques described in memos and interrogation plans. Lynndie England could claim she was performing her duty as detailed: she had her detainee in a shameful and uncomfortable position.

After asserting the spontaneous nature of the abuses, the secretary addressed the problem of separating them from policy. He had commissioned investigations. One such was an investigation that did shift away from the Taguba Report's emphasis on intentional and systematic abuses, which set the conditions for investigations. On May 12, 2004, Rumsfeld had appointed former secretary of defense James Schlesinger to head an independent review panel. This panel reported in August 2004 and pointed to the deviance of the individual abusers: "The events of October through December 2003 on the night shift of Tier 1 at Abu Ghraib prison were acts of brutality and purposeless sadism. . . . The pictured abuses . . . were not part of authorized interrogations nor were they even directed at intelligence targets. They represent deviant behavior and a failure of military leadership and discipline."[63] There was less emphasis on intentions and systematic abuse, although the report concedes that some abuses, which were not photographed, occurred during interrogation sessions.[64] The main conclusions of the report were that those involved had engaged in purposeless sadism at a precise time and location and that there was a local principal-agent problem.

The report also shifted some blame to other agencies. It noted that the presence of private contractors created particular oversight problems.[65] Schlesinger made a point of stating that his panel did not have access to information that would have allowed it to investigate the role of the CIA.[66] The report claimed that the secretary of defense faced an information asymmetry problem: "good news travels up the chain of command quickly; bad news generally does not."[67] In this way, the report corroborated the secretary of defense's "million people-midnight shift" point.

As mentioned, another report on Abu Ghraib was ordered by the commander in Iraq, Lieutenant General Sanchez, and released in August, 2004. The Jones/Fay Report, as it was called, pointed to the corrupt few, while noting the complexities of the situation.[68] This report did provide some detail on the CIA's activities at Abu Ghraib. It discussed the death in custody of detainee 28, Manadel al-Jamadi, who was "butt-stroked" on the side of his head by a special forces (Navy SEAL Team 7) member during the process of arrest and then was taken to a shower room at Abu Ghraib by two CIA agents. Forty-five minutes later, detainee 28 was found dead, face down and handcuffed, with a sandbag over his head.[69] The corpse was featured in some of the Abu Ghraib photographs next to American soldiers giving a "thumbs-up." The emphasis of the Jones/Fay investigation was on deviance and the influence of other agencies.

On May 25, 2004, Secretary Rumsfeld commissioned a report specifically directed at the authorized interrogation techniques. Admiral Albert Church's major finding, delivered in March 2005, was unequivocally supportive of the secretary. His report said that "we found, without exception, that the DoD officials and military commanders responsible for the formulation of interrogation policy evidenced the intent to treat detainees humanely, which is fundamentally inconsistent with the notion that such officials or commanders ever accepted that detainee abuse would be permissible."[70] Here, then, blame was shifted to the bottom on the perceived intent of leaders.

The Church Report's claim that the abuses had nothing to do with the policies of the administration were met with disbelief by human rights groups: "This is simply untrue. The abuses evident in the photos included the use of military working dogs, hooding, and forced nudity. All of these techniques were approved interrogation policy at some point by various U.S. government officials."[71] The Church Report addressed the speculation that "undue pressure for actionable intelligence contributed to the abuses at Abu Ghraib."[72] It dismissed both this speculation and the idea that the secretary of defense might have given "back channel" permission for the use of interrogation techniques. At the same time, it stated that the Department of Defense and military commanders had made direct requests for information to officials at Abu Ghraib. These direct requests showed that the interrogations at Abu Ghraib were of interest to senior officials. According to those in the chain of command in Iraq, there were "calls coming in from Washington, and the message was: produce, produce, produce."[73] One prisoner at Abu Ghraib was of such interest to the secretary of defense that he held telephone conversations with the head of military intelligence at the prison, Colonel Pappas, "several times a week."[74] There is evidence of particular interest in prisoners held at Abu Ghraib and an active line of communication with Washington.

As these investigations reported, the administration consistently denied that the United States practiced torture. In his September 6, 2006, statement concerning the secret CIA prisons, the president stated, "I want to be absolutely clear with our people, and the world: The United States does not torture. It's against our laws, and it's against our values. I have not authorized it—and I will not authorize it."[75] In 2008, Attorney General Michael B. Mukasey refused to say whether the techniques were torture.[76] Stephen Grey, in his investigation of the rendition program, quoted a former CIA official: "Saying *we don't do torture* is as bad as President Clinton saying *I didn't have sex with that woman.*" The official went on to admit that "of course we do torture. Imagine putting President Bush's head under water and telling him to raise his hand when he thinks he's being tortured . . . he'd be raising his hand straight away . . . we need to be honest about what we are doing."[77] It is the agent's view. Similarly, Sir Arthur Harris wanted politicians to provide an account in plain English of the strategic bombing offensive at Dresden.

When the nature of the harm done to the detainees was exposed, when the immediate worldwide disgust was apparent, when the size of the self-inflicted defeat in the struggle for legitimacy within and outside Iraq became clear, the blame dropped to the bottom. When it hit the bottom, Rumsfeld and other administration officials voiced outrage at the behavior of American personnel. At his confirmation hearing for U.S. attorney general, in 2005, Alberto Gonzalez still pursued the line that the abuse was not related to interrogations and said that he was horrified at Abu Ghraib, if a little uncertain: "what you see in the pictures—the most horrific of the abuses that we see, the ones that we all, you know, condemn and abhor . . . those were not related to interrogations. . . . This is simply people who were morally bankrupt having fun. And I condemn that."[78] As White House counsel, Gonzalez was one of the legal architects of the policy on interrogation.[79] He readily blamed those at the bottom. Officials' outrage put distance between them and the abuse. But what you see in the pictures was what, in 2002, the CIA's lawyer had known you would see. The pictures would be, in his word, ugly, even for "legal" techniques.[80]

In the political aftermath, the smiles and poses of the guards both cost and benefited the administration. The benefit was that they provided evidence of an intent—purposeless sadism—that was independent of the administration's policy decisions to use nakedness, stress positions, and dogs in interrogating prisoners. Goal variance, despite the way it is commonly understood by economists, political scientists and court-martial judges, does not necessarily imply that there are conflicting interests. In other words, both the agents and the leadership can arrive at the same policy actions. But they may be taken there by different motivations, bestial and strategic. Goal variance is conventionally understood as a problem for policymakers, but it may also provide an opportunity for them. The prosecutor in Lynndie England's case stated that "the accused knew what she was doing. . . . She is enjoying, she is participating, all for her own sick humor."[81] The selfishness on the faces of the guards allowed those above to delegate the blame to them.

Administration officials had the International Committee of the Red Cross (ICRC) reports of prisoner abuse from the beginning of the conflict. The ICRC is a neutral monitoring body that visits detainees and prisoners of war and ensures that they are receiving the protections of the Geneva Conventions. In 2003, the ICRC alerted the U.S. government to allegations of ill treatment of detainees that suggested torture.[82] Because it collected this information on allegations of ill treatment and deaths in custody over a period of time, the ICRC concluded that it might be evidence of accepted practice.[83] The ICRC reports are confidential. Things began to unravel for the Bush administration only in January 2004, when a soldier sounded the alarm. Joseph Darby informed the U.S. Army Criminal Investigation Division, leading the Pentagon to initiate the internal, classified investigation by General Taguba.

The various investigations agree that there was a failure to react to the reports of abuse.[84] According to the Jones/Fay Report, there were fifty-four soldiers and civilian contractors with some level of involvement in the abuse.[85] In Thomas Ricks's view, the abuses were the responsibility of commanders.[86] Of the bad-apples claim, he says, "to anyone who knew the military that just didn't sound right." He quotes the chief of staff to Secretary of State Colin Powell: "As former soldiers, we knew that you don't have this kind of pervasive attitude out there unless you've condoned it. And whether you did it explicitly or not is irrelevant."[87] When the actions of the U.S. personnel were displayed in the media, the administration admitted to a control problem, denied it was part of a larger pattern of abuse, and handed over its "morally bankrupt" agents.

Consequences

The Bush administration did not deliver a "plain English" account of the violations committed by American forces. It manipulated the definition of torture to permit the use of its chosen techniques and claimed to learn of the violations only when the media obtained the evidence, not when officials received reports of abuse. It then claimed that the treatment was unrelated to interrogations and the obtaining of information. Only those at the bottom suffered punishment. Denial and delegation were the central components of blame management. Donald Rumsfeld was succinct. When asked about Abu Ghraib in 2005, he said, "People have been punished and convicted in a court-martial. So the idea that there's any policy of abuse or policy of torture is false. Flat false."[88] This conception is the zero-sum conception of the blame: the more blame is transferred to someone else, the less you leave for yourself.

In July 2008, retired General Taguba provided the preface to the Physicians for Human Rights report on the use of torture by U.S. forces in Iraq. This report details the treatment of eleven detainees at Abu Ghraib and is based on medical and psychological evidence. The report describes a "systematic regime of torture" authorized by the president and his officials. Taguba mentions the damage done to U.S. honor, to the country's institutions, and to its healing professions. According to Taguba, the "only question that remains to be answered is whether those who ordered the use of torture will be held to account?"[89] This question remains.

President Bush was reelected to serve a second term after Abu Ghraib. His autobiography reveals that he "felt blindsided" by Abu Ghraib. Rumsfeld told him of an investigation, but Bush had "no idea how graphic or grotesque the photos would be. . . . I was not happy with the way the situation had been handled."[90] Rumsfeld offered to resign "anytime you feel it would be helpful to you," but Bush did not "blame him for the misconduct of the soldiers . . . and I didn't want to turn him into a scapegoat." The chairman of the Joint Chiefs of Staff, General Richard Myers, was a better choice. According to Rumsfeld's account of this episode, the president asked him "if there was anyone else he should hold accountable by firing them, and he raised General Myers as a possibility," but Rumsfeld opposed placing the blame at that level: "Mr. President you would be firing the wrong person."[91] The blame was with the soldiers. Bush was "sick" at the way the soldiers had behaved, "in defiance of their orders and military law." He noted that those responsible were court-martialed, but "America's reputation took a severe hit."[92] Evidence suggests that his own reputation, as measured by presidential approval ratings and his reelection, was not severely hit by this event.[93]

Donald Rumsfeld survived Abu Ghraib. He left his office only after the midterm election reversals in 2006. In his autobiography, he discusses his offer to resign in 2004 in order to demonstrate accountability and to help the administration and the Iraqis get over the scandal. Looking back, he says his mistake was not to insist on resigning. The blame for the abuse, Rumsfeld still maintains, lies with a "small group of disturbed individuals."[94] He reasserts that the scandal was not linked to interrogation and faults poor training and inadequate oversight of the prison by General Sanchez's understaffed headquarters. His memoir suggests that Sanchez was out of his depth as commander of ground forces in Iraq, and he notes that he does not recall participating in Sanchez's "inexplicable selection," speculating that it may have been made by the Army's Central Command in the belief that Sanchez "would be operating in a postwar environment in which an international peacekeeping force could maintain security."[95] As a former Navy pilot, Rumsfeld regrets that the Navy's tradition of linking authority to responsibility and accountability is not shared by the other services,[96] and he describes a simple agency problem for which military superiors have some responsibility.

Officers got off lightly in comparison to their subordinates. The commander at Abu Ghraib, General Karpinski, on orders from President Bush, was demoted to colonel in May 2005 for dereliction of duty and also for not disclosing a shoplifting charge.[97] Colonel Pappas was fined $8,000. Lieutenant Colonel Steven Jordan was the one officer court-martialed. He seemed a surprising choice as he makes only a brief appearance in the Senate report, averring the normality of nakedness for detainees. He got a reprimand, not a criminal conviction, and seemed to view himself as a scapegoat of a higher rank.[98] Lieutenant General Sanchez, who retired in 2006, was not held responsible for his role in taking the gloves off at Abu Ghraib. He was not grateful for this; in fact, he was reportedly bitter that he had not received further promotion under Donald Rumsfeld. Major General Miller, who retired that same year, did rather better. He had encouraged aggression, advocated the use of dogs at Abu Ghraib and dispatched "tiger teams" of Guantanamo interrogators to train Abu Ghraib personnel.[99] Nonetheless, Miller received the Distinguished Service Medal at his retirement ceremony.

This award was too much for the *New York Times*. The paper was caustic about the general's role in the treatment of detainees and the administration's decision to reward him.[100] In the heat of the legal action, Miller had left his soldiers to take the blame. The jersey apparently could come off when the heat was on. Miller had refused to testify at the court-martial of one of the Abu Ghraib dog handlers for fear of self-incrimination. He chose to testify in another case and then denied advising that dogs be used as an interrogation technique.[101] Others in the chain of command behaved similarly. Colonel Pappas, who had authorized the use of dogs at Abu Ghraib, received immunity from prosecution and testified against the dog-handling soldiers.[102] Those higher up the chain are positioned to drop the blame on those below.

Eleven sergeants, specialists, and privates were court-martialed and convicted for the Abu Ghraib abuses. The charges included maltreatment, dereliction, indecent acts, and assault and battery. Sentences ranged from a fine or a dishonorable discharge to ten years in prison. Lynndie England was found guilty of conspiracy, maltreatment of detainees, and commission of an indecent act. She served two and half years of a three-year sentence, became a mother, and is unemployed at the time of writing.

9

Baghdad to Basra

The toughest test of a democracy's commitment to the rule of law is whether it is willing to hold its own people to account. The American poet laureate Charles Simic says democracies fail this test: "What unites many countries in the world, both the ones that don't give a fig about human rights and the ones that profess they do is their unwillingness to punish their war criminals."[1] Simic says that "when it comes to accountability, instances of confronting their own guilt are exceedingly rare among nations . . . there's an unwritten understanding that crimes committed by the United States and a few other Western powers go unpunished."[2] The poet is right and wrong.

For the sexual humiliation and abuse of prisoners at Abu Ghraib, eleven American soldiers received convictions. The woman photographed with the smile, the thumbs-up signal, and Manadel al-Jamadi's battered corpse got six months. The puzzle is why no one was punished for beating him to death. British military justice works similarly. As we will see in this chapter, for the sexual humiliation and abuse of prisoners at Camp Breadbasket, near Basra, four British soldiers received prison terms of six months to two years; for beating Baha Mousa to death, one soldier received a sentence of one year. We will find out that, for a British or American soldier in Iraq, it is more dangerous to strike a pose than a prisoner.

In May 2004, Britain had a total of 8,600 troops in Iraq and the United States had 138,000.[3] As their governments remind us, if we consider the numbers of soldiers involved in the conflict, the number of cases of unlawful killing and abuse, as best we can tell, is very small. But what happens when crimes are committed? We know about Abu Ghraib. But we do not know as much about how the other cases of abuse and unlawful killing by American and British soldiers have been managed.

The expectation is that those on top go unpunished. The theory of the fall guy suggests that in a democracy the prospect for those below is more uncertain. Leaders do not want to accept personal blame for initiating or for failing to prevent wrongful actions. Nor do they normally want to punish an agent, because doing so may affect the loyalty of others. The agent confidence factor influences the management of abuse and atrocity. Punishment creates as well as corrects noncompliance. This element of the theoretical argument was illustrated in what happened after the killing of an Iraqi man on New Year's Day 2004. A British Special Air Service (SAS) corporal chased, shot, and killed Gatteh al-Roomi. Iraqi investigators and family members said he was a civilian returning from a wedding, not an insurgent. Celebration shots had been fired at the wedding, and those shots had drawn the attention of the soldiers. Family members said Gatteh al-Roomi was shot in the back, not the front, as the soldier claimed. Yet, twenty of the corporal's regimental comrades threatened to resign if he was prosecuted for murder.[4] The case was not pursued.

Whether a democratic leader is gripped by a neoconservative agenda, as was President George W. Bush, or by an "ethical foreign policy," as was Prime Minister Tony Blair, he will seek public support and the loyalty of officials. A democratic leader is expected to "back his women and men." Under these pressures, a leader is loath to admit abuse and reluctant to administer punishment. When abuse is exposed, the calculation shifts. Punishment now offers the political benefit of putting distance between the unlawful act and those up the chain of delegation. If punishment is administered, it will not fall on all those responsible. It will fall to the lowest plausible level, to the fall guy. This act of leadership carries with it the expected cost of the alienation of other agents. There are two ways to try to reduce this cost: like General Dyer, one can administer a token punishment, or one can isolate the agent from the others as singularly deserving of punishment.

With the exposure of abuse, when denial is no longer an option, the trick for the leader is to reconcile the personal desire to shift blame and the need to maintain agent commitment with the demand for accountability. For the agent, the prospect of lenient treatment improves if the variance between the motivation for the violation and the strategic mission is perceived as small. If the violation arises from some sense of duty, misplaced though it may have been, the chances of going unpunished improve. The prospect of lenient treatment recedes if the act is attributed to a private benefit. The clearest cases of agent-motivated, rather than strategically motivated, violations are cases of sexual violence or indecent acts. It is clear that strategic rationales for such behavior are available. They have been around from the first syllable of recorded time, if the poets have it right. According to Homer, the Greek commander

Agamemnon used the prospect of the ill treatment of the women of Troy to encourage his troops.

> So now let no man hurry to sail for home, not yet . . .
> not till he beds down with a faithful Trojan wife,
> payment in full for the groans and shocks of war
> we have all borne for Helen.[5]

Yet, most obviously, there is simply a selfish motivation at work. Ancient Greeks aside, sexual violence is an action that other agents and the wider public will recognize as something that merits punishment. If any defendant in a court-martial is likely to be punished severely, it is one who clearly betrays a private motive for the violation. Trophy photographed abuse will not go unpunished.

This argument frames expectations about accountability for violations, the pattern of sentencing, and even the severity of punishment. Accountability in the sense of appropriate punishment for those responsible is unlikely. To the degree that punishment is within the control of those within the hierarchy, and where offenses are punished, punishment falls on those at the bottom. Heavy punishment is usually the result of a display of goal variance. Those at high risk of punishment are those with a clearly selfish content to their wrongdoing and without high rank.

Alternatively, if one accepts the accountability claims of the democracy literature, one expects punishment to be commensurate with the violation, distributed across ranks, and comparable across democracies.[6] If what matters is not just democratic institutions but the particular leader's grip on principled ideas, one expects leaders with that commitment to oversee a robust accountability regime. There were clear differences in commitment to human rights between the Bush and the Blair governments. How did this commitment influence the management of operations in Iraq?

The United States, the United Kingdom, and Iraq

British soldiers first patrolled the streets of Basra in 1914. With the defeat of the Ottoman Empire at the end of World War I, Britain accepted the Iraq mandate from the League of Nations. Its obligation was to prepare the country for freedom and independence. Eighty years later, it blithely assumed the obligation again. Whether displacing Saddam Hussein or the Ottoman Empire, British governance in the cradle of civilization provoked unrest. The mood at home was little better.

By 1922, the British press was uniformly hostile. The recently appointed secretary of state for the colonies, Winston Churchill, wrote to the prime minister, Lloyd George, that "in my own heart I do not see what we are getting out of it . . . we are paying eight millions a year for the privilege of living on an ungrateful volcano out of which we are in no circumstances to get anything worth having."[7] It is an odd metaphor. But it is clearly an uncomfortable place to be. Churchill scrambled together some short-term fixes, anticipating solutions arrived at later by the United States.

To substitute for economically and politically expensive British troops, Churchill relied on technology and the recruitment of local forces. "Air policing," as the bombing of insurgents and their villages was called, and "Iraq Levies" addressed the cost problem. The historian David Omissi describes how commanders tried to use these forces to restore law and order while avoiding "the frightfulness of General Dyer."[8] Omissi quotes a report compiled by the commander of 45 Squadron in Iraq: "they now know that within 45 minutes a full sized village can be practically wiped out and a third of its inhabitants killed or injured by four or five machines which offer them no real target, no opportunity for glory as warriors."[9] It sounds somewhat like the "shock and awe" benefits of bombing Baghdad many years later. Omissi says that "this was too much even for the Air Ministry, who underlined some of the unpleasant passages, notably that which claimed 'we now cause real casualties . . . that produce a real, as opposed to a purely moral effect.'" Omissi says that "in the ruins of this dying village one can dimly perceive the horrific firestorms of Hamburg and Dresden, for the report was written by Squadron Leader Arthur Harris."[10] The policy of air policing caused "disquiet" among the British public, according to the historian Toby Dodge.[11] There were questions in the House of Commons about the casualties inflicted. Answers were unforthcoming. George Lansbury, a Labour MP, asked how many casualties had been suffered by the Air Force and how many suffered by the local people. He was informed of five bombing operations in a five-month period in 1924; not less than two days' warning was given in four operations (the other case was in response to an attack on native police). The minister said that there were no Air Force casualties. Lansbury did not get a reply on local casualties.[12] Information on civilian casualties is as scarce today.

Unsurprisingly, T. E. Lawrence advocated the use of local forces. In a letter to the *Times* on July 23, 1920, he pointed to the naiveté of politicians and the press for thinking that an occupation with good intentions would be met with gratitude. Lawrence of Arabia went on to ask why the government would sacrifice British or Indian soldiers when it could raise local forces.[13] Kurds, Marsh Arabs, and the highly regarded Assyrians were used, instead. The Assyrians had fought with the Russians against the Turks in World War I. Their record of service with the British was not unblemished.

In May 1924, Assyrians, in lupine form,[14] killed fifty to one hundred Muslims in Kirkuk. An adviser to the British High Commissioner in Iraq, Gertrude Bell, described this event in a letter home: "there never would have been any incident if British or Indian troops had been there."[15] After the massacre, the local troops were put on trial. A special court composed of civilian judges, both Iraqi and British, the regent for the titular King of the Assyrian nation, and Squadron Leader F. H. W. Guard (RAF) sentenced eight Assyrians to life sentences of penal servitude.[16] Local troops did not go unpunished.

This earlier episode suggests that, despite its intentions, no occupier should expect local gratitude for its military presence. Despite the advantages of removing one's own troops from the violence, one must know the risks involved in enlisting local militias. Despite Gertrude Bell's confidence in British troops, it is prudent to anticipate that they too will kill civilians and create incidents.

Iraq 2003

The invasion of Iraq by the United States and Britain in 2003 and the actions of some of their soldiers provide a common arena for comparing crime and punishment. This conflict offers one of those "naturally occurring experiments" for the study of accountability in two liberal democracies.

At the time of the invasion, President Bush and Prime Minister Blair had contrasting positions on human rights. Independent judicial processes place prosecution and criminal penalties beyond the control of political leaders. But political leaders can signal their priorities, provide protection for their agents, and influence the performance of the chain of command. President Bush "un-signed" the 1998 Rome treaty setting up the International Criminal Court (ICC) to try violations of humanitarian and human rights law. His government pursued bilateral agreements with other countries to limit the reach of the court. These countries agreed not to surrender U.S. personnel to the ICC without U.S. consent.[17] Bush also raised the possibility of the misuse of international law for political purposes and questioned the applicability of the Geneva Convention to the war in Afghanistan, although he allowed that it applied in Iraq; he also removed protections for detainees. His officials notified Congress of the "gloves off" approach.[18] Administration lawyers also sought to define torture in a way that was consistent with the administration's new national security priorities.

Prime Minister Blair's government had other priorities. It ratified the treaty establishing the ICC and declared "an ethical foreign policy." In 1998, the Human Rights Act incorporated the European Convention on Human Rights into domestic law. In Northern Ireland, Blair sought the truth about older atrocities and set up the Saville Inquiry into the killing of civilians in Londonderry. The destruction of the World Trade Center and the other atrocities of 9/11 may have brought the leaders closer, but their policy paths to Iraq were quite different. If a leader's commitments shape his government's priorities and the process of accountability, this should be evident in the patterns of punishment for British and American soldiers who committed atrocities in Iraq. Contrary to gravitational theory, each government's commitment to principle should be evident: for a given type of offense, we should expect more severe punishment for British violators than for American violators.

For members of the armed forces, punishment is decided by military courts. Under the British system, the military police submit a report of an incident to the commanding officer and to the Army Prosecuting Authority (APA). The APA decides whether there should be a court-martial. The court-martial has a civilian judge advocate and between three and eight officers or warrant officers. A civilian lawyer represents the defendants.[19] Under the American system, the commanding officer investigates and decides whether to refer the case to a court-martial. Before a court-martial is convened, there is a hearing (an Article 32 hearing) to see whether there is enough evidence to go ahead. The court-martial has a military judge and at least five other members, including officers, warrant officers, and enlisted men or women. If the defendant is enlisted, then he or she may request that at least one-third of the members of the court-martial be enlisted, as well. The defendant is entitled to a military lawyer, or he or she can retain a civilian lawyer.[20]

The British system has been faulted for the unwillingness of officers to convict other officers. A weakness of the American system is the discretion accorded the commanding officer. For example, in one case, after a roadside bomb exploded, a sergeant shot a mother and two female children. One of the children died. His commander let it go. After this event, the sergeant and a soldier detained a cowherd, and the soldier shot the handcuffed cowherd in the back of the head. He said the cowherd had lunged at the sergeant. The soldier was tried and convicted of manslaughter. He served two years of a three-year sentence before being released.[21] Under any system of justice, there are contentious cases, so, within the limits of the available information, it is worth taking a more general approach to the analysis of the management of military forces and the response to unlawful killing and abuse in Iraq.

The overall number of unlawful killings and cases of abuse committed by the coalition forces in Iraq is, in Donald Rumsfeld's phrase, a known unknown. It is fair to say that he wanted it that way. A 2009 United Nations (UN) report criticized the United States for not recording this information. It described the failure to "systematically compile statistics on civilian casualties in its operations in Afghanistan and Iraq," saying that "in relation to deaths in military custody, operational difficulties cannot be used to justify a failure to compile statistics."[22] Information on the response to civilian killings by coalition forces is similarly scarce. It is difficult to obtain comprehensive information on the numbers of individuals charged with abuses and killings. The UN report noted that "it is remarkably difficult for the U.S. public, victims' families, or even commanders to obtain up-to-date information on the status of cases" and recommended the creation of a "centralized system for reporting and providing public information about all courts-martial and non-judicial proceedings relating to civilian casualties."[23] In an effort to address the lack of information, in 2006, the *Washington Post* conducted an analysis of unlawful killings. It cautioned that there were likely to be many more cases of soldiers involved in unlawful killings than the thirty-nine it found and quoted an army officer's comments on the general reluctance to report cases up the chain of command.[24] In contrast to civilian crimes and homicide data, where, as the UN report noted, there are records on the victims, we have little information on the overall number of offenses and unlawful killings of civilians in Iraq. Professor Gary Solis and others make similar observations about unreported cases during the Vietnam War, with the My Lai massacre only the most well-known of the atrocities.[25] It is not known whether Britain has a worse or better record than the United States for unreported cases. Because commanders and government leaders have little incentive to submit accurate accounts of abuse and atrocity, it is very difficult to obtain good information.

From a search of publicly available media reports and court-martial documents between March 2003 and September 2009, some 109 American and 35 British soldiers faced allegations that they unlawfully killed or abused Iraqi civilians or detainees. The last case retrieved in this search was that of an American 101st Airborne soldier for the murder of Ali Mansur Muhammad near Beiji, Iraq in May 2008.[26] These cases are listed in Appendix 9.1. It is likely that only the most egregious cases get investigated. Even these do not carry a high probability of conviction, and those convicted tend to receive light sentences. In its review of American cases between 2003 and 2006, the *Washington Post* found that thirty-nine soldiers had been charged with unlawful deaths, of whom twelve went to prison.[27] It concluded that most American soldiers were acquitted; those who were found guilty were often convicted of reduced charges.[28] When we extend the review of cases to 2009 and include British cases, the pattern of light sentences, reduced charges, and acquittals holds. If we look at just the 107 American and British soldiers allegedly involved in cases of unlawful killing and put aside those accused of the abuse or ill treatment of detainees, we find that 55 percent had the charges dropped or were acquitted. A further 22 percent were convicted on reduced charges (not murder or manslaughter).

The particular context of an incident may provide an excuse for what occurred. It is relevant to know whether the killing or abuse occurred under combat conditions, in the heat of the action, and in situations where the soldier's own safety was at issue. These are circumstances that are likely to produce tragic mistakes, as well as intentional violations. To judge from the descriptions of the cases that were investigated, it seems that many of the victims of unlawful killings or abuse did not pose an obvious threat to the soldiers who killed them. They were unarmed, in custody, or handcuffed. Some lay wounded.

The Heat of the Action

The British Army's Aitken Report into cases of abuse by British soldiers, released in January 2008, discussed four cases involving the deaths of Iraqis.[29] In separate incidents, Ahmed Jabber Kareem, age fifteen, and Sa'eed Shabram drowned after allegedly being forced into the Shat' Al Arab canal. In the first incident, four soldiers were acquitted of murder by the court-martial. The Shabram incident, which was investigated by the APA, resulted in no legal proceedings. In another case, Nadhem Abdullah was allegedly beaten to death with rifle butts, and seven soldiers were charged with the crime and faced a court-martial. The charges were later dismissed, although the judge "concluded that there was sufficient evidence to show that Nadhem had died as a result of an assault carried out by the Section of which all seven defendants were members."[30] In another case, an Iraqi prisoner was beaten to death on a Royal Air Force helicopter. There were no reliable witnesses, and no charges were brought.[31] Although there was conflicting testimony, in two of the cases the circumstances suggest that the heat of the action played a role and that the soldier's safety was at issue. One of these cases is the 2004 case of the SAS corporal, referred to earlier, who shot and killed someone who was either a wedding guest or an insurgent. That case provoked agent loss of confidence and resignation threats. The charges were dropped. In the other case, a soldier was acquitted of charges that he had shot dead an Iraqi civilian who was driving a car that might have been going toward some soldiers.

The best-known of the British cases is the death in custody of Baha Mousa. Mousa, a hotel receptionist, was arrested in September 2003. The soldiers went to the hotel to seize weapons said to be stored there, and Mousa and six others were taken into custody. Over a period of a day and a half, he was beaten to death by soldiers of the Queen's Lancashire Regiment. Baha Mousa's father said that his son had informed on some soldiers who had stolen from the hotel safe and that the soldiers were taking revenge.[32] The soldiers hooded the detainees and put them in "stress positions," beating them when they did not maintain the positions. The Royal Air Force pathologist reported that the nature and number of injuries suggested beating.[33] Among the soldiers was a diary keeper who was a member of another unit but who was serving with the Queen's Lancashire Regiment. Diary entries include an incident on July 25, 2003: "leg and winged [threw] Ali Baba into Shat al Arab [Shatt al-Arab canal] for stealing wood. Piss funny." The entry for September 15, 2003, is: "still conditioning the terrorists. . . . The fat bastard [believed to be Baha Mousa] who kept taking his hood off and escaping from his plasticuffs got put in another room. He resisted [words scribbled out]. He stopped breathing. Then we couldn't revive him. [words scribbled out] What a shame."[34] The diarist turned witness for the prosecution. But in court he forgot the incidents so memorably entered in his diary. The court-martial in the Baha

Mousa case was clear about the widespread involvement of soldiers and demonstrated that the soldiers were unconcerned about monitoring and correction by the chain of command for the treatment of detainees. An indeterminate number of soldiers were involved in beating Baha Mousa, and seven appeared at the court-martial. One, Corporal Payne, was convicted. He was sentenced to twelve months on reduced charges.

Similarly, in the American cases, the victims were often in custody or for other reasons were unlikely to present a direct threat to soldiers. One captain claimed that he had shot a wounded Iraqi out of pity for his wounds. The shooting was caught by a surveillance drone. The captain was convicted of the lesser charge of assault with intent to commit voluntary manslaughter and was sentenced to dismissal from the army.[35] Perhaps the most well-known killing of an unarmed, wounded Iraqi occurred in a mosque during the intense combat in Fallujah, on November 13, 2004. The fatal shooting was filmed by a journalist, Kevin Sites, whose patriotism was questioned when he released his video of the event to NBC News, for which he received death threats. Sites described what happened in the mosque in a letter he wrote to the Marines following the event.

> "He's fucking faking he's dead. He's faking he's fucking dead." . . . I can see the Marine raise the muzzle of his rifle in the direction of the wounded Iraqi. There are no sudden movements. . . . However, the Marine could legitimately believe the man poses some kind of danger. Maybe he's going to cover him while another Marine searches for weapons. Instead, he pulls the trigger. There is a small splatter against the back wall and the man's leg slumps down. "Well he's dead now," says another Marine in the background. . . . I get up after a beat and tell the Marines again what I had told the lieutenant: this man, and all of these wounded men, were the same ones from yesterday. They had been disarmed, treated and left here.[36]

No charges were brought against the unidentified Marine corporal.

British and American Punishment

The general pattern of light sentencing and acquittals holds across the conflict and the forces involved. Both the British and the American systems have produced similar outcomes of light or no sentencing. In both systems, soldiers have sometimes received more severe punishment for nonlethal offenses of ill treatment than for killing civilians or detainees. While there is a limited number of cases to compare, the record suggests that the British are more likely to drop charges or impose light sentences for the unlawful killing of Iraqis than are the Americans. If we examine only the most serious violations, we find that eighty American soldiers were alleged to be involved in unlawful killings, of whom 41 percent were not convicted and a further 28 percent were convicted of a lesser offense.[37] Of the twenty-seven British soldiers allegedly involved in unlawful killings, there was one conviction—Payne's conviction on the lesser offense of inhumane treatment. Other British convictions have come in cases of abuse.

Beyond conviction, what are the sentencing outcomes for soldiers? For both democracies, the majority of those investigated for killing and abuse received no prison time or received sentences of twelve months or less. Of those convicted, 67 percent of British defendants and 53 percent American defendants fall into this category. The surprising finding is the particular weakness of the British regime. There are fewer British cases to compare, but the British cases are not obviously less serious.

One feature of the British cases has been the difficulty of obtaining evidence to support convictions. Soldiers are more or less successful at hiding their actions. Information from confessions and other soldiers is critical for a successful prosecution; if the soldiers cooperate with each other and limit the flow of information about the case, they can reduce the likelihood of punishment.

No Dilemma for Military Prisoners

In the area of military justice, soldiers have gone some way to solving the proverbial prisoner's dilemma of whether to inform on one's partner in crime.[38] It is a tale told by social scientists, often not with real prisoners in mind, to illustrate the difficulties rational individuals face in achieving cooperation, even when it is in their overall interest to cooperate. Two prisoners, held separately, are expected to accept the prosecutor's offer of immunity or reduced charges in exchange for confession and testimony against the other. Now suppose that the prosecutor lacks information to convict you or your partner in crime on anything but a lesser charge. If you both remain silent, you will be charged with this lesser offense. If your partner remains silent and you inform, you will receive immunity. If your partner informs, you can inform as well, gaining some mitigation for doing so. After solitary consideration of their options, both prisoners inform. Each chooses what is individually advantageous, but the overall outcome is worse than if they both had held their tongues. The prisoners' problems are information and trust. They lack knowledge of what the other is going to do, and they do not have sufficient trust to compensate for the lack of knowledge. That said, the expectation of informing may not extend to circumstances where different cultural norms are influential and reinforce trust. Economists say that "how private incentives interact with cultural norms of behaviour might be the next important step of research."[39] Institutions with powerful and specific cultural norms include army regiments. There, one may find that it is a cultural norm to care more about the well-being of your fellow soldiers than about your own well-being.

British authorities have complained specifically about cooperation rather than defection among their soldiers. In the Baha Mousa case, the judge complained of a "wall of silence."[40] He said that "none of those soldiers has been charged with any offence, simply because there is no evidence against them as a result of a more or less obvious closing of ranks."[41] At the court-martial, the lawyer for the one individual convicted in the case said that "in the light of what we all know about what occurred . . . there is I suggest something a little distasteful about the sight of Don Payne standing here alone before you as the man—the only man—to be singled out for punishment for this sorry episode."[42] In another case, the killing of Nadhem Abdullah, Parachute Regiment soldiers were unwilling to testify against one another. As a result, there was insufficient evidence to proceed. These two cases account for fourteen of the twenty-seven British soldiers who have faced charges for unlawful killing. The British Army's Aitken Report sees the problem of getting soldiers to provide information to investigators as the central issue and specifically notes the importance of the value of loyalty to the army as an organization. It goes on to say that "the challenge is to educate our people to understand that lying to the Service Police, or having selective memory loss in court, in order to protect other members of their unit, are not forms of loyalty, but rather a lack of integrity . . . courage includes having the moral courage to challenge unacceptable behaviour whenever it is encountered."[43] Clearly, this is a complex but important challenge.

In the British case that resulted in the longest sentences, the Camp Breadbasket case involving the sexual humiliation and abuse of some Iraqis detained for looting, one soldier did inform. A lawyer for the other soldiers said that the informer had "offered up their scalps in order to save his own skin."[44] While the small number of British cases makes comparisons tentative, a review of U.S. prosecutions suggests that they have been more successful in securing defection. Appendix 9.1 includes some cases where there was information that the charges were modified in exchange for testimony or some form of cooperation. The sexual assault and murder case by soldiers of the 502nd Infantry came from information from a soldier. In another example, in April 2006, a sergeant in the Marines and his squad killed Hashim Ibrahim Awad near Hamdania, Iraq. According to the *New York Times*, a member of the squad testified that the sergeant had praised the squad for committing the murder without being caught.[45] The sergeant received fifteen years for unpremeditated murder.

Fall Guys

One way to think about the difference in performance between the United States and the United Kingdom is to consider the inability of the British to punish. The difference in performance also may reflect the comparative incentives to punish; perhaps the British government was more sensitive than the U.S. government to the need to pay attention to Hume's agent confidence factor. There was greater domestic opposition to the war in Britain than in the United States and greater reluctance to place troops in a difficult place. Leaving aside the larger human rights principles that may have motivated the government in other areas and at other times and staying with the theoretical argument, while British leaders had a disincentive to press a rigorous accountability regime on their soldiers, American leaders, at least after the spring of 2004, had a greater incentive to punish some bad apples. American leaders had been more directly engaged in the introduction and justification of the use of violence and humiliation to extract information from detainees and therefore had more incentive to put distance between themselves and the abuses. As the *Economist* was to put it in describing the abuse by British and American soldiers in Iraq, "Geoff Hoon [the British defense secretary] is no Donald Rumsfeld."[46] The Bush administration had a greater level of complicity; it had announced that it was taking the gloves off. Once the ugly appearance of abuse became clear and a major international scandal was created, the administration had an incentive to shift the blame downward and demonstrate a commitment to justice and the rule of law. The Blair government, although criticized for its acquiescence during these years, took a less aggressive position. Exposed at Abu Ghraib, the Bush administration vigorously asserted that the treatment of detainees in Iraq was a simple agency problem. President Bush promised that the perpetrators would be punished. And, as noted in the previous chapter, Secretary Rumsfeld pointed out that there was no policy of abuse because individuals had been punished.[47] Those individuals punished were, however, at the bottom of the chain of command.

Privilege of Rank

In her analysis of war crimes in the Vietnam War, Deborah Nelson reports that of "284 suspects in war crimes other than My Lai . . . [o]fficers represented roughly 30 percent of the suspects but just 14 percent of those convicted."[48] The figures for Iraq are consistent with that, with the advantageous position of officers yet more pronounced. For both British and American forces, officers made up 14 percent of those facing allegations and 8 percent of those convicted. Few officers are investigated, and fewer still are convicted. The higher one's rank, the less likely one is to be convicted. Those officers who were convicted, all Americans, were low in the chain of command—three lieutenants, two captains and a major. Three served time.

Of the cases reviewed, the only American officer to receive a substantial sentence was a lieutenant. He was the 101st Airborne soldier who killed Ali Mansur Muhammad. His sentence, initially twenty-five years, was shortened to fifteen years (reduced by five years by his commanding general and by another five years by the Army Clemency Board). Military prosecutors accused the lieutenant of stripping a detainee naked in the desert north of Baghdad, interrogating and shooting him. A soldier under his command set fire to the body and later testified against the lieutenant. Professor Solis's analysis of cases from Vietnam pointed to a practice of "military justice" qualified by "civilian clemency," where sentences were reduced "by clemency boards and politically appointed under secretaries of the Army and Navy."[49] This practice fits with my theoretical argument and the influence of the agent-confidence factor.

No British officers have been convicted. In the Baha Mousa case, the commanding officer, Colonel Jorge Mendonca, a recipient of the Distinguished Service Order who had twenty-five years of service to his credit, was charged with negligently performing his duty and failing to protect civilians. Major Michael Peebles, his subordinate, was similarly charged. The court-martial heard how prisoners were "conditioned" with the use of hooding, stress positions, and sleep deprivation. The use of stress positions (standing with knees bent and arms outstretched), hooding, and noise were standard practice; they had apparently been used by another regiment before and were used with the knowledge of senior officers and with Brigade approval. The treatment of prisoners was observed by officers.[50] The court-martial made it clear that senior officers had authorization for the use of stress positions and the hooding of detainees but left us in the dark on one critical issue: when did these techniques, banned in the aftermath of Bloody Sunday, become part of the British interrogation repertoire once again? The Aitken Report into cases of abuse by the British army in Iraq noted this question but saw it as beyond the boundaries of its inquiry.[51] According to Prime Minister Edward Heath, prime ministerial and parliamentary approval for these techniques should have been obtained before they could be reintroduced.

The court-martial was informed that there was a perception that the British were underperforming as interrogators and that they were pressured by the Americans to do better in this regard. The head of the army's Intelligence Corps testified that the Americans had been critical of the amount of information obtained by the British.[52] The conditioning process was designed to maintain "the shock of capture" and to induce cooperation from the detainees. For the soldiers ordered to implement the conditioning process, the problem was that the detainees, quite naturally, would not keep themselves in stress positions or deprive themselves of sleep. The Queen's Lancashire Regiment solved these problems by kicking and punching the detainees when they slumped or slept. The British soldiers referred to "the choir" to describe noises made by the detainees when they assaulted them. The choir performed for visiting British military personnel at the base, but not, apparently, within earshot of officers and Colonel Mendonca. He denied hearing screaming from the building in which the detainees were beaten. The prosecution accepted that his hearing might have deteriorated but observed that "he is in the Crown's submission on the evidence . . . by no means deaf."[53] Deafness aside, the colonel relied on delegation. He explained to the court-martial that the responsibility for the treatment of detainees rested with Major Peebles:

> Had people been placed in the stress position for that period of time, yes, that would have been inhumane and that is why we have the judgment of a field officer. A major is expected to operate in these circumstances because I was not personally supervising this process. I had a battalion to run. . . . I placed my confidence in a major who had this process to work through and common sense dictates that he is responsible for making sure that the requirements of tactical questioning are balanced against the needs of humanity and decency and all the things that you and I expect and hope our soldiers to behave by. I delegate responsibility. I delegate tasks to various people and they are responsible for the completion of those tasks successfully and properly.[54]

The prosecution pointed out that, as commander, he was responsible for the actions of his subordinates and that the use of the conditioning techniques had been going on for months, not just with Mousa.

Major Peebles had briefed his soldiers that the detainees might be responsible for murdering three Royal Military Police in Basra on August 23, 2003. This briefing may have increased the risk of abuse for Mousa and the others arrested just three weeks later. Major Peebles agreed with the prosecution that he had ordered conditioning of the prisoners, while at the same time not specifying the techniques to be used. His lawyer pointed out that the major had no formal training in handling detainees, had been in his post for only two weeks, and was too junior to question arrangements already in place.[55] Peebles was acquitted.

The judge ruled that Colonel Mendonca had no case to answer. It had been confirmed with Brigade headquarters that maintaining the shock of capture by conditioning, including stress positions and hooding, was authorized. The lawyer for the guilty corporal saw it this way: "You may think that there is something deeply unattractive, deeply unfair, about a prosecution which applies one set of rules to the junior ranks—those operating at the sharp end—and a different set to those higher up the chain of command."[56] Corporal Payne pleaded guilty to inhumane treatment and was acquitted of manslaughter; as we have seen, he was sentenced to twelve months. In addition to killing Baha Mousa, soldiers under Colonel Mendonca's command inhumanely treated eight other detainees, two of whom required hospitalization.

An Opportunity for Accountability:
Trophy Photos and Goal Variance

I have suggested that those who are motivated by a desire for selfish grati-fication in their misconduct are likely to receive more severe punishment. Trophy photos of detainee abuse and humiliation capture goal variance. In some cases, strategic harm is done by the soldier's selfishness. In oth-ers, selfish acts may be seen to contribute a strategic good such as the extraction of information. Varying goals do not necessarily mean conflict-ing goals. But it is evidence of a selfish motivation, not necessarily the gravity of the case, that creates an opportunity for accountability and sen-tencing, should there be pressure to deliver that.

To represent this idea in the analysis, it is possible to isolate cases where there are allegations of sexual violence or indecency, which draw attention to the agent-centered nature of the abuse. These cases include the abuse of prisoners by British soldiers at Camp Breadbasket. The camp had been the target of looters. In order to arrest and deter other looters, the camp commander, Major Dan Taylor, launched Operation Ali Baba. It was a choice of name that did not augur well for the humane treat-ment of those caught. He ordered his men to "work them hard." Others testified that Major Taylor had briefed his soldiers that the looters needed "thrashing" and "beasting" (*sic*) and that "the Iraqis should be given a good kicking," which the major denied.[57] Those detained were humili-ated and abused. They were stripped, forced to simulate oral and anal sex for the camera, and dangled from a forklift truck. One soldier took pictures and, on returning home, got them developed. The shop assistant called the police. Inadvertently, this soldier informed on himself. Then he informed on the others. The soldier and three corporals appeared at the court-martial. In mitigation, his lawyer referred to orders: "No doubt Major Taylor when he told the police . . . that his instructions were that they were to be given a hard time did not anticipate quite how hard a time they would have been given, nevertheless that was his instruction."[58] The soldier pleaded guilty to disgraceful conduct of a cruel kind. In giving his reasons for sentencing the three corporals involved in the Camp Bread-basket abuse, the judge stated: "What you did was done, we find, for a key reason of producing trophy photographs. . . . You chose to behave as you did, and it has never been claimed by anyone that you behaved as you did because you were following orders."[59] The judge's identification of the soldiers' selfish motivations seems safe enough. The court-martial left it at that. The abuse was a *can't control* problem. Yet, the imprecise orders, the suggestion that the men use harsh treatment, and the lack of oversight left the agents with substantial discretion in carrying out the operation. Sentences in this case were more severe than in the Baha Mousa death in custody case. The soldiers got between nine and twenty-four months.

Some fifteen of the American and British cases we have reviewed involve charges with sexual or indecent content. They fit this narrow interpretation of goal variance. For these cases, the conviction rate was more than 90 percent (in contrast to the 47 percent conviction rate for incidents without a sexual or indecent content). Those convicted received prison sentences substantially heavier than would have been likely without such obvious goal variance.

Where the selfish motivation is revenge, agents can expect a lower level of accountability and sentencing. Captain Eric Paliwoda, a well-liked officer of the 4th Infantry Division, died in a mortar attack on January 2, 2004. This division, under Major General Raymond Odierno, had a reputation for aggressive operations, according to the journalist and author Thomas Ricks.[60] In responding to this attack the next day, 4th Infantry soldiers arrested Zaidoun Hassoun and his cousin at a checkpoint. There was no evidence linking them to the mortar attack. The soldiers took the cousins to the Tigris and forced them into the river, and Zaidoun Hassoun drowned. In the proceedings that followed, a sergeant received a six-month sentence and a lieutenant forty-five days for assault. The lieutenant received a lighter sentence in exchange for his testimony. Both the lieutenant and the sergeant were acquitted of manslaughter.

On the same night, January 3, 2004, 4th Infantry soldiers entered Naser Ismail's home and shot him dead. A sergeant told his soldiers when they got to Ismail's house that "we're going to kill this motherfucker."[61] The killing was investigated after a soldier confided in his army psychologist, who then alerted investigators.[62] The court-martial documents described how, prior to the killings, an officer, who had been at West Point with Paliwoda, had given a briefing. At this briefing, the officer had listed individuals linked to the mortar attack and said that these individuals "were not to come back alive."[63] Ismail was on the list. The officer who gave the briefing faced a charge of solicitation of murder. Despite the lieutenant's testimony, the charge was dismissed. The soldier who shot Ismail claimed that he had acted in defense of another soldier. The court found the soldiers not guilty.

If the motivation for an atrocity can be connected to self-defense or to some conception of duty, rather than selfishness, then the soldier is on safer ground. A case in point is that involving an Iraqi general, Abed Hamed Mowhoush, who surrendered to the U.S. Army on November 10, 2003, and was detained at Al-Qaim detention facility. He was beaten, shoved headfirst into a sleeping bag, sat upon, and suffocated. A soldier was charged, found guilty of negligent homicide, fined, and sentenced to two months' house, office, and church confinement. His lawyer's interpretation of the outcome of the trial was that the court had agreed with the argument that his client was doing what he thought was his duty in the absence of detailed instructions from his commander. The lawyer urged that we must back our soldiers when they have risked their lives.[64] The soldier had authorization from a major to use a sleeping bag in interrogation. The major said she did not know that the interrogation would also involve the victim being tied up and sat upon.[65] The soldier saw what he did as fulfilling his moral duty to protect other American soldiers.[66] In other words, he asserted that there was no goal variance. At that time, American commanders had shifted actionable intelligence to the top of their priorities as they scrambled to deal with the unanticipated insurgency.[67] If abuse or killing can be associated with duty, misconceived as it might be, then blame will not fall too heavily on the perpetrator. Those most at risk of severe punishment are those whose own selfish motivations for their actions are clear.

Accountability

Crimes do not go entirely unpunished. But the poet laureate is right about the general pattern of accountability in Western democracies. Where it is administered, punishment falls to the lowest plausible level and tends to be light.

In one other case from Iraq, a Danish captain and four military police accused of breaching the Geneva Conventions in interrogations of Iraqis were all acquitted.[68] "Command responsibility" had career implications for General Karpinski at Abu Ghraib; she was demoted. The sentencing data offer little evidence of officers being held accountable for negligence, solicitation, or the behavior of those under their command. Those officers who have been punished were personally involved in shooting, drowning, or abusing the victims. In general, those soldiers most likely to be punished, and to be punished severely, were those who displayed clear evidence of goal variance.

In the light of the Blair government's firm commitment to a human rights agenda, the most surprising finding is the weakness of the British record. British soldiers have been involved in fewer cases of abuse and unlawful killing than Americans, and all occurred in 2003 and 2004. But these cases mostly went unpunished. In the British cases, there was difficulty in obtaining evidence, and, as discussed earlier, there was less incentive to punish.

The Baha Mousa case continues to occupy the government. In a legal action separate from the court-martial, the Mousa case was taken to the House of Lords on appeal. The issue was whether the United Kingdom Human Rights Act of 1998 applied abroad. In *Al-Skeini and others v. Secretary of State for Defence*, the government argued that it did not apply and opposed an independent public inquiry. The House of Lords disagreed, ruling that the Human Rights Act applied abroad to those detained by British forces. As a consequence, the Ministry of Defense announced that a public inquiry would be held and that compensation would be paid to the Mousa family and to the other Iraqis abused by the British soldiers.[69] The report of the inquiry was to be published in the autumn of 2011. The government's actions in this case suggest that it had preferred to leave accountability at the result arrived at by the court martial—one soldier serving twelve months.

At the Mousa inquiry, there were questions about how the secretary of state for defense and the minister of state for the armed forces had exercised their responsibilities. The minister of state for the armed forces, Adam Ingram, was questioned about statements he had provided to Parliament in 2004. At that time, the minister denied being aware of the use of hooding for interrogations. However, it was revealed that he had been briefed on the use of this technique. The minister blamed his civil servants: "it would have been better if the department had reminded me of all the documentation."[70] On a separate occasion, Ingram wrote to the chair of Parliament's Joint Human Rights Committee in June 2004, stating: "I should make absolutely clear that hooding was only used during the transit of prisoners; it was not used as an interrogation technique." Rabinder Singh, counsel for Mousa's family, questioned Ingram about this denial.

SINGH: It is just not accurate, is it?

INGRAM: That's correct.

SINGH: You knew, by this time, of Baha Mousa having been hooded for something like 24 hours in September 2003, didn't you?

INGRAM: Albeit not continually.

SINGH: He was not in the process of transit, was he?

INGRAM: That's correct.[71]

Although committed to human rights, the Labor government behaved much like any other government when confronted with human rights violations by its own forces.

The question of ministerial responsibility was raised with the secretary of state for Defense, Geoff Hoon, in May 2004. Hoon told the House of Commons that, of thirty-three cases of deaths, injuries, and ill treatment, in fifteen there had been "no case to answer" and that, at that point, six were under investigation.[72] He discussed a February 2004 report by the International Committee of the Red Cross on the treatment of detainees in Iraq. The report included mention of the Mousa case and the use of hooding by British forces. Like Minister of State Ingram, Hoon shifted responsibility down to his department. He claimed that the report had been looked at by officials and that ministers had not seen the report until "very recently." A Conservative member of Parliament noted that "if the recent allegations against British soldiers are found to be true, they must be proceeded against with the full rigour of military law" and then said, "Is the Secretary of State really being serious in telling the House that neither he nor any other Minister . . . was made aware of the ICRC report until very recently because it was given to the British Government in confidence?"[73] A week later, the Commons returned to the issue and questioned whether Hoon could "use his officials as a bombproof shelter for him and his fellow Ministers. . . . It should have been blindingly obvious that those reports should have been at the top of the Secretary of State's agenda."[74] Hoon told the House that the Conservatives were not going to turn this case "into some sort of ministerial responsibility."[75] The *Economist* discussed the claim that only officials, not ministers, had seen the Red Cross report: "It seems extraordinary that . . . they did not think to warn their political masters that they were sitting on such damaging material. The impression conveyed is not so much of attempted cover-up, as some have suggested, but of incompetence."[76] In the House of Commons, MPs sought reassurance in the more widespread allegations of violations by American soldiers. They called for Donald Rumsfeld to resign.

The record of American and British war crimes and punishment in Iraq illustrates the heaviness of the decision to commit soldiers to a conflict where they are in close contact with the civilian population. Democratic politicians take this decision. It then exposes them to conflicting pressures of which they may have only a dim awareness when taking the decision to deploy. The principles associated with democracy are likely to conflict with the ability to maintain the loyalty and commitment of those who serve. Even if leaders are not complicit in the abuse or atrocity, accountability is a demanding test.

APPENDIX 9.1.

Cases Involving Unlawful Killing or Abuse of Iraqi Civilians or Detainees, 2003–2008

RANK OF ACCUSED	MAIN ALLEGATION	MAIN OUTCOME
UNITED KINGDOM CASES		
2003		
Unknown	detainee death on helicopter	charges dropped or acquitted
Unknown	detainee death on helicopter	charges dropped or acquitted
Unknown	detainee death on helicopter	charges dropped or acquitted
Fusilier	disgraceful/indecent conduct, Camp Breadbasket	9 months
Corporal	disgraceful/cruel conduct, Camp Breadbasket	18 months
Corporal	assault/indecent conduct, Camp Breadbasket	2 years
Corporal	assault/indecent conduct, Camp Breadbasket	6 months
Guardsman	drowning of Ahmed Jabar Karheem	charges dropped or acquitted
Corporal	drowning of Ahmed Jabar Karheem	charges dropped or acquitted
Guardsman	drowning of Ahmed Jabar Karheem	charges dropped or acquitted
Sergeant	drowning of Ahmed Jabar Karheem	charges dropped or acquitted
Private	murder of Nadhim Abdullah	charges dropped or acquitted
Private	murder of Nadhim Abdullah	charges dropped or acquitted
Private	murder of Nadhim Abdullah	charges dropped or acquitted
Private	murder of Nadhim Abdullah	charges dropped or acquitted
Private	murder of Nadhim Abdullah	charges dropped or acquitted
Private	murder of Nadhim Abdullah	charges dropped or acquitted
Corporal	murder of Nadhim Abdullah	charges dropped or acquitted
Officer	drowning of Said Shabram	charges dropped or acquitted
Soldier	drowning of Said Shabram	charges dropped or acquitted
Soldier	drowning of Said Shabram	charges dropped or acquitted
Private	wounding of 13-year-old	fined £750
Trooper	murder of Hassan Abbad Said	charges dropped or acquitted
Corporal	murder of civilian in car	charges dropped or acquitted
Corporal	inhuman conduct, Baha Mousa case	charges dropped or acquitted
Kingsman	inhuman conduct, Baha Mousa case	charges dropped or acquitted
Colonel	negligence, Baha Mousa case	charges dropped or acquitted
Major	negligence, Baha Mousa case	charges dropped or acquitted

RANK OF ACCUSED	MAIN ALLEGATION	MAIN OUTCOME
Sergeant	assault, Baha Mousa case	charges dropped or acquitted
Warrant Off.	negligence, Baha Mousa case	charges dropped or acquitted
Corporal	manslaughter, Baha Mousa case	12 months
2004		
Corporal	murder of Gatteh al-Roomi	charges dropped or acquitted
Unknown	abuse and assault	charges dropped or acquitted
Unknown	abuse and assault	charges dropped or acquitted
Corporal	abuse and assault	charges dropped or acquitted

UNITED STATES CASES

2003		
Private	assault of detainees	2 months
Private	assault of detainees	12 months
Sergeant	assault of detainees	15 months
Private	assault of detainees	8 months
Sergeant	mistreatment of Iraqi POWs	military discharge
Sergeant	mistreatment of Iraqi POWs	military discharge
Sergeant	mistreatment of Iraqi POWs	military discharge
Specialist	mistreatment of Iraqi POWs	military discharge
Captain	assault	45 days
Corporal	maltreatment of detainees	3 months
Corporal	homicide of Nagem Hatab	charges dropped or acquitted
Major	dereliction of duty in Nagem Hatab case	military discharge
Sergeant	abuse in Nagem Hatab case	60 days of extra duties
Private	involved in Nagem Hatab case	immunity for testifying
Major	dereliction of duty	charges dropped or acquitted
Corporal	maltreating detainees	4 months
Lieutenant	assault in Manadel al-Jamadi case	charges dropped or acquitted
Lieutenant	conduct unbecoming an officer, striking three prisoners	fined $12,000
Sergeant	murder of wounded 16-year-old	12 months
Sergeant	murder of wounded 16-year-old	12 months
Lieutenant	murder of wounded 16-year-old	charges dropped or acquitted
Lt. Colonel	mistreatment of a detainee, staging a "mock execution"	relieved of command
Specialist	fatal shooting of Obeed Radad	military discharge
Corporal	negligent homicide	18 months
Sergeant	maltreatment of detainees, Abu Ghraib	6 months

RANK OF ACCUSED	MAIN ALLEGATION	MAIN OUTCOME
Private	maltreatment of detainees, indecent act, Abu Ghraib	3 years
Specialist	maltreatment of detainees, Abu Ghraib	fine
Sergeant	use of dog for abuse, Abu Ghraib	90 days hard labor
Specialist	maltreatment of detainees, Abu Ghraib	8 months
Sergeant	maltreatment of detainees, indecent act, Abu Ghraib	8 years, released on parole after 3 years
Specialist	maltreating detainees, indecent act, Abu Ghraib	10 years
Specialist	maltreatment of detainees, indecent act, Abu Ghraib	6 months
Lt. Colonel	failure to train and supervise, Abu Ghraib	letter of reprimand
Specialist	maltreatment of detainees, Abu Ghraib	10 months
Specialist	maltreatment of detainees, Abu Ghraib	12 months
Sergeant	maltreatment of detainees, indecent act, Abu Ghraib	6 months
Specialist	murder of General Mowhoush	immunity for testifying
Sergeant	murder of General Mowhoush	immunity for testifying
Warrant Off.	negligent homicide of General Mowhoush	immunity for testifying
Warrant Off.	negligent homicide of General Mowhoush	2 months (restricted to house, office, and church)
2004		
Specialist	assault of Zaidoun Hassoun	charges dropped or acquitted
Sergeant	drowning of Zaidoun Hassoun	charges dropped or acquitted
Sergeant	drowning of Zaidoun Hassoun	6 months
Lieutenant	drowning of Zaidoun Hassoun	45 days
Captain	solicitation of murder	charges dropped or acquitted
Sergeant	murder of unarmed Iraqi	charges dropped or acquitted
Private	manslaughter, shooting Iraqi in the back of the head	3 years
Lieutenant	murder of two Iraqis	charges dropped or acquitted
Specialist	murder of Iraqi after consensual sex	25 years
Private	murder of two Iraqis	5 years
Sergeant	murder of two Iraqis	25 years
Private	manslaughter, shot woman from roof	6 months
Sergeant	murder of hand-cuffed detainee	7 years

RANK OF ACCUSED	MAIN ALLEGATION	MAIN OUTCOME
Corporal	fatal shooting wounded Iraqi in a mosque	charges dropped or acquitted
Sergeant	manslaughter, two Iraqi insurgents	charges dropped or acquitted
Sergeant	murder, two Iraqi insurgents	reduced in rank after plea
Sergeant	murder, two Iraqi insurgents	charges dropped or acquitted
Specialist	manslaughter, shooting of translator	18 months
Specialist	manslaughter, shooting of translator	3 years
2005		
Sergeant	attempted murder	charges dropped or acquitted
Captain	shooting of wounded Iraqi	military discharge
Sergeant	maltreatment of detainees	5 months
Sergeant	maltreatment of detainees	12 months
Sergeant	maltreatment of detainees	6 months
Lt. Colonel	dereliction of duty, Haditha	charges dropped or acquitted
Sergeant	murder, Haditha	immunity for testifying
Lieutenant	obstruction of justice, Haditha	charges dropped or acquitted
Captain	failure to investigate, Haditha	immunity for testifying
Captain	failure to investigate, Haditha	charges dropped or acquitted
Corporal	murder, Haditha	charges dropped or acquitted
Corporal	murder, Haditha	immunity for testifying
Sergeant	manslaughter, Haditha	court-martial postponed
2006		
Specialist	manslaughter	charges dropped or acquitted
Sergeant	obstruction of justice	reduced in rank
Specialist	sexual assault, murder	life sentence
Sergeant	sexual assault, murder	life sentence
Private	sexual assault, murder	life sentence
Specialist	sexual assault, murder	5 years
Private	sexual assault, murder	life sentence
Sergeant	lookout in sexual assault, murder	immunity for testifying
Petty Off.	murder of disabled victim	1 year
Sergeant	murder of disabled victim	15 years
Corporal	murder of disabled victim	21 months (reduced charges, agreed to testify)
Private	murder of disabled victim	18 months
Corporal	murder of disabled victim	15 months
Corporal	murder of disabled victim	15 months
Corporal	murder of disabled victim	21 months
Corporal	murder of disabled victim	reduced in rank, bad conduct discharge

RANK OF ACCUSED	MAIN ALLEGATION	MAIN OUTCOME
Private	murder of three prisoners	18 years
Sergeant	murder of three prisoners	10 years
Specialist	murder of three prisoners	9 months
Specialist	murder of three prisoners	18 years
2007		
Sergeant	murder of four prisoners	40 years
Sergeant	murder of four prisoners	20 years
Sergeant	murder of four prisoners	20 years
Sergeant	murder of four prisoners	charges dropped or acquitted
Specialist	murder of four prisoners	7 months (reduced charges, agreed to testify)
Specialist	murder of four prisoners	8 months (reduced charges, agreed to testify)
Sergeant	murder of three civilians	10 years
Specialist	murder of three civilians	5 months (reduced charges, agreed to testify)
Sergeant	murder of three civilians	5 months
Medic	attempted murder	charges dropped or acquitted
Sergeant	murder of wounded Iraqi	charges dropped or acquitted
Corporal	accessory to murder	charges dropped or acquitted
Sergeant	murder	charges dropped or acquitted
Specialist	murder of Iraqi national	75 days
Sergeant	manslaughter, sniper killing of two civilians	charges dropped or acquitted
2008		
Lieutenant	murder of Ali Mansur Muhammad	25 years
Sergeant	murder of Ali Mansur Muhammad	17 months (reduced charge, agreed to testify)

⫻ 10 ⫻

A Tale of a Few Cities

Better Leaders, Better Institutions,

or a Better Audience?

The times when it must confront guilt are the worst of times for democracy. Submitting an accurate account and admitting responsibility for wrongdoing or for failing to control those who commit it is an option. Whether in the routine cases of unlawful killing or abuse or in the case of the notorious events in Baghdad, Beirut, or Londonderry, leaders choose not to take that option. If blame is assigned, it goes to the fun-seekers on the midnight shift at Abu Ghraib, to the revenge-seekers of the Christian Militia, or to the ill-disciplined soldiers of 1 Para. If punishment is administered, it tends to be light. Such acts of leadership carry no political penalty.

From time to time, democratic leaders face difficult choices in preserving national security, restoring the rule of law, and protecting the community from terrorism. But, when things go wrong, whether through a calculated policy or carelessness, leaders evade accountability and transfer the blame. There is a simple explanation. They act opportunistically to avoid personal blame or damage to their ability to govern. Leaders must have the loyalty of officials, above all security officials, if they are to govern. It turns out that, despite the conventional view that it is democracy's defining feature, accountability is a surprisingly tough test for a democracy. We must not mistake the presence of the mechanisms of accountability—elections, inquiries and so forth—for the delivery of accountability. Years later, we may obtain a fuller account, too late to sanction those responsible or to redistribute the load of blame if that is merited.

Accountability is a procedure that happens once a violation has occurred. It requires a timely and accurate account of actions and policies and how they meet relevant standards.[1] The everyday usage of the word includes the requirement that consequences follow for those responsible for wrongful actions. It is expected that democracies will deliver accountability. The literature emphasizes the importance of the rule of law and accountability. Leaders in democracies profess to follow these principles. But the cases considered here provide little evidence that these leaders live up to them. The cases fit gravitational logic.

One might quarrel with the argument that leaders try to deflect responsibility by questioning the evidence base. There are other cases. The murders at My Lai, from the Vietnam War, have been discussed at length elsewhere. This case would seem to fit the general theory. At the same time, it is clear that gravity may fail in the political world. A refrain across the cases studied has been that, instead of hoping to get away with their failures, leaders would have been better off coming forward with a more honest account. Senator Susan Collins raised this question with Donald Rumsfeld, a journalist raised it with Ariel Sharon, and Montagu had to address it in the House of Commons. Gravity is a resistible force. Things could be different. But the grounds for optimism are scant. The expectation is that going down with the ship is a nautical, not a political, tradition. Whether or not there are doctrines of ministerial or command responsibility, leaders in democracies do not take responsibility for war crimes and violations of human rights. Nor are they held responsible. The challenge is to find counterexamples where the internal moral compass overcame opportunism's pull. This idea bears a similarity to the empirical quest launched by the statement that democracies do not make war on each other, which has led political scientists to search for counterexamples to the "democratic peace."[2] The search has not had much success without stretching the central concepts of democracy and war. The "cod war" between Britain and Iceland in the 1970s, for example, stretched the concept of war.

With accountability, we begin on firmer footing. In contrast to the democratic peace, the search for accountability starts with the logic and then proceeds to the evidence. But there are also conceptual pitfalls. For example, the claims about democracy's blameless leaders—they do not take responsibility for abuse and atrocity and they are not held responsible—would not be undermined by the taking of notional responsibility in the "man-at-the-top-not-man-at-fault" style of Richard Nixon. For counterexamples to those considered in this book and as a direction for future research, one might examine the performance of other stable democracies with some history of conflict. France in the 1950s fought in Vietnam and Algeria.[3] Australia as well as America committed troops to the Vietnam conflict in the 1960s and 1970s. For the investigation of court-martial data, one might extend the analysis to Afghanistan (2001–).

It is worth addressing the failure of accountability for all concerned. The failure of accountability is bad for victims and for survivors, who bear the highest costs. It is bad for the fall guy, who carries an unfair share of the blame. It is also bad for democrats, whose politics is not working as it says on the package. It is bad for the past, present, and future stewards of our institutions, most especially for those in the armed services, who are left with stains, untreated, on otherwise proud traditions. Failures of accountability may even be bad for the one who evades the blame, if uneasy lies his head. In this chapter, I distill the major findings of this book and think about what they imply for a remedy in this most serious of policy areas.

The Performance of Leaders and Institutions

In the wake of atrocity, political leaders resort to denial, delay, diversion, and delegation. They do so even when they have not been complicit in the abuse and atrocity. They are concerned about protecting their agents and also protecting themselves from charges of incompetence. When leaders are complicit and not simply negligent, the failure of accountability is severe. Aware that the killing of civilians or abusing detainees violates humanitarian and human rights law, rational leaders avoid formal links between their policy pronouncements and the behavior in question. As the philosopher Larry May says, "It is often very hard to find evidence of orders to torture or kill. Instead, the norm seems to be that there are generalized orders, such as the order to 'secure an area' or 'clear civilians from an area.'"[4] Relying on the willingness of agents and on informal understandings, as Ben-Gurion is said to have done in 1948[5] or as Henry II and his squad of French knights are said to have done when they murdered Archbishop Thomas Becket in his cathedral in 1170, makes degrees of complicity hard to determine. Without being able to coordinate documentary evidence and reliable testimony from the leaders and agents involved, it is difficult to come to firm conclusions about the true location of blame. In the absence of the information, sorting out whether the action was calculated policy requires a difficult judgment. For the leader who wants to jump ship rather than go down with it, the chance that the action represented a simple agency problem is the life raft of reasonable doubt.

In any organization, there are problems of control. Those employed to carry out tasks misbehave. Some abuse of prisoners by security forces is a simple agency problem; the difficulty is distinguishing a case of *can't control* from a case of *won't control*. We can make two mistakes in deciding which is which.[6] In the first case, the conspiracy theorist mistakenly categorizes every killing as a case of *won't control*. Worldly-wise, she rejects all official statements as untrue. In the second case, the loyal apologist mistakenly categorizes every killing as a case of *can't control*. He naively accepts all official statements as true. Accountability requires that we avoid both mistakes.

Of the cases discussed in this book, it is easiest to rule out complicity in the massacre at Amritsar. This was a violation initiated by an individual. A combination of incompetence and vanity is the likely explanation. General Dyer's civilian counterpart in the city hurriedly distanced himself from the event, and his immediate superiors in the Punjab gave approval after the event, encouraging Dyer to think he would receive credit, not blame, for the action. But, when external pressure mounted—not when they first had information about the event—political leaders in London condemned the "frightfulness" of the massacre. Responsibility for the massacre belongs at a higher level only for those whose analytical focus shifts away from individual actions to the wider and more abstract landscape of geopolitical structures and relationships and who picture Dyer as a fall guy for imperial rule. But if the massacre was an individually initiated violation, the timing of the accountability process as a response to Indian political pressure and the token and equivocal nature of the punishment imposed by the institutions of this representative democracy reflect the competing audience demands.

In contrast to Amritsar, it is least easy to rule out complicity in the cases of Dresden and Abu Ghraib. In those cases, there is some documentary evidence of the involvement of leaders. The blame for the terror bombing and for the abuse was shifted to those below. In the other two cases, Londonderry and Beirut, the documentary evidence is patchier. There is some evidence that political and military leaders calculated that there were strategic benefits—avoiding further casualties, changing the demography, using shooting as a last-ditch effort to end the conflict—to be derived from putting the civilian population at mortal risk. Against the advice of other officers or intelligence officials, in both Londonderry and Beirut, military and political leaders knowingly placed militia or regular units with a prior reputation for brutal behavior among the civilian population. They then failed to properly supervise and control these units. The members of these units took the blame for breach of discipline (in the case of Londonderry, after the Saville Report in 2010) and unusually poor combat morality (in the case of Beirut). But, at the bottom, only those involved at Abu Ghraib, where their selfish motivations for the violations were on display, served time in prison.

Democratic folklore refers to ministerial responsibility and the buck stopping in the highest office. But it has things upside down. Democracies do not hold those in leadership positions accountable for policy disasters involving the killing and abuse of civilians. Disaster is not too strong a category for these policies. Even ignoring the disgrace of killing or abusing civilians and detainees, the net effect of these actions was probably counterproductive for security goals. These actions motivated backlash violence and unrest, alienated groups and communities, and reassured tyrants elsewhere.

Instead of shifting blame to the lowest plausible level, a commitment to accountability requires timely and accurate information about an action. A dimension of justice requires proper recognition of a wrong. Those injured in the cases cited did not get this from democracy's blameless political leaders. The results of congressional investigations and public inquiries were mixed in terms of putting it right. The punishment consequences, if any, were generally light.

Political scientists expect presidential systems to produce more transparency than parliamentary systems for several reasons.[7] In presidential systems, the executive has less control of the legislature. The legislature's committees are powerful. The members of political parties in the legislature are less under the discipline of their party leaders than are their parliamentary counterparts. Finally, officials are responsive to both the legislature and the president. In the language of analysis, these officials have multiple principals, giving greater access across the different branches of government to information. But transparency takes time to develop. Five years after the events at Abu Ghraib grabbed worldwide attention, in April 2009, the Senate Armed Services Committee released its declassified report (completed in November 2008). A Democratic senator from Michigan, Carl Levin, described the committee's report as putting the record straight and emphatically rejected the idea that blame belonged at the bottom: "Attempts by senior officials to portray [the bad apples scenario] to be the case while shrugging off any responsibility for abuses are both unconscionable and false. Our investigation is an effort to set the record straight on this chapter in our history that has so damaged both America's standing and our security. America needs to own up to its mistakes."[8] The report of this committee described the counterproductive nature of the action; it tracked the transfer of techniques from Afghanistan to Iraq and made clear leaders' responsibility for the abuse and their use of fall guys.

Parliamentary systems have a mixed record on providing information. There is ample evidence of the importance of parliamentary questioning in raising the issue of accountability; Richard Stokes before and after the Dresden bombing, Merlyn Rees after Bloody Sunday, and Shimon Peres in the Israeli Knesset asked telling and important questions. But parliamentary exchanges did not produce an accurate account. Responsibility for that task was delegated to public inquiries, except in the case of Dresden.[9] Months before that city was obliterated, Churchill had the authority to dismiss a bombing survey as a "sterile" exercise. Fortunately, sterile exercises appeal to historians.

While government leaders seek a "safe pair of hands" to conduct investigations, inquiries vary in their composition, rules, terms of reference, and appearance of impartiality. This variability is an indicator of the pressures leaders feel on an issue. Pressure comes from the personal wish of leaders to avoid blame, from their officials, and from the external domestic and international audiences. Any form of inquiry is recognition of a level of external pressure (Menachem Begin considered it an admission of guilt). The background of the members of the inquiry—for example, whether they are former soldiers—may reflect sensitivity to this pressure. In the cases considered here, the number of members on the tribunal was itself a crude barometer of government sensitivity to pressure. The greater the sensitivity to the external audience, the more members the government was willing to appoint. The greater the sensitivity to the agent confidence factor or to personal concern to avoid blame, the more likely the government was to ask the chair of the inquiry to sit alone, as Begin tried with Kahan and Heath succeeded with Widgery. Generally speaking, the fewer the members, the easier it is for leaders to maintain control of the inquiry. The greater the efforts in the direction of impartiality, the more members were likely to be appointed. Inquiry panels may also have an international component or include representatives of the affected population (e.g., the Indian representation on the Hunter Committee). Such a composition is an indication that the the pressure felt by leaders weighed most heavily on the side of the external audience. The appointment of the Hunter Committee and the Saville Inquiry occurred in the context of broader policy agendas. Ministers at the time needed the cooperation of Indians in reforming imperial relations and from the Irish government in brokering an end to the conflict in Northern Ireland. The Widgery Tribunal was at the other end of the scale. In that case, the prime minister declared that propaganda was a priority. The three-person Kahan Commission in Israel was more independent. Begin, like Heath, wanted to control the proceedings and wanted Kahan to conduct a limited inquiry. But his initial crude mismanagement of the blame, along with public and IDF pressure, Israeli coalition politics, and Kahan himself, presented obstacles to this. Begin waited ten days to name an investigator, allowing criticism to grow within his own coalition and demonstrations to be organized. The prime minister's unwillingness to permit an inquiry itself became a focus of criticism.[10] Consequently, he conceded more control of the inquiry. In contrast, Heath acted immediately to appoint his Lord Chief Justice to lead the inquiry into Bloody Sunday.

Begin got an inquiry that had more powers than he wanted. It went further than he anticipated and examined ministerial responsibility. But the damage was, from a blame management perspective, limited. The international lawyer Richard Falk says of the Kahan investigation that "in the end the Israeli leadership is censured for its carelessness, and that alone."[11] For Israeli democracy, the Kahan Commission report acted as a restorative. The Saville Inquiry might have followed Kahan's example, not just by finishing the inquiry in six months. It, too, might have given systematic minister-by-minister consideration to the question of ministerial responsibility for the "carelessness" of placing ill-disciplined troops with a known record of brutal behavior in a volatile situation..

The lack of consequences for those at the top puts Western democracies in a difficult position. Perhaps you recall that MP's question in the Amritsar debate about how to tell off Turks for what they did to the Armenians. How do we tell off the Serbs for what they did to the Bosnians? The political leader of the Bosnian Serbs, Radovan Karadžić, was arrested in 2008 and is on trial at the International Criminal Tribunal for the Former Yugoslavia in the Hague. Charges include failure to investigate and take corrective action against members of Serb forces who committed atrocities in Bosnia. It is doubtless irritating to compare what happened in Iraq or Northern Ireland with the war in the former Yugoslavia. There is a vast difference, for example, between the number of victims in Londonderry and the number killed in the various shooting and shelling incidents in the Balkans, as there was between the number killed in the massacre in Amritsar and in the Armenian genocide. The situations are not equivalent, but we should expect some unwelcome parallels to be drawn. Paragraph 35 of the 2009 indictment of Karadžić reads as follows:

> Radovan Karadžić failed to take the necessary and reasonable measures to prevent the commission of crimes by members of the Bosnian Serb Forces and/or Bosnian Serb Political and Governmental Organs and/or to punish the perpetrators thereof . . . his failure to take such necessary and reasonable measures include: (a) his failure to order or initiate genuine or adequate investigations into credible allegations of the commission of crimes by Bosnian Serb Forces and/or Bosnian Serb Political and Governmental Organs; (b) his failure to report information about the commission or possible commission of crimes by Bosnian Serb Forces and/or Bosnian Serb Political and Governmental Organs to the appropriate authorities; (c) his failure to discipline, dismiss, demote or refrain from promoting or rewarding members of the Bosnian Serb Forces and/or Bosnian Serb Political and Governmental Organs who were involved in the commission of crimes and/or who failed to prevent or punish the commission of crimes by their subordinates; and/or (d) his failure to issue the orders that were necessary and reasonable in the circumstances to prohibit or put a stop to the commission of crimes by Bosnian Serb Forces and/or Bosnian Serb Political and Governmental Organs.[12]

The Bosnian Serb leader was faulted for promoting and rewarding and for not preventing, investigating, and punishing. In Northern Ireland, whether or not there was a plan to shoot hooligans and retake the "no go" areas in Londonderry, officers failed to prevent or to punish the unjustified shooting by their subordinates. Key officers present on Bloody Sunday were promoted or honored. There was a failure to initiate an adequate investigation into credible allegations of crimes by British forces. No British political leader took responsibility.

In contrast, ministerial responsibility does operate where there is a sexual or financial content to the wrongdoing. In those cases, ministers resign. Why is punishment likely in these cases? When an individual minister seeks sexual or financial reward, the task is less easily delegated to someone else. And such cases exhibit clear evidence of goal variance: the individual is driven by a desire for personal gain. Misleading the House of

Commons is risky behavior. Ministers lose their posts for that. But, even with that, it is whether they have done so for personal gain that seems the central issue. Secretary for War John Profumo resigned in 1963 for misleading the House of Commons about his private life. The political scientists Keith Dowding and colleagues say that "the cardinal sin for ministers is to be found to have misled parliament: a minister who makes a statement to the House that he knows to be wrong, or should have been briefed not to have made, will except in the most unusual circumstances have to resign."[13] After Bloody Sunday, the home secretary, Reginald Maudling, and the minister of state for defense, Lord Balniel, made statements that they should have been briefed not to make. The statements were based on lists reportedly compiled from the false accounts of privates, corporals, and sergeants who had done the shooting. The statements were contradicted by the credible accounts of the mainstream press, religious leaders, and others who witnessed the event. At the time, Maudling was accused of lying. There was no other consequence than that he had his face slapped by his accuser, Bernadette Devlin, the member for Mid-Ulster.

In the cases examined here, the leaders were not seeking private gain from the killing or abuse. Although the action in question may have been counterproductive, the leaders had a conception of national security. They were seeking an end to a conflict, actionable intelligence, or perhaps the removal of a suspect population. The actions, mistaken though they may have been, were done in the name of the people of Britain, the United States, or Israel. If leaders were complicit in the actions, it was not for some personal advantage. And they were not held to account. The closest any political leader came to political accountability was Ariel Sharon, who changed his seat in the cabinet (and pointed out that he had not been fired). He later went on to become prime minister. If there was any loss for the leaders, it was felt through the softer forms of accountability. But loss of sleep and image are dependent on the personal and public mood. No one doubts the authenticity of Macbeth's pain, but these forms of accountability are not singularly democratic ones, are difficult to measure, and are too intangible to offer a satisfactory basis for claims of democratic accountability.

Some would argue that it is appropriate that a leader of Sharon's caliber did not get derailed by Beirut. Even human rights conventions allow governments some latitude in living up to their human rights obligations "in times of public emergency," although there is no derogation from the prohibitions on killing and torture. But if there are no tangible consequences for leaders, that decision must be made on the basis of informed deliberation by citizens and their legislatures. They must know how their leaders understand their responsibility for national security and be aware of the policies pursued in their interest.

The Theory of the Fall Guy: Extending and Testing the Argument

The argument that leaders seek to avoid accountability in any of the several ways that I have described applies to cases involving the use of armed forces, the killing of civilians, and the violation of human rights and humanitarian law. Beyond extending the search for counterexamples where accountability was delivered for these kinds of rights violations, distinguishing in our measures of violations between individual and state initiated violations and cases of *can't control* or *won't control*, analyzing public opinion for the public's tolerance for our own war crimes, and investigating whether voters ever punish their elected representatives for cases of abuse and atrocity or reward them for exposing them, there is also the question of whether the argument applies to other policy areas and institutions. A way to think about this question is to consider the incentives involved. What are the incentives to participate in the accountability process?[14] According to the argument, human rights violations typically provide strong incentives to cheat and weak incentives to deliver.

The strong incentives to cheat reflect the high and concentrated costs of being held to account. Wrongdoing in this policy area raises issues of criminal liability, as well as political survival. As the Allies insisted at Nuremberg and the Western democracies have insisted more recently, there is now individualized responsibility in this area at the level of military and political leaders. Adding to the costs is countries' dependency on security forces to enforce policy. The policy domain is occupied by those agents that Hume says leaders can least afford to cross. Although agents are formally subordinate to elected representatives, leaders' need to retain their confidence. This factor takes on increased magnitude during armed conflict. The strength of these agents' position rests with their monopoly on the means of violence. They cannot easily be replaced. In addition, these agents, in contrast to social workers, for example, have special resonance with the domestic public in the U.S., British, and Israeli democracies. The public do not want their troops "vilified," in the words of Lord Balniel in 1972. If a particular issue of accountability poses lower individual costs and involves easily substitutable agents, it may be easier for leaders to resist the temptation to cheat.

On the other side, it is the victims and their families who seek the benefits of accountability. For them, the benefits are concentrated and intense. For ordinary voters, on the other hand, the benefits are likely to be more diffuse (only at Londonderry were victims voters). Voters are concerned about the troops that politicians have sent to difficult places. They may prefer to focus on the aberrant and anomalous nature of the violation and move on, rather than be forced to dwell on the unpleasant details by a process of accountability. Where benefits are thinly spread across voters, there is less incentive to participate in the political process. Consequently, for opposition party candidates, human rights violations represent an issue that can backfire. Such issues are better avoided.

Only in cases of personal involvement in some act of selfishness are leaders likely to be vulnerable to processes of accountability. Somewhat surprisingly, research suggests that, even when corruption is involved and there is clear evidence of goal variance, "elections have proved rather ineffective in pruning governmental institutions of their corrupt members" and that voters do not exercise their responsibility very reliably.[15] The type of election system and whether candidates themselves are exposed to a selection procedure is likely to influence the way voters exercise their responsibilities.

In addition to unethical behavior associated with corruption and sex, leaders may improperly seek a narrow political advantage. President Richard M. Nixon, in the early 1970s, denied involvement with a burglary organized by his 1972 reelection campaign and its aftermath. He was undone by the "smoking gun" tape, on which he was heard agreeing to use the pretext of national security and the CIA to obstruct justice. Unable to disguise his selfish intent, he eventually resigned to avoid impeachment. As with Clinton's impeachment by the House of Representatives over his relationship with Monica Lewinsky and questions of whether he had lied under oath about it, there was clear goal variance, despite the "national security" pretext, and there was direct participation, rather than delegation.[16] In this case, research by Gerald Wright suggests that, after Watergate, voters did punish Nixon loyalists on the House Judiciary Committee. However, his analysis also shows that the incentives to pursue wrongdoing are less clear. Voters in congressional elections did not reward Democrats on the committee for voting to impeach Nixon.[17]

Beyond government, the argument should have application to the management of blame for unlawful acts in other hierarchical institutions. Corporations or churches are obvious examples. In the handling of cases of abuse, members of a church hierarchy are likely to act opportunistically. They wish to avoid personal blame and to maintain the loyalty of their officials. The officials are not easily substitutable. If denial fails, they will arrange a soft landing for those left with the blame. Critical questions involve whether the abuse was a result of a *can't control* or a *won't control* leadership and how much the faithful want to know—not much, if the Grand Inquisitor is correct. According to Dostoyevsky's fable, humankind does not want freedom and knowledge. It wants "miracle, mystery, and authority."[18] Under these conditions and with this audience, wrongdoing is likely to take some time to expose. With corporations, however, shareholders may be more assertive in exposing it.

Remedies: Individual, Institutional, International, and Moral

This book's purpose has been to examine and explain how democracies manage blame after cases of abuse and atrocity. Swept up in the drama of a particular event, we seem not to notice that the failure of accountability is systemic. The puzzle is why, despite democratic mechanisms and norms, leaders are able to evade accountability. In addressing this puzzle, this analysis has implications for how to remedy the situation. The primary implication is that the situation is not easily remedied; perhaps we make the association between accountability and democracy too easily. The reasoning is along the following lines. It is not that the institutional levers to lift blame to the appropriate level are missing. We have at our disposal elections and votes of confidence in the legislature; in addition, leaders can lose the confidence of their cabinet colleagues (as Margaret Thatcher found out in 1990, when her eleven-year tenure as prime minister came to an end). These levers are in place. The problem is that, when it comes to abuse and atrocity, we apparently lack the will to pull them. Pulling them requires a commitment to informed and responsible decision making, to upholding human rights commitments, and to the rule of law. But, as a French philosopher says, our remembrance is selective: "Yet the essence of a nation is that all individuals have many things in common; and also that they have forgotten many things. . . . Every French citizen has to have forgotten the massacre of Saint Bartholomew."[19] It is difficult to motivate democratic leaders if the audience prefers oblivion, not the truth, about Saint Bartholomew's Day. In other words, we cannot expect politicians to behave properly if voters are indifferent to the exercise of control. As the failure of accountability and the search for scapegoats have been with us all along, as they are features of parliamentary and presidential democracies, and as there is little evidence that we are getting better, there are not good grounds for optimism. On the other hand, this failure is a choice, there is analysis, and so there is the possibility of learning and improvement.

Better Leaders?

The failure of accountability is not a failure of a singularly poor leader or of a particular institutional arrangement. Of course, not all leaders are equally poor. Not all have to weather charges of abuse and atrocity. Some choose not to resort to harsher measures, vague commands, unplain English, or untrustworthy militias or to invade another country in the first place. Some can remind us of good days in office and of the difference they made. But when they face charges of abuse or atrocity, leaders are alike. They give in to the temptation to let others bear the blame. For war crimes and human rights violations, there is a failure of accountability across both parliamentary and presidential systems and over time. Indeed, if anthropologists are right, failed accountability is the human condition. Sir James Frazer tells us that "the notion that we can transfer our guilt and sufferings to some other being who will bear them for us is familiar to the savage mind."[20] He goes on to describe the use of scapegoats in classical antiquity. Athenians "regularly maintained a number of degraded and useless beings [bad apples] at public expense; and when any calamity . . . befell the city, they sacrificed two of these outcasts as scapegoats."[21] The contemporary leader retains a savage mind.

Better Institutions?

If it is unrealistic to expect better leaders, we still expect institutions to tame the leaders we have. Both parliamentary and presidential systems fail in this task. What is more, there is little evidence of learning. When it comes to ministerial responsibility, we are where Professor Finer was in the 1950s. As far as inquiries go, there was a loss of learning between the 1920 Hunter

Committee into the Amritsar massacre and the 1972 Widgery Inquiry into Bloody Sunday. Inaccurate accounts and the refusal to recognize the harm that has been done, the transference of blame and the token punishment, remain characteristic of the management of these events.

Better International Institutions?

When domestic institutions fail, it is tempting to turn to the expanding international public sector. Some advise that nations delegate responsibility for delivering accountability to international legal institutions. The International Criminal Court promises to individualize responsibility before impartial judges who apply a common standard to past and present political and military leaders. But we should also be aware that there are some serious drawbacks to shifting responsibility in this way. Such a delegation shifts a democratic responsibility to a legal institution. It reduces accountability to legal accountability, where the legal position may not be clear. Churchill condemned it after the fact, but the legality of bombing Dresden is still disputed. There was and is no convention on aerial warfare. As Arthur Harris pointed out, civilian deaths can also result from blockades and embargoes. Even where the legal context is clear, shifting responsibility to international institutions is unlikely to answer. In particular, such institutions are less able to bring to account the powerful Western democracies that are at the center of this analysis.

International institutions incorporate a bias that frustrates accountability. This bias results from the fact that they are dependent on the cooperation of nation states. The operation of these institutions reflects disparities in the power of states. Were all nations to ratify the 1998 Rome Statute that set up the International Criminal Court, there would likely remain a bias in implementation reflecting the international distribution of power. A decade on, the ICC's caseload was entirely African. Western democracies are unlikely to cooperate where their own forces are concerned. As political scientists Ruth Grant and Robert Keohane observe, there is great variability in the responsiveness of states to external accountability mechanisms.[22]

Whatever their inadequacies or their strengths, the fact remains that shifting responsibility to international institutions is not a substitute for the exercise of democratic accountability. The key question for a democracy is the one posed by Richard Stokes MP. After Dresden, he asked, "Is terror bombing—perhaps the Minister will answer me—now part of our policy . . . why is it that the British people are the only people who may not know what is done in their name?"[23] Similarly, the Israeli and American people need to know what hidden actions are taken and what policies are followed in their name. In his *Considerations on Representative Government*, John Stuart Mill says that "the first question in respect to any political institution is how far they tend to foster in the members of the community the various desirable qualities, moral and intellectual."[24] If one thinks of democracy as something more than a set of procedural devices, citizens and their representatives ought not be relieved of the burden of active participation in delivering accountability.

Better Soldiers?

The political and military dimensions of the issue are comparable. There are mechanisms in place to hold both officers and soldiers accountable. In Iraq, the American system delivered more punishment than the British, but to those at the lowest levels in the hierarchy. The British Army's Aitken Report into wrongdoing by British soldiers in Iraq observed that the idea for going into that country was to improve the people's welfare.[25] It described the abuse as counterproductive and said that it was a consequence of soldiers and commanders abandoning the army's core values.[26] As the Aitken Report suggested, countering the insurgency depended on winning both the military and the "propaganda" wars. Beyond the obvious strategic consideration, those who served honorably want to distance themselves from those who did not. Nevertheless, it is a tough challenge to put qualifications on soldiers' loyalties to each other and to communicate a distinction between good and bad forms ("selective memory loss") of loyalty.[27] A major problem, as we saw in the British abuse cases, was the lack of information. If, as this report argues, soldiers are motivated by core values (selfless commitment, courage, discipline, integrity, loyalty, respect for others), the mechanisms of accountability may become effective. Furthermore, those core values provide soldiers with insulation from manipulation by *won't control* commanders. Adherence to these values would protect them from vague general orders to "work detainees hard," entrapment into committing violations, and the prospect of being left with the blame. These values provide a basis on which to question such exercises of authority. Like loyalty, rule following is double-edged. Like the predisposition to transfer guilt, a predisposition to demonstrate obedience seems to be the human condition. In a famous experiment at Yale University, the psychologist Stanley Milgram demonstrated people's willingness to inflict harm on command for trivial purposes. In his journal article on his research, he ended his analysis with the plea that we question authority.[28] Milgram's article belongs in the kitbag.

Better Audiences?

Years after Bloody Sunday, General Sir Mike Jackson, British chief of the General Staff from 2003 to 2006, emphasized in his memoirs and in the context of Iraq how damaging abuse is to a soldier's self-respect and the importance of the rule of law.[29] Similarly, the analysis here suggests that adherence to core values, not new mechanisms, is the likely path to reform. The theoretical argument assumes that when we enter policy domains where the stakes are very high, principle is left behind, and leaders act opportunistically. It is not that values are unimportant; it is that they are unlikely to provide guidance to leaders under these pressures. As the literature suggests, if accountability is to work, it will do so through adherence to democratic values. The rectitude of individuals is a property developed in relation to others.[30] Officials, with the right esprit de corps, and electoral audiences committed to the rule of law are the democratic remedy and are likely to lead to better leaders. Again, John Stuart Mill gives authority to this point: "if the public, the mainspring of the whole checking machinery, are too ignorant, too passive, or too careless and inattentive to do their part, little benefit will be derived from the best administrative apparatus. . . . Publicity, for instance, is no impediment to evil, nor stimulus to good, if the public will not look at what is done."[31] Both the quality of leadership and the operation of institutional mechanisms depend on properly motivated audiences. That is where to find the will to pull the levers to lift blame to the right level.

But finding the right audience is not an easy prescription. We know that leaders sometimes win popular support for authoritarian policies. President Vladimir Putin of Russia did.[32] In contrast, in established democracies, we expect such policies to be less popular. Yet, democratic publics may accept that the goal of ending the conflict or shifting a suspect population justifies resort to authoritarian means. General Dyer received considerable domestic support, as did Begin and Sharon. Why did not the electorate punish George W. Bush for the policy of abuse that produced the worldwide scandal of Abu Ghraib in 2004? He sought a second term as the scandal broke. The man behind the successful reelection campaign knew our deep-seated aversion to knowing about our own soldiers' atrocities. Karl Rove, Bush's political adviser, singled out some advertisements that targeted John Kerry and the Vietnam War and made it clear that he was not responsible for these advertisements; the Swift Boat Veterans for Truth launched them. "The most powerful attack," Rove said, was "a tape of Kerry testifying before the Senate Foreign Relations Committee in 1971. . . . Kerry said that his comrades in America's military had 'raped, cut off ears . . . randomly shot civilians, razed villages in a fashion reminiscent of Genghis Khan' . . . it was very effective because it used Kerry's own face and words to show him attacking the U.S. military."[33] Kerry's "slandering of his Vietnam comrades," Rove said, also "raised the question of whether the Left would force us to lose another war we could win and for which America had already made considerable sacrifices."[34] The Kerry campaign concurred with Rove in the recognition that abuse by coalition forces in Iraq was not a promising campaign issue. It made this choice even when there was evidence that tied the abuse to the policy decisions of the Republican administration. David Bromwich's review of Rove's autobiography puts it this way: "His point is that you cannot speak of a war crime by Americans and get elected in America."[35] While a central feature of democracy is the claim of accountability, the mechanism of accountability is unlikely to operate when a democracy's troops are responsible for unlawful killings or abuse. If these issues are out of bounds in the competition between political parties, the mechanism will not be engaged.

Some argue that democratic institutions require political leaders to make good policy. Their political survival depends on it.[36] In contrast to authoritarian systems, where leaders hand out a few personal benefits ("Swiss bank accounts") to key supporters, leaders in democracies need a large "winning coalition" in order to hold onto office: "With many supporters demanding rewards, the costs of personal benefits required to keep their loyalty are just too high. Instead, whether leaders are civic-minded or not, those who rely on a large coalition emphasize the production of goods that benefit everyone in their society."[37] Noting that specific definitions of the range of goods may vary, scholars identify a bundle of public goods of universal value. These core public goods include civil liberties, political rights, transparency, peace, and prosperity. Of the types of democratic systems on offer, presidential systems are likely to do best in delivering the goods. Presidents—needing a majority vote—are likely to be dependent on a somewhat larger winning coalition than are prime ministers, whether the parliament is elected through a first-past-the-post system or by a system of proportional representation.[38] With this analytical apparatus, one can detect an "invisible hand" in the political market ("he intends only his own gain, and he is in this, as in many other cases, led by an invisible hand to promote an end which was no part of his intention").[39] The politician seeking office where there is a requirement of a large winning coalition benefits us all, whether or not she is well meaning. She delivers the core public goods to maintain her competitive position in the market for votes. It is an elegant account and a reasoned defense of the importance of representative democracy. Yet, Rove demonstrated the limits of the salutary effect of large winning coalitions. Opposition candidates are ill advised to campaign on abuse and atrocity; doing so may be viewed as evidence of disloyalty. To induce good security policy, the values binding the winning coalition must extend to the rule of law. The electorate must not want to forget their own nation's atrocities. As Mill says, however good the mechanisms, the public must care. Or, put another way, until political leaders calculate that at least they will not lose elections by raising the question of war crimes, democracies will have a deficit of accountability.

The flow of messages from leaders and the media influences the views of voters.[40] In an analysis of American news media coverage of the Abu Ghraib scandal, W. Lance Bennett, Regina Lawrence, and Steven Livingston ask "why the press reported reality during the Iraq years largely as the Bush administration had scripted it?"[41] These authors argue that the label "torture" was appropriate for what had happened at Abu Ghraib. Nevertheless, the press deferred to the administration's descriptions. It did so because of the lack of a strong political opposition willing to claim that there was a policy of torture and in the absence of corroborating evidence from other institutions. Neither the trials of soldiers nor the investigations revealed "bright lines connecting Rumsfeld's policy decisions with the treatment of prisoners photographed at Abu Ghraib."[42] If there was general deference, there were also some examples of independent reporting. As the references to the cases considered in this book show, some journalists provided timely information and analysis that got directly at accountability. Not all deferred. Watchdogs barked. But, as the Middle Eastern adage goes, the caravan moved on.

Political opponents, legislative committees, and even public inquiries draw on news stories not only for information but also for the resolve to push for accountability on an issue. And the journalists from the major newspapers and media outlets have a reciprocal need for support in order to sustain stories critical of the government.[43] The highly critical domestic reporting of the Beirut massacre was sustained by the criticism of Israel's role that developed within the Israeli army. According to one account, pressure from the reserve units and notably the paratroops "finally roused the press to confront Sharon."[44] The combined pressure generated a public inquiry. In the Israeli case at least—and in contrast to what we know of the Bloody Sunday episode—there were a few cabinet colleagues who protested the government's actions and sounded the alarm. No one listened, yet they set an example. Whether it is more realistic to expect a better audience than it is to expect better leaders is arguable. The question is what forces we can harness to oppose gravity. Without underestimating the challenge, we can finish with thinking about how things might be improved.

The Rewards of a Virtuous Action: There is something to be said for putting one's own house in order. There is the incentive of collective self-respect to be had from the self-regulation of the exercise of power. In the aftermath of an atrocity, it is an opportunity for at least a small entry on the credit side of the moral reckoning that would be relinquished if cleaning up were left to an international institution. For example, there are few worse episodes in human history than the slave trade. British business interests dominated this trade in the eighteenth century. The decision to abolish the trade by act of Parliament in 1807 and to enforce the abolition on the high seas allowed for some redemption. That is how the British saw it at the time. A member of Parliament wrote: "We want parliament and the country to practise a notable piece of self-denial, and to do a magnificent act of justice—to pass a kind of self-denying ordinance, and we can only hope that parliament will do this heroic deed in some fit of heroism."[45] Democratic accountability offers the opportunity to retrieve some dignity from the indignity of the atrocious event (human rights conventions commonly recognize inherent human dignity as a starting point). Credit in the moral reckoning is an incentive. But it is likely a weak force beside the short-term desire to transfer blame.

Know the Techniques of Evasion: If there is to be learning, it starts with clarifying the record of accountability. This requires understanding what is going on, valuing plain English, and enumerating the techniques of evasion. We would be better for reading George Orwell's essay "Politics and the English Language."

Rewards for Watchdogs: Dana Priest won a Pulitzer Prize in 2006 for reporting on the Bush administration's secret prisons, and Thomas Friedman won one for his coverage of the Beirut massacre. Our own war crimes must not go unreported. But journalists are under pressure to defer to the government.

Core Values and Won't Control: As recommended in the military context, a reinforcement of core value in politics would likely improve the prospect for accountability. After World War II, Germans, unlike the French and the rest of us, defined nationhood by remembering rather than forgetting. Admittedly, postwar Germany is a special case. There was outside tutelage in the form of occupation, the sins could be linked to another Germany, to the Third Reich, and there was the uniqueness of the Holocaust to concentrate minds on confronting their own guilt.

In leadership circles, accountability requires cabinet ministers and members of the legislature committed to the rule of law and to making of command more than a hollow responsibility for what happens on their watch. These commitments would have to trump the narrower demands of, in this case, party or administration loyalties. As Mrs. Thatcher learned in 1990, motivated cabinet ministers can summon the energy to unseat powerful prime ministers. For motivation, we require audiences that reward candidates for opposing war crimes.

Use of Force: Perhaps the prospect of more immediate progress does lie with the military. Only a small number of the troops who serve faced allegations of misbehavior. Most serve with honor. A soldier intervened on the side of the victims at My Lai. Others raised the alarm in Beirut, Baghdad, and in Londonderry. An emphasis on core values, on Cromwellian pride in their profession, and on command responsibility reduces the chances of abuse and atrocity. Meanwhile, it is best not to place soldiers in these difficult situations, if there is choice in the matter.

Notes

PREFACE

1. House of Commons, *Parliamentary Debates*, July 8, 1920, 131, c. 1720.

CHAPTER ONE

1. Joseph S. Nye Jr., *The Powers to Lead* (Oxford: Oxford University Press, 2008), 122.
2. The case remains the subject of a public inquiry at the time of writing.
3. See Ruth Grant and Robert Keohane, "Accountability and Abuses of Power in World Politics," *American Political Science Review* 99 (February 2005): 29.
4. Priscilla B. Hayner, *Unspeakable Truths: Facing the Challenge of Truth Commissions* (New York: Routledge, 2001).
5. Mark Gibney, Rhoda E. Howard-Hassmann, Jean-Marc Coicaud, and Niklaus Steiner (eds.), *The Age of Apology: Facing Up to the Past* (Philadelphia: University of Pennsylvania Press, 2007).
6. John L. Austin, "A Plea for Excuses," *Philosophical Papers* (1961): 123–152; Morris P. Fiorina, "Group Concentration and Delegation of Legislative Authority," in Roger G. Noll (ed.), *Regulatory Policy and the Social Sciences* (Berkeley: University of California Press, 1985); R. Kent Weaver, "The Politics of Blame Avoidance," *Journal of Public Policy* 6 (October 1986): 371–398. Kathleen McGraw, "Managing Blame: An Experimental Test of the Effects of Political Accounts," *American Political Science Review* 85 (December 1991): 1133–1157. See also Christopher Hood, "The Risk Game and the Blame Game," *Government and Opposition* 31 (Winter 2002): 15–37; Christopher Hood, "What Happens When Transparency Meets Blame-Avoidance," *Public Management Review* 9 (2007): 191–210; Arjen Boin, Paul't Hart, Eric Stern, and Bengt Sundelius, *The Politics of Crisis Management: Public Leadership Under Pressure* (Cambridge: Cambridge University Press, 2005).
7. Margaret Keck and Kathryn Sikkink, *Advocacy Beyond Borders* (Ithaca: Cornell University Press, 1998); Todd Landman, *Protecting Human Rights: A Global Comparative Study* (Washington, DC: Georgetown University Press, 2005); Thomas Risse, Stephen C. Ropp, and Kathryn Sikkink, *The Power of Human Rights: International Norms and Domestic Change* (Cambridge: Cambridge University Press, 1999). See also Clifford Bobb, *The Marketing of Rebellion* (Cambridge: Cambridge University Press, 2005).
8. Gary J. Bass, *Stay the Hand of Vengeance: The Politics of War Crimes Tribunals* (Princeton: Princeton University Press, 2000), 14, 7.

9. Landman, *Protecting Human Rights*; Beth Simmons, *Mobilizing for Human Rights*, (Cambridge: Cambridge University Press, 2009).

10. Bruce Bueno de Mesquita, George W. Downs, Alastair Smith, and Feryal Marie Cherif, "Thinking Inside the Box: A Closer Look at Democracy and Human Rights," *International Studies Quarterly* 49 (September 2005): 439. See also Christian Davenport and David A. Armstrong II, "Democracy and the Violation of Human Rights: A Statistical Analysis from 1976 to 1996," *American Journal of Political Science* 48 (July 2004): 538–554; David L. Richards and Ronald D. Gelleny, "Good Things to Those Who Wait? National Elections and Government Respect for Human Rights," *Journal of Peace Research* 44 (July 2007); Todd Landman and Marco Larizza, "Inequality and Human Rights: Who Controls What, When, and How," *International Studies Quarterly* 53 (September 2009).

11. Christian Davenport, *State Repression and the Domestic Democratic Peace* (New York: Cambridge University Press, 2007), 176.

12. Boin et al., *The Politics of Crisis Management*, 152.

13. Karl Rove, *Courage and Consequence: My Life as a Conservative in the Fight* (New York: Threshold Editions, 2010), 78.

14. Ze'ev Schiff and Ehud Ya'ari, *Israel's Lebanon War* (London: Unwin Paperbacks, 1986), 284.

15. Frank Newman and David Weissbrodt, *Selected International Human Rights Instruments* (Cincinnati, OH: Anderson, 1996), 198.

16. Winston Churchill, House of Commons, *Parliamentary Debates*, July 8, 1920, 131, cc. 1728–1729.

17. Charles Webster and Noble Frankland, *The Strategic Air Offensive Against Germany, 1939–1945* (London: Her Majesty's Stationery Office, 1961), III, 112.

18. Peter Pringle and Philip Jacobson, *Those Are Real Bullets, Aren't They?* (London: Fourth Estate, 2001), 3.

19. One widely used measure of democracy is provided by the Polity Scale. A score of between eight and ten on the ten-point scale is taken as a full democracy. The literature on human rights violations suggests that only these regimes have been found to reduce the likelihood of violations. South Africa and Britain had scores of four at the time of the Sharpeville and the Peterloo massacres. Britain had crossed the full-democracy threshold by the time of Amritsar massacre, when it scored an eight on the Polity Scale (women were not fully enfranchised). See Polity IV, http://www.systemicpeace.org/polity/polity4.htm.

20. See Richard Rose, "A Model Democracy?," in Richard Rose (ed.), *Lessons from America: An Exploration* (New York: Wiley, 1974), 131.

21. W. Philips Shively, *Power and Choice* (New York: McGraw-Hill, 2003), 317. France's involvement in colonial wars and its shifting between a parliamentary and a hybrid presidential system invites investigation. But it is less of a test of the argument. During its "savage war of peace" in Algeria, France's failure of accountability could be attributed to its not being among the ranks of stable democracies; see Alistair Horne, *A Savage War of Peace: Algeria 1954–1962* (New York: New York Review of Books Classics, 2006).

22. Arend Lijphart, *Patterns of Democracy: Government Forms and Performance in Thirty-Six Countries* (New Haven: Yale University Press, 1999), 9.

23. For a discussion of research design criteria, see Gary King, Robert O. Keohane, and Sidney Verba, *Designing Social Inquiry: Scientific Inference in Qualitative Research* (Princeton: Princeton University Press, 1994).

24. Quoted in Russell Watson, Milan Kubic, and Joyce Barnathan, "Sharon Takes the Rap," *Newsweek*, February 21, 1983, 30.

25. See Goldman as quoted in ibid., 30.

26. See Bass, *Staying the Hand of Vengeance*, 14.

27. Gabriel Sheffer, *Moshe Sharett: Biography of a Political Moderate* (Oxford: Clarendon Press, 1996), 686.

CHAPTER TWO

1. General Sir Mike Jackson, Hearing Transcript, Day 100, 154, http://www.bahamousainquiry.org/baha_mousa_inquiry_evidence/evidencev1.htm.

2. Neil J. Mitchell, *Agents of Atrocity: Leaders, Followers and the Violation of Human Rights in Civil War* (New York: Palgrave Macmillan, 2004). For further empirical analysis of the argument, see Robert J. Brym and Yael Maoz-Shai, "Israeli State Violence During the Second Intifada: Combining New Institutionalist and Rational Choice Approaches," *Studies in Conflict and Terrorism* 32, 7 (2009): 611–626.: Todd Landman and Anita Godhes, "Principals, Agents and Atrocities: The Case of Peru 1980–2000" (unpublished paper).

3. See Sabine Carey, "The Use of Repression as a Response to Domestic Threat," *Political Studies* 58 (February 2009).

4. See Kenneth J. Arrow, "The Economics of Agency," in John W. Pratt and Richard J. Zeckhouser (eds.), *Principals and Agents: The Structure of Business* (Boston: Harvard Business School Press, 1985); Jean-Jacques Laffont and David Martimort, *The Theory of Incentives: The Principal-Agent Model* (Princeton: Princeton University Press, 2001); for applications of this approach to public policy see John Brehm and Scott Gates, *Working, Shirking, and Sabotage* (Ann Arbor: University of Michigan Press 1997); Richard W. Waterman, Amelia A. Rouse, and Robert L. Wright, *Bureaucrats, Politics and the Environment* (Pittsburgh: University of Pittsburgh Press, 2004).

5. See Arrow, "The Economics of Agency"; Jeffrey S. Banks and Barry R. Weingast, "The Political Control of Bureaucracies Under Asymmetric Information," *American Journal of Political Science* 36 (May 1992): 509–524.

6. See Theodor Meron, "Shakespeare's Henry the Fifth and the Law of War,"*American Journal of International Law* 86 (1992): 1–45; and Mitchell, *Agents of Atrocity*.

7. William Shakespeare, *Henry V*, Act 3 Scene, 3.

8. Ibid.

9. Quoted in Friedrich Schiller, *The History of the Thirty Years' War in Germany*, trans. A. J. W Morrison (Boston: Francis A. Nicolls, 1901), 178–179. See Mitchell, *Agents of Atrocity*, for an analysis of this event.

10. See Arrow, "The Economics of Agency."

11. Pranab Bardhan, "Corruption and Development: A Review of Issues," *Journal of Economic Literature* 35 (1997): 1320–1346.

12. See Arrow, "The Economics of Agency."

13. For a development of this argument see Stephan Poth and Torsten Selk, "Principal Agent Theory and Artificial Information Asymmetry," *Politics* 29 (June 2009): 137–144.

14. Wolfgang C. Müller, Torbjörn Bergman, and Kaare Strøm, "Parliamentary Democracy: Promise and Problems," in Kaare Strøm, Wolfgang C. Müller, and Torbjörn Bergman (eds.), *Delegation and Accountability in Parliamentary Democracies* (Oxford: Oxford University Press, 2006), 21.

15. Poth and Selck, "Principal Agent Theory and Artificial Information Asymmetry," 138–141.

16. Morris P. Fiorina, "Group Concentration and Delegation of Legislative Authority," in Roger G. Noll (ed.), *Regulatory Policy and the Social Sciences* (Berkeley: University of California Press, 1985), 187.

17. Laffont and Martimort, *The Theory of Incentives*, 28.

18. Fiorina, "Group Concentration and Delegation of Legislative Authority," 187.

19. Weaver, "The Politics of Blame Avoidance," 372.

20. See Matthew McCubbins, Roger G. Noll, and Barry R. Weingast, "Administrative Procedures as Instruments of Political Control," *Journal of Law Economics and Organization* 3 (1987): 243–277.

21. Kirk Semple, "Iraq Hearing on Rape and Murder Opens," *New York Times*, August 7, 2006, 9.

22. Sarah Childress and Michael Hirsh,"An Itchy Finger," *Newsweek*, August 7, 2006, http://www.msnbc.msn.com/id/14097559/site/newsweek/.

23. George Akerlof, "The Market for Lemons: Quality Uncertainty and Market Mechanism," *Quarterly Journal of Economics* 84 (August 1970): 488–500.

24. Cromwell: "I raised such men as had the fear of God before them, as made some conscience of what they did. And from that day forward I must say to you, they were never beaten." Wilbur Cortez Abbott (ed.), *Writings and Speeches of Oliver Cromwell* (Cambridge, MA: Harvard University Press, 1947), IV: 471.

25. For an analysis of the role of pro-Serbian militias and the links to the government in Belgrade, see James Ron, *Frontiers and Ghettos: State Violence in Serbia and Israel* (Berkeley: University of California Press, 2003), 58. Ron quotes a journalist: "Can you imagine anyone stupid enough to write down an ethnic cleansing order?"

26. Ruth Grant and Robert Keohane, "Accountability and Abuses of Power in World Politics," *American Political Science Review* 99 (February 2005): 29.

27. See Arjen Boin, Paul't Hart, Eric Stern, and Bengt Sundelius, *The Politics of Crisis Management: Public Leadership Under Pressure* (Cambridge: Cambridge University Press, 2005), chapter 5, for a discussion of playing the blame game. Blame involves harm, agency (not an act of God), and the attribution of responsibility.

28. See Mitchell, *Agents of Atrocity*.

29. See Jeffrey S. Banks and Barry R. Weingast, "The Political Control of Bureaucracies," *American Journal of Political Science* 36 (May 1992): 509–524; Beth Simmons, *Mobilizing for Human Rights* (Cambridge: Cambridge University Press, 2009); Todd Landman, *Protecting Human Rights: A Comparative Study* (Washington, DC: Georgetown University Press, 2005); Emilie M. Hafner-Burton and Kiyoteru Tsutsui, "Human Rights in a Globalizing World: The Paradox of Empty Promises," *American Journal of Sociology* 110, 5 (2005): 1373–1411.

30. James D. Fearon, "Domestic Political Audiences and the Escalation of International Disputes," *American Political Science Review* 88 (September 1994) 577.

31. See the discussion of "reactive strategies" in McCubbins, Noll, and Weingast, "Administrative Procedures as Instruments of Political Control," 249.

32. David Hume, "Of the First Principles of Government," in *Hume's Moral and Political Philosophy*, ed. Henry D. Aiken (New York: Hafner Press, 1948), 307.

33. Niccolo Machiavelli *The Prince*, trans. Robert M. Adams (New York: W. W. Norton, 1977), 22.

CHAPTER THREE

1. See Kaare Strøm, Wolfgang C. Müller, and Torbjörn Bergman (eds.), *Delegation and Accountability in Parliamentary Democracies* (Oxford: Oxford University Press 2006).

2. See, for example, Ruth W. Grant and Robert O. Keohane, "Accountability and Abuses of Power in World Politics," *American Political Science Review* 99 (February 2005): 29.

3. See Weaver, "The Politics of Blame Avoidance," *Journal of Public Policy* 6 (October 1986): 385. Weaver distinguishes a variety of blame avoiding strategies, including delegation ("find a scapegoat" and "pass the buck") and diversion ("redefining the issue"). More recently, Christopher Hood distinguishes three broad blame-avoiding strategies, including delegation ("agency strategies"), justifications ("presentational strategies"), and policy strategies. See Hood, "The Risk Game and the Blame Game," *Government and Opposition* 31 (Winter 2002): 15–37.

4. See Kathleen M. McGraw, "Managing Blame: An Experimental Test of the Effects of Political Accounts," *American Political Science Review* (December 1991).

5. See Rupert Furneaux, *Massacre at Amritsar* (London: George Allen and Unwin, 1963), 109–110.

6. See Stanley Cohen, *States of Denial: Knowing About Atrocities and Suffering* (London: Polity Press, 2001), for a discussion of types of denial.

7. Jacobo Timmerman, *Prisoner Without a Name, Cell Without a Number* (New York: Vintage Books, 1982). See also Alison Brysk, *The Politics of Human Rights in Argentina: Protest, Change, and Democratization* (Stanford: Stanford University Press, 1994).

8. Council of Europe Committee on Legal Affairs and Human Rights, "Secret Detentions and Illegal Transfers of Detainees Involving Council of Europe Member States: Second Report," Council of Europe, June 7, 2007, 46, http://www.coe.int/T/E/Com/Files/Events/2006-cia/.

9. Amnesty International, "Off the Record: U.S. Responsibility for Enforced Disappearances in the War on Terror," http://web.amnesty.org/library/Index/ENGAMR510932007.

10. Council of Europe, "Secret Detentions and Illegal Transfers of Detainees,"15.

11. Ibid., 24.

12. Ibid., 26.

13. Ibid., 51–53.

14. Amnesty International, "Off the Record."

15. Raymond Bonner, "The CIA's Secret Torture," *New York Review of Books*, January 11, 2007, 29.

16. Ibid., 29.

17. See http://www.state.gov/g/drl/.

18. Bureau of Democracy, Human Rights, and Labor, U.S. Department of State, http://www.state.gov/g/drl/hr/.

19. Steven C. Poe, Sabine C. Carey, and Tanya C. Vazquez, "How Are These Pictures Different? A Quantitative Comparison of the U.S. State Department and Amnesty International Human Rights Reports, 1976–1995," *Human Rights Quarterly* 23, 3 (2001): 650–677.

20. Barry Lowenkron, "On the Record Briefing on the State Department's 2006 Country Reports," http://www.state.gov/g/drl/rls/rm/2007/81468.htm#bfl.

21. See Raanan Sulitzeanu-Kenan, "Scything the Grass: Agenda Setting Consequences of Appointing Public Inquiries in the UK: A Longitudinal Analysis," *Policy and Politics* 35 (2007): 629–650.

22. Marilyn Friedman, "How to Blame People Responsibly" (unpublished manuscript, 13).

23. Hans-Heinrich Jescheck, "The General Principles of International Criminal Law Set Out in Nuremberg, as Mirrored in the ICC Statute," *Journal of International Criminal Justice* 2 (2004): 52.

24. Quoted in Benny Morris, *1948 and After: Israel and the Palestinians* (Oxford: Clarendon Press, 1990), 133.

25. "President Discusses Military Commissions," September 6, 2006, http://www.whitehouse.gov/news/releases/2006/09/20060906-3.html.

26. Ibid.

27. See Gary Lafree, Laura Dugan, and Raven Korte, "The Impact of British Counter-Terrorist Strategies on Political Violence in Northern Ireland: Comparing Deterrence and Backlash Models?" *Criminology* 47 (February 2009): 17–45.

28. John Austin, "A Plea for Excuses," *Philosophical Papers* (1961): 124.

29. McGraw, "Managing Blame," 1138.

30. Ibid., 1141.

31. Austin, "A Plea for Excuses," 125, and see McGraw, "Managing Blame."

32. For a discussion of the Iran-Contra episode, see James M. McCormick, *American Foreign Policy and Process* (Itasca, IL: F. E. Peacock, 1992).

33. Lawrence E. Walsh, "Political Oversight, the Rule of Law, and Iran-Contra," *Cleveland State Law Review* 42 (1994): 593.

34. Ibid., 596.

35. McCormick, *American Foreign Policy*, 420.

36. Quoted in Milton, "The Tenure of Kings and Magistrates," in Don M. Wolfe (ed.), *Complete Prose Works of John Milton* (New Haven: Yale University Press, 1962), III: 205–206.

37. For a discussion of seven "mechanisms of accountability," including legal and public reputational accountability, see Grant and Keohane, "Accountability and Abuses of Power in World Politics," 36.

38. Geoffrey Robertson, *Crimes Against Humanity: The Struggle for Global Justice* (London: Penguin Press, 1999), 216.

39. See Amnesty International, "The Conviction of Fujimori—A Milestone in the Fight for Justice," http://www.amnesty.org/en/for-media/press-releases/peru-conviction-fujimori-%E2%80%93-milestone-fight-justice-20090407.

40. The Statute of the International Criminal Tribunal for the Former Yugoslavia, Article 7 (September, 2009), http://www.un.org/icty/.

41. "ICC Prosecutor presents case against Sudanese President, Hassan Ahmad AL BASHIR," Press Release, ICC-OTP-20080714-PR341 (July 14, 2008), http://www.un.org/apps/news/story.asp?NewsID=27361&Cr=Darfur&Cr1.

42. Grant and Keohane, "Accountability and Abuses of Power in World Politics," 39.

43. Ibid., 30.

44. David Cingranelli and Mikhail Filippov, "Electoral Rules and Incentives to Protect Human Rights," *Journal of Politics* 72 (January 2010): 243.

45. James D. Fearon, "Electoral Accountability and the Control of Politicians: Selecting Good Types versus Sanctioning Poor Performance," in Adam Przeworski, Susan C. Stokes, and Bernard Manin (eds.), *Democracy, Accountability, and Representation* (Cambridge: Cambridge University Press, 1999), 83.

46. Helmut Norpoth, *Confidence Regained* (Ann Arbor: University of Michigan Press, 1992), 2.

47. The evidence on how well voters hold governments accountable even for economic performance is surprisingly mixed. See, for example, Jose Antonio Cheibub and Adam Przeworski, "Democracy, Elections, and Accountability for Economic Outcomes," in Adam Przeworski, Susan C. Stokes, and Bernard Manin (eds.), *Democracy, Accountability, and Representation* (Cambridge: Cambridge University Press, 1999).

48. Ernest Renan, "What Is a Nation?" Sorbonne Lecture, March 11, 1882, http://www.nationalismproject.org/what/renan.htm; Karl Rove, *Courage and Consequence: My Life as a Conservative in the Fight* (New York: Threshold Editions, 2010), 78.

49. Weaver, "The Politics of Blame Avoidance," 392

50. Herman Finer, quoted in Torbjörn Bergman, Wolfgang C. Müller, Kaare Strøm, and Magnus Blomgren, "Democratic Delegation and Accountability: Cross-national Patterns," in Kaare Strøm, Wolfgang C. Müller, and Torbjörn Bergman (eds.), *Delegation and Accountability in Parliamentary Democracies* (Oxford: Oxford University Press, 2006), 168.

51. Kaare Strøm, "Parliamentary Democracy and Delegation," in Kaare Strøm, Wolfgang C. Müller, and Torbjörn Bergman (eds.), *Delegation and Accountability in Parliamentary Democracies* (Oxford: Oxford University Press 2006), 95.

52. Oonagh Gay and Thomas Powell, "Individual Ministerial Responsibility—Issues and Examples," *House of Commons Research Paper* 04/31 (April 5, 2004), 6–7.

53. Quoted in ibid., 25.

54. Margaret Thatcher, *The Downing Street Years* (London: HarperCollins, 1993), 185–186.

55. S. E. Finer, "The Individual Responsibility of Ministers," *Public Administration* 34 (Winter 1956): 377–396.

56. Keith Dowding and Won-taek Kang, "Ministerial Resignations 1945–1997," *Public Administration* 76 (Autumn 1998): 421–423; see also Matthew Flinders, "The

Enduring Centrality of Individual Ministerial Responsibility Within the British Constitution," *The Journal of Legislative Studies* 6, (2000): 73–92.

57. Finer, "The Individual Responsibility of Ministers," 393; note also the greater difficulty of resigning now than in the nineteenth century. This point is made by Grant Jordan, who quotes the following: "Our ministers do not break their hearts when they lose office. They are rich . . . and distinguished persons, occupying a fine position in the most agreeable society in the world . . . sending him back to his friends, his estates, his sports, his studies, and his recreations" Grant Jordan, *The British Administrative System: Principles versus Practice* (London: Routledge, 1994), 219.

58. Report of the Commission of Inquiry into the Events at the Refugee Camps in Beirut, February 8, 1983, published as Kahan Commission, *The Beirut Massacre: The Complete Kahan Commission Report* (New York: Karz-Cohl, 1983), 64.

59. Ibid., 64.

60. Joseph S. Nye Jr., *The Powers to Lead* (Oxford: Oxford University Press, 2008).

61. Parker has argued that the rewards of a good reputation may restrain a politician's opportunism. He considers both the electoral and the future employment effects of reputation. Glenn R. Parker, *Self-Policing in Politics: the Political Economy of Reputational Controls on Politicians* (Princeton: Princeton University Press, 2004).

62. "Foes Raise Voices to Stop Blair's EU President Bid," http://www.euractiv.com/en/future-eu/foes-raise-voices-blair-eu-president-bid/article-186332.

63. It is a heavy price for Cassio in Othello: "I have lost my reputation! I have lost the immortal part of myself, and what remains is bestial." Iago sees it differently: "Reputation is an idle and most false imposition: oft got without merit, and lost without deserving. You have lost no reputation at all, unless you repute yourself such a loser." *Othello*, Act II, Scene II.

64. Hood, "The Risk Game and the Blame Game," 23.

65. Adam Smith, *The Theory of Moral Sentiments* (New York: Prometheus Books, [1759] 2000), 173.

CHAPTER FOUR

1. House of Lords, *Parliamentary Debates*, July 20, 1920, 41, cc. 314–315.

2. *Report of the Committee Appointed by the Government of India to Investigate the Disturbances in the Punjab* (London: His Majesty's Stationery Office, 1920), Cmd. 681, 28–29.

3. Ibid., 29.

4. See Nigel Collett, The *Butcher of Amritsar: General Reginald Dyer* (London: Hambledon Continuum, 2005), 246, 259.

5. *Report of the Committee*, 29.

6. Ibid., 112–113.

7. Ibid., 28

8. Ibid., 112–113.

9. Ibid.,, 25.

10. Ibid., 83.

11. Ibid., 83.

12. Helen Fein, *Imperial Crime and Punishment: The Massacre at Jallianwala Bagh and British Judgement 1919–1920* (Honolulu: University Press of Hawaii, 1975), xiii.

13. House of Lords, *Parliamentary Debates*, July 20, 1920, 5 Series, 41, col. 359.

14. Report of the Committee, 83.

15. Quoted in Rupert Furneaux, *Massacre at Amritsar* (London: George Allen and Unwin, 1963), 79.

16. Quoted in ibid., 80.

17. Quoted in ibid., 109–110.

18. Ibid., 111.

19. Montagu quoted in ibid., 41.

20. Report of the Committee, 30.

21. Ibid., 30–31.

22. Ibid., 115

23. Ibid., 114.

24. Ibid., 113.

25. Ibid., 30.

26. Ibid., 31.

27. Statement by Brigadier-General Dyer, Cmd. 771, July 3, 1920, 110; Fein remarks, "Dyer changed his story and style completely . . . in June 1920 he presented a systematic and sophisticated defense before the Army Council—a defense made to fit the regulations for the use of firepower against civilians" (131).

28. Derek Sayer, "British Reaction to the Amritsar Massacre 1919–1920," *Past and Present* 131 (May 1991): 131–132.

29. Fein, *Imperial Crime and Punishment*, xiii.

30. Ibid., xiii.

31. See Sayer, "British Reaction to the Amritsar Massacre,"133.

32. Ibid., 133

33. Quoted in ibid., 133.

34. Report of the Committee, 115–116.

35. Furneaux, *Massacre at Amritsar*, 120.

36. Sayer, "British Reaction to the Amritsar Massacre," 145.

37. V. N. Datta, *Jallianwala Bagh* (Ludhiana Bhopal-Chandigarh-Kurukshetra: Lyall Book Depot, 1969), 108.

38. "Peers and General Dyer," *Manchester Guardian*, July 21, 1920, 7.

39. Sayer, "British Reaction to the Amritsar Massacre," 150.

40. Quoted in ibid., 148

41. Ibid., 150.

42. Ibid., 145.

43. Fein, *Imperial Crime and Punishment*, 104; Datta, *Jallianwala Bagh*, 108–109.

44. Quoted in Datta, *Jallianwala Bagh*, 109.

45. Ibid., 109.

46. Ibid., 121–123.

47. House of Commons, *Parliamentary Debates*, December 16, 1919, 123, c. 240.

48. House of Commons, *Parliamentary Debates*, December 22, 1919, 128, c. 1231–1232.

49. Fein, *Imperial Crime and Punishment*, 130.

50. "The Amritsar Tragedy," *Observer*, December 21, 1919, 18.

51. "Defiant Crowd at Amritsar," *Times* April 22, 1919, 1.

52. Datta, *Jallianwala Bagh*, 107.

53. House of Commons, *Parliamentary Debates*, May 22, 1919, 116, c. 628, 635–636.

54. House of Commons, *Parliamentary Debates*, December 16, 1919, 123, cc. 240–242.

55. "Letters to the Editor." *Observer*, November 15, 1925, 18.

56. Sayer, "British Reaction to the Amritsar Massacre," 159.

57. Fein, *Imperial Crime and Punishment*, 135.

58. See Sayer, "British Reaction to the Amritsar Massacre," 56.

59. House of Commons, *Parliamentary Debates*, July 8, 1920, 131, cc. 1708–1709.

60. Ibid., c. 1715.

61. Ibid.

62. Ibid., c. 1719.

63. Sir William Sutherland quoted in Martin Gilbert, *Winston S. Churchill*, Vol. IV: 1917–1922 (London: Heinemann, 1975), 402–404.

64. House of Commons, *Parliamentary Debates*, July 8, 1920, 131, cc. 1719–1733.

65. Ibid., c. 1727.

66. House of Commons, *Parliamentary Debates*, July 8, 1920, 131, cc. 1728–1729.

67. Ibid., c. 1731.

68. Gilbert, *Winston S. Churchill*, 410.

69. House of Commons, *Parliamentary Debates*, July 8, 1920, 131, c. 1734.

70. House of Lords, *Parliamentary Debates*, July 20, 1920, 41, c. 320.

71. Ibid., c. 331.

72. House of Lords, *Parliamentary Debates*, July 20, 1920, 41, c. 316.

73. House of Commons, *Parliamentary Debates*, July 8, 1920, 131, c. 1730.

74. House of Lords, *Parliamentary Debates*, July 20, 1920, 41, c. 366.

75. Quoted in Fein, *Imperial Crime and Punishment*, xii.

76. Collett, *The Butcher of Amritsar*, 419.

77. Sayer, "British Reaction to the Amritsar Massacre," 159.

78. Ibid., 159.

CHAPTER FIVE

1. Anthony Trollope, *Phineas Redux* (London: Penguin Books, 2003), 87.

2. Frederick Taylor, *Dresden: Tuesday 13 February 1945* (London: Bloomsbury Publishing, 2005), xiii.

3. Charles Webster and Noble Frankland, *The Strategic Air Offensive Against Germany, 1939–1945* (London: Her Majesty's Stationary Office, 1961), III: 109.

4. Report by the Police President of Hamburg on the raids on Hamburg in July and August 1943, dated December 1, 1943, appendix 30, in Webster and Frankland, *The Strategic Air Offensive Against Germany*, IV, Annexes and Appendices, 310–315.

5. Report by the Police President of Hamburg, 314.

6. See Frederick Taylor, "How Many Died in the Bombing of Dresden?' Spiegel Online, October 2, 2008, http://www.spiegel.de/international/germany/0,1518,581992,00.html; see also Martin Gilbert, *Churchill: A Life* (New York: Henry Holt, 1991), 824; Max Hastings, *Bomber Command* (New York: Dial Press, 1979), 397.

7. For an analysis of the legal and moral issues, see A. C. Grayling, *Among the Dead Cities* (London: Bloomsbury, 2006).

8. Webster and Frankland, *The Strategic Air Offensive Against Germany*, III: 113.

9. House of Commons, *Parliamentary Debates*, June 21, 1938, 337, cc. 937–938.

10. See Stanley Milgram, "Some Conditions of Obedience and Disobedience to Authority," *Human Relations* (1965).

11. Webster and Frankland, *The Strategic Air Offensive Against Germany*, III: 25–28.

12. Note by the Chief of the Imperial General Staff for the Chiefs of Staff Sub-Committee on the memorandum by the Chief of Air Staff, May 16, 1928 Appendix 2 in Webster and Frankland, *The Strategic Air Offensive Against Germany*, IV: 79–81.

13. Note by the Chief of the Naval Staff for the Chiefs of Staff Sub-Committee on the memorandum by the Chief of Air Staff, May 21, 1928, Appendix 2 in Webster and Frankland, *The Strategic Air Offensive Against Germany*, IV: 83.

14. Memorandum by Marshal of the Royal Air Force Lord Trenchard on the Present War Situation, May 19, 1941, Appendix 10 in Webster and Frankland, *The Strategic Air Offensive Against Germany*, IV, 195.

15. Trenchard on the Present War Situation, May 19, 1941, 194–195.

16. Note by Sir Charles Portal, Chief of the Air Staff, on Lord Trenchard's memorandum, June 2, 1941, Appendix 10 in Webster and Frankland, *The Strategic Air Offensive Against Germany*, IV: 200.

17. See Air Vice-Marshal N. H. Bottomley to Air Marshal Sir Richard Peirse, July 9, 1941, Appendix 8 in Webster and Frankland, *The Strategic Air Offensive Against Germany*, IV: 136.

18. Air Vice-Marshal N. H. Bottomley to Air Marshal A. T. Harris, May 5, 1942, Appendix 8 in Webster and Frankland, *The Strategic Air Offensive Against Germany*, IV: 148.

19. Combined Chiefs of Staff, Directive for the Bomber Offensive from the United Kingdom, January 21, 1943, Appendix 8 in Webster and Frankland, *The Strategic Air Offensive Against Germany*, IV: 153.

20. Webster and Frankland, *The Strategic Air Offensive Against Germany*, III: 52–54.

21. Ibid., III, 54–55.

22. Ibid., III: 100.

23. Ibid., III: 103.

24. Ibid., III: 103.

25. Ibid., III: 103.

26. Ibid., III: 103–104.

27. Alex Danchev and Daniel Todman (eds.), *Fieldmarshal Lord Alanbrooke, War Diaries 1939–1945*, (Berkeley: University of California Press, 2001), 546-547.

28. Webster and Frankland, *The Strategic Air Offensive Against Germany*, III: 79–80.

29. Hastings, *Bomber Command*, 407.

30. Tami Davis Biddle, *Rhetoric and Reality in Air Warfare: The Evolution of British and American Ideas About Strategic Bombing, 1914–1945* (Princeton: Princeton University Press, 2002), 246.

31. Reports by Speer to Hitler on the Effects of the Attacks on Oil, Appendix 32 in Webster and Frankland, *The Strategic Air Offensive Against Germany*, IV: 325.

32. Interrogation of Albert Speer, former Reich Minister of Armaments and War Production (6th Session—15.00–17.00 hours, 30 May 1945), Appendix 37 in Webster and Frankland, *The Strategic Air Offensive Against Germany*, IV: 374–375.

33. Interrogation of Albert Speer, former Reich Minister of Armaments and War Production (July 18, 1945), Appendix 37 in Webster and Frankland, *The Strategic Air Offensive Against Germany*, IV: 383.

34. Michael Horowitz and Dan Reiter, "When Does Aerial Bombing Work? Quantitative Empirical Tests, 1917–1999," *Journal of Conflict Resolution* 45 (April 2001): 164.

35. See Grayling, *Among the Dead Cities*, 272

36. Michael Walzer, *Arguing About War* (New Haven: Yale University Press, 2004), 46; See also John Rawls, *The Law of Peoples* (Cambridge Mass: Harvard University Press, 2001), 99.

37. House of Commons, *Parliamentary Debates*, July 8, 1920, 131, c. 1732.

38. Biddle, *Rhetoric and Reality in Air Warfare*, 219.

39. House of Lords, *Parliamentary Debates*, February 9, 1944, 130, cc. 737–743.

40. Ibid., cc. 747–748

41. House of Commons, *Parliamentary Debates*, March 6, 1945, 408, cc. 1899–1901.

42. Biddle, *Rhetoric and Reality in Air Warfare*, 273.

43. Ibid., 257.

44. Arthur T. Harris, *Bomber Offensive* (London: Collins, 1947), 58.

45. House of Lords, *Parliamentary Debates*, February 9, 1944, 130, cc. 751–752.

46. House of Commons, *Parliamentary Debates*, March 6, 1945, 408, cc. 1989–1990.

47. House of Commons, *Parliamentary Debates*, March 31, 1943, 388 c. 155.

48. House of Commons, *Parliamentary Debates*, December 1, 1943, 395, c. 338.

49. Webster and Frankland, *The Strategic Air Offensive Against Germany*, III: 116.

50. Sir Archibald Sinclair to the Chief of Air Staff, Sir Charles Portal, October 28, 1943, AIR 19/189: BOMBING POLICY.

51. Webster and Frankland, *The Strategic Air Offensive Against Germany*, III: 116.

52. Sinclair to Portal, October 28, 1943.

53. House of Commons, *Parliamentary Debates*, May 27, 1943, 389, cc. 1731.

54. Ibid., cc. 1730–1731.

55. Ibid.

56. Webster and Frankland, *The Strategic Air Offensive Against Germany*, III: 113.

57. Ibid., III: 105.

58. Ibid., III: 112.

59. Ibid., III: 115.

60. Frank Newman and David Weissbrodt, *Selected International Human Rights Instruments* (Cincinnati, OH: Anderson, 1996), 198.

61. Taylor, *Dresden: Tuesday 13 February 1945*, 431.

62. Ibid., 434.

63. Webster and Frankland, *The Strategic Air Offensive Against Germany*, III, 117.

64. Ibid., III: 119.

65. See Kathleen McGraw, "Managing Blame: An Experimental Test of the Effects of Political Accounts," *American Political Science Review* 85 (December 1991): 1133–1157.

66. John Lukacs, *Five Days in London: May 1940* (New Haven: Yale University Press, 2001), 129.

67. Joseph P. Lash, *Roosevelt and Churchill 1939–1941: The Partnership That Saved the West* (New York: W.W. Norton & Co., 1977), 146.

68. Lukacs. *Five Days in London*, 75–76.

69. Quoted in Lash, *Roosevelt and Churchill 1939–1941*, 145.

70. Lukacs, *Five Days in London*, 112.

71. Ibid., 2.

72. Alanbrooke, *War Diaries 1939–1945*, xxi.

73. Webster and Frankland, *The Strategic Air Offensive Against Germany*, III: 113.

74. Mark Franklin and Matthew Ladner, "The Undoing of Winston Churchill: Mobilization and Conversion in the 1945 Realignment of British Voters," *British Journal of Political Science* 25 (1995): 452.

75. Taylor, *Dresden: Tuesday 13 February 1945*, 442–443.

76. Ibid., 443–445.

77. Quoted in Martin Gilbert, *Winston S. Churchill: 1945–1965* (London: Heinemann, 1988), 259.

78. Winston. S. Churchill, *Triumph and Tragedy* (Boston: Houghton Mifflin, 1953).

79. "Mr Lely, I desire you would use all your skill to paint my picture truly like me, and not flatter me at all; but remark all these roughnesses, pimples, warts, and everything as you see me, otherwise I will never pay a farthing for it." Oliver Cromwell quoted in Antonia Fraser, *Cromwell: The Lord Protector* (New York: Alfred A. Knopf, 1973), 472.

80. Webster and Frankland, *The Strategic Air Offensive Against Germany*, III: 116–117.

81. Richard Overy, *Why the Allies Won* (London: Pimlico, 2006), 137.

82. Harris, *Bomber Offensive*, 88-89.

83. Ibid., 242.

84. Biddle, *Rhetoric and Reality in Air Warfare*, 197.

85. Ibid., 214.

86. House of Commons, *Parliamentary Debates*, July 8, 1920, 131, c. 1729.

87. "Even much stronger mortals than Fred Vincy hold half their rectitude in the mind of the being they love best. 'The theatre of all my actions is fallen,' said an antique personage when his chief friend was dead; and they are fortunate who get a theatre where the audience demands their best." George Eliot, *Middlemarch* (New York, Bantam Books, 1992), 219.

CHAPTER SIX

1. Arthur Harris, *Bomber Offensive* (London: Collins, 1947), 31. Note that the city is referred to as Londonderry or Derry. Londonderry is the official name and preferred by Unionists.

2. Micháel Ó Siochrú, *God's Executioner: Oliver Cromwell and the Conquest of Ireland* (London: Faber and Faber, 2008), 1.

3. Wilbur Cortez Abbott, *The Writings and Speeches of Oliver Cromwell* (Cambridge, MA: Harvard University Press, 1939), II: 126.

4. Ibid., II: 127, fn 60.

5. Antonia Fraser, *Cromwell: The Lord Protector* (New York: Alfred A. Knopf, 1973), 278.

6. Abbott, *The Writings and Speeches of Oliver Cromwell*, I: 552.

7. See Neil J. Mitchell, "Resisting Machiavelli: Reducing Collective Harm in Conflict," in Donelson R. Forsyth and Crystal L. Hoyt (eds.), *For the Greater Good of All: Perspectives on Individualism, Society, and Leadership* (New York: Palgrave Macmillan, 2011).

8. Paul Arthur, *Governance and Politics of Northern Ireland* (Burnt Mill, Essex: Longman, 1984), 12.

9. For accounts of Bloody Sunday see Peter Pringle and Philip Jacobson, *Those Are Real Bullets, Aren't They?* (London: Fourth Estate, 2001); Graham Dawson, *Making Peace with the Past? Memory, Trauma and the Irish Troubles* (Manchester: Manchester University Press, 2007); and Eamon McCann, *Bloody Sunday in Derry: What Really Happened* (Dingle: Brandon, 1992).

10. Pringle and Jacobson, *Those Are Real Bullets, Aren't They?*, 39.

11. Ibid., 79.

12. Statement by General Sir Robert Ford quoted in Loden Hearing Transcript, Bloody Sunday Inquiry, June 18, 2003, 7. Hearing transcripts for all the Saville Inquiry Bloody Sunday witnesses can be found at http://www.bloody-sunday-inquiry. org/.

13. Report of the Bloody Sunday Inquiry, Vol. 1, 3.50.

14. Report of the Bloody Sunday Inquiry, Vol. 1, 3.66.

15. As home secretary in 1911, Churchill was the victor of the "Siege of Sydney Street." He had ordered out the artillery to subdue an anarchist, Peter the Painter. So he might, nevertheless, understand missteps in this area.

16. Richard Norton-Taylor, "Bloody Sunday: The Final Reckoning Begins," *Guardian*, November 22, 2004.

17. Bishop Edward Daly, Hearing Transcript, Bloody Sunday Inquiry, February 6, 2001, 37.

18. General Sir Mike Jackson, "Bloody Sunday Victims Innocent," http://news.bbc. co.uk/1/hi/northern_ireland/6699729.stm.

19. CS7-58 Closing Submission of Counsel to the Inquiry, Sector 5, The Shooting of Patrick Doherty, Bloody Sunday Inquiry, December 13, 2004.

20. Brian Cashinella, "March Ends in Shooting," *Times*, January 31, 1972, 1.

21. Statement of David Houston Capper, Bloody Sunday Inquiry, February 5, 2001, M9-18; quoted in Soldier 162, Hearing Transcript, Bloody Sunday Inquiry, May 15, 2003, 240.

22. Soldier 027 quoted in Soldier F, Hearing Transcript, Bloody Sunday Inquiry, October 1, 2003, 127.

23. "The New Tragedy in Ulster," *Times*, January 31, 1972.

24. Sir Edward Heath, Hearing Transcript, Bloody Sunday Inquiry, January 27, 2003.

25. House of Commons, *Parliamentary Debates*, February 1, 1972, 830, c. 267.

26. Ibid., cc. 325–326.

27. Major General Andrew "Patrick" MacLellan, Hearing Transcript, Bloody Sunday Inquiry, November 19, 2002, 24.

28. Desmond Hamill, *Pig in the Middle: The Army in Northern Ireland 1969–1984* (London: Methuen, 1985), 88.

29. Ford, Statement, Bloody Sunday Inquiry, 1998, 1208-071.

30. James Ron interviewed a Belgrade journalist: "Can you imagine anyone stupid enough to write down an ethnic cleansing order . . . . Everyone knew this was a crime. You will never find an official or officer who put his name to an order to kill or ethnically cleanse." *Frontiers and Ghettos: State Violence in Serbia and Israel* (Berkeley: University of California Press, 2003), 58. See also the Beirut chapter and the discussion of earlier Israeli wars on this issue.

31. Report of the Bloody Sunday Inquiry, Vol. 1, 9.771.

32. Ibid.

33. Heath, Hearing Transcript, Bloody Sunday Inquiry, January 15, 2003, 58–59.

34. Ford, Hearing Transcript, Bloody Sunday Inquiry, October 29, 2002, 51.

35. Ford, Statement, Bloody Sunday Inquiry,1998, 1208-030.

36. Heath, Hearing Transcript, Bloody Sunday Inquiry, January 28, 2003, 101

37. Ford, Statement, Bloody Sunday Inquiry, 1998, 1155-017.

38. Soldier K, Hearing Transcript, Bloody Sunday Inquiry, September 15, 2003.

39. Ford, Hearing Transcript, Bloody Sunday Inquiry, October 30, 2002, 54.

40. Ford, Hearing Transcript, Widgery Tribunal, Witness Statement, Bloody Sunday Inquiry B1123 01, 1174.

41. Ford, Hearing Transcript, Bloody Sunday Inquiry, November 12, 2002, 3–4.

42. Ibid.

43. Ford, Hearing Transcript, Bloody Sunday Inquiry, November 11, 2002, 97.

44. Soldier 027, Hearing Transcript, Bloody Sunday Inquiry, October 16, 2002, 28.

45. Cashinella, "March Ends in Shooting," 2.

46. Ford, Hearing Transcript, Bloody Sunday Inquiry, November 11, 2002, 100.

47. Wilford, Hearing Transcript, Bloody Sunday Inquiry, March 27, 2003, 39.

48. Wilford, Hearing Transcript, Bloody Sunday Inquiry, April 10, 2003, 54.

49. Wilford, Statement, Bloody Sunday Inquiry B944-1, 1067,

50. Ford, Statement, Bloody Sunday Inquiry B1123 01.

51. Antony Virnier, *Financial Times*, Statement, Bloody Sunday Inquiry.

52. Colonel Dalzell-Payne, Witness Statement, Bloody Sunday Inquiry, 24.

53. Report of the Bloody Sunday Inquiry, Vol. 1, 9.515.

54. Colonel Dalzell-Payne, Witness Statement, Bloody Sunday Inquiry, 24.

55. Pringle and Jacobson, *Those Are Real Bullets, Aren't They?*, 3.

56. Michael Carver, *Out of Step* (London: Hutchinson, 1989), 419.

57. Rod Thornton, "Getting It Wrong: The Crucial Mistakes Made in the Early Stages of the British Army's Deployment to Northern Ireland (August 1969 to March 1972)," *Journal of Strategic Studies* 30 (February 2007): 85.

58. Heath, Hearing Transcript, Bloody Sunday Inquiry, January 29, 2003, 34.

59. Ibid., 5–7.

60. Ibid., 6.

61. Alexander B. Downes, "Desperate Times, Desperate Measures: The Causes of Civilian Victimization in War," *International Security* 30 (Spring 2006): 170.

62. The Yellow Card, which British soldiers carried, provided the rules for opening fire. They were required to give a warning, "never to use more than the minimum necessary force to enable you to carry out your duties . . . fire only aimed shots." Under some circumstances "you may fire without warning . . . either when hostile firing is taking place in your area, and a warning is impracticable, or when any delay

could lead to death or serious injury to people whom it is your duty to protect or to yourself; and then only: a) against a person using a firearm against members of the security forces or people whom it is your duty to protect; or against a person carrying a firearm if you have reason to think he is about to use it for offensive purposes."

63. Heath, Hearing Transcript, Bloody Sunday Inquiry, January 14, 2003, 89.

64. Heath, Hearing Transcript, Bloody Sunday Inquiry, January 28, 2003, 101.

65. Report of the Bloody Sunday Inquiry, Vol. 1, 9.494: "Edward Heath, Lord Carrington and Robert Armstrong all gave evidence that they . . . were not made aware of the possibility of a shooting war. There is nothing in the GEN 47 minutes or elsewhere in the material considered by the Inquiry to suggest this evidence of these individuals should be rejected and in our view it accurately reflected the position."

66. Heath, Hearing Transcript, Bloody Sunday Inquiry, January 28, 2003, 131–132.

67. Ibid., 102.

68. Simon Winchester, "13 Killed as Paratroops Break Riot," *Guardian*, January 31, 1972.

69. Edward Heath, *The Course of My Life* (London: Hodder and Stoughton, 1998), 641.

70. Philip Ziegler, *Edward Heath: The Authorised Biography* (London: Harper Press, 2010), 568.

71. House of Commons, *Parliamentary Debates*, July 13, 1989, Vol. 156, c 1176.

72. Edward Heath quoted in Ziegler, *Edward Heath*, 568–569.

73. Ibid., 569.

74. House of Commons, *Parliamentary Debates*, February 1, 1972, Vol. 830, c 311.

75. Sir John Peck in David McKittrick and David McVea, *Making Sense of the Troubles* (London: Penguin Books, 2001), 78.

76. Heath, Hearing Transcript, Bloody Sunday Inquiry, January 29, 2003, 47.

77. Quoted in McKittrick and McVea, *Making Sense of the Troubles*, 67.

78. Quoted in Laura K. Donohue, *The Cost of Counterterrorism: Power, Politics, and Liberty* (Cambridge: Cambridge University Press, 2006), 43.

79. ITN News, http://www.youtube.com/watch?v=ODQ11bo_roU.

80. Ford, Hearing Transcript, Widgery Tribunal, Witness Statement, Bloody Sunday Tribunal, B1123 01, 1185.

81. Ibid., 1188.

82. Colonel Dalzell-Payne, Hearing Transcript, Bloody Sunday Inquiry, October 15, 2002, 30.

83. Michael Mansfield: "only one soldier so far even recalls being interviewed by Major Loden; do you follow?" General Sir Mike Jackson, Hearing Transcript, Bloody Sunday Inquiry, October 15, 2003, 31.

84. For a copy of the "shot list" see Richard Norton-Taylor, "Army Chief Questioned over 'Shot List,'" *Guardian*, October 16, 2003.

85. Jackson, Hearing Transcript, Bloody Sunday Inquiry, October 15, 2003, 11.

86. Ibid., 29–30.

87. Jackson quoted in Norton-Taylor, "Army Chief Questioned over 'Shot List.'"

88. Report of the Bloody Sunday Inquiry, Vol. 1, 3.82.

89. House of Commons, *Parliamentary Debates*, February 1, 1972, 830, c 33.

90. Ibid., cc 270–279.

91. Pringle and Jacobson, *Those Are Real Bullets*, 3.

92. House of Lords, *Parliamentary Debates*, February 1, *1972, 327, c 690.*

93. Ibid., cc 774–776.

94. Heath, Hearing Transcript, Bloody Sunday Inquiry, January 29, 2003, 82–83.

95. Norton-Taylor, "Bloody Sunday: The Final Reckoning Begins."

96. *Lord Widgery's Report of Events in Londonderry, Northern Ireland on 30 January 1972* (London: The Stationary Office [1972] 2001), 39.

97. Ibid., 44.

98. Rosie Cowan, "Bloody Sunday Soldier's Horror at Killings," *Guardian*, October 17, 2002, and see Hearing Transcript, Bloody Sunday Inquiry, October 16, 2002.

99. Soldier S, Hearing Transcript, Bloody Sunday Inquiry, May 14–15, 2003, 62.

100. Richard Norton-Taylor, "Censored Journalists to Give Evidence on Army Shootings in Derry," *Guardian*, June 10, 2002.

101. *Lord Widgery's Report of Events in Londonderry*, 57.

102. Ibid., 92.

103. Ibid., 95.

104. Ibid., 99.

105. Stanley Cohen, *States of Denial: Knowing About Atrocities and Suffering* (London: Polity Press, 2001), 62.

106. Report of the Bloody Sunday Inquiry, Vol. 8, 154.1.

107. David Cameron's statement to the House of Commons, http://www.bbc.co.uk/news/10322295.

108. House of Commons, *Parliamentary Debates* February 17, 1972, Vol. 831, c 595.

109. Report of the Bloody Sunday Inquiry, Vol. 1, 4.4.

110. Report of the Bloody Sunday Inquiry, Vol. 1, 5.4–5.5.

111. Report of the Commission of Inquiry into the Events at the Refugee Camps in Beirut, February 8, 1983 published as Kahan Commission, *The Beirut Massacre: The Complete Kahan Commission Report* (New York: Karz-Cohl, 1983), 72–73.

112. Lord Carrington, Hearing Transcript, Bloody Sunday Inquiry, December 19, 2002, 55.

113. Heath, Hearing Transcript, January 14, 2003, 139–140.

114. House of Commons, *Parliamentary Debates, February 1, 1972, Vol. 830, c 276.*

115. Sir Geoffrey Johnson-Smith, Hearing Transcript, Bloody Sunday Inquiry, December 18, 2002, 10.

116. Ibid., 67.

117. Lord Carrington, Hearing Transcript, Bloody Sunday Inquiry, December 19, 2002, 56.

118. Ibid., 56–57.

119. See Heath, Hearing Transcript, January 14, 2003, 139.

120. Heath, Hearing Transcript, January 15, 2003, 59-60.

121. Report of the Bloody Sunday Inquiry, Vol. 1, 9.494.

122. Soldier F, Hearing Transcript, October 2, 2003, 7-9.

123. Report of the Bloody Sunday Inquiry, Vol. 1, 4.11–4.12.

124. Report of the Bloody Sunday Inquiry, Vol. 8, 169.23.

125. Report of the Bloody Sunday Inquiry, Vol. 1, 4.18.

126. General Sir Mike Jackson, *Soldier: The Autobiography* (London: Bantam Press, 2007), 71–72.

127. Ibid., 67.

128. Report of the Bloody Sunday Inquiry, Vol. 7, 165.7

129. Report of the Bloody Sunday Inquiry, Vol. 8, 165.10–165.19.

130. Report of the Bloody Sunday Inquiry, Vol. 1, 5.4–5.5.

131. "Colonel Wilford: 'Don't Blame My Soldiers,'" http://news.bbc.co.uk/1/hi/in_depth/northern_ireland/2000/bloody_sunday_inquiry/673039.stm (accessed April 22, 2008).

132. John Mullin, "I Was Made the Scapegoat," *Guardian*, July 7, 1999.

133. Soldier S, Hearing Transcript, Bloody Sunday Inquiry, May 15, 2003, 99.

CHAPTER SEVEN

1. Michael Bar-Zohar, *Ben-Gurion* (London: Weidenfeld and Nicholson, 1977), 206; see Yaacov Bar-Siman-Tov, "Ben-Gurion to Sharett: Conflict Management and Great Power Constraints in Israeli Foreign Policy," *Middle Eastern Studies* 24 (1988), for the distinction between activists and moderates, and Neil J. Mitchell, *Agents of Atrocity: Leaders, Followers and the Violation of Human Rights in Civil Wars* (New York: Palgrave Macmillan, 2004).

2. Bar-Siman-Tov, "Ben-Gurion to Sharett," 330.

3. For a careful empirical analysis of Israel's use of violence and the application of rational choice and institutionalist accounts, see Robert J. Brym and Yael Maoz-Shai, "Israeli State Violence During the Second Intifada: Combining New Institutionalist and Rational Choice Approaches," *Studies in Conflict and Terrorism* 32, 7 (2009) 32: 611–626.

4. See Ze'ev Schiff and Ehud Ya'ari, *Israel's Lebanon War* (London: Unwin Paperbacks, 1986), 39.

5. "Israel: The Rise of Ariel," *Economist*, August 8, 1981, 27.

6. Angus Deming with Patricia J. Sethi, John. J. Lindsay, and Milan Kubic, "A Vote Against Israel," *Newsweek*, June 29, 1981, 40.

7. See Arthur Max, "Lebanon Missile Crisis Is Heated Israeli Election Issue," Associated Press, May 24, 1981.

8. Martin Gilbert, *Israel: A History*, (London: Black Swan, 1998), 503.

9. See Schiff and Ya'ari, *Israel's Lebanon War*, 69.

10. Ze'ev Schiff, "The Green Light," *Foreign Policy* 50 (Spring 1983): 78–79.

11. This militia is also referred to as the Lebanese Forces. This description relies on the Report of the Commission of Inquiry into the Events at the Refugee Camps in Beirut, February 8, 1983, published as Kahan Commission, *The Beirut Massacre: The Complete Kahan Commission Report* (New York: Karz-Cohl, 1983).

12. Thomas L. Friedman, "The Beirut Massacre: The Four Days," *New York Times*, September 26, 1982, 19.

13. *The Beirut Massacre: The Complete Kahan Commission Report*, 22.

14. Ibid., 23.

15. Ibid., 23.

16. Ibid., 29.

17. Ibid., 24–25.

18. Ibid., 93.

19. Ibid., 94–96.

20. David Shipler, "In Israel, Anguish over the Moral Questions," *New York Times*, September 23, 1982, 1.

21. See David Shipler, "Evidence Suggests Israelis Were Aware of Killings," *New York Times*, September 21, 1982, 1.

22. *The Beirut Massacre: The Complete Kahan Commission Report*, 27.

23. Ibid., 28.

24. Ibid., 29.

25. Ibid., 30.

26. Ibid., 31.

27. Ibid., 35.

28. Ibid., 97–98.

29. Ibid., 33.

30. Ibid., 36–38.

31. Schiff and Ya'ari, *Israel's Lebanon War*, 272.

32. *The Beirut Massacre: The Complete Kahan Commission Report*, 45.

33. Ibid., 46.

34. Ariel Sharon, "Sharon's Knesset Address," September 22, 1982, in BBC Summary of World Broadcasts, September 24, 1982.

35. Leon Dash, "Christian Militia Unit Vows It Won't Enter Moslem West Beirut," *Washington Post*, August 11, 1982, A17.

36. See Shipler, "Evidence Suggests Israelis Were Aware of Killings."

37. See David Shipler, "Army's Anger at Sharon Said to Grow," *New York Times*, September 24, 1982, 5.

38. Herbert Denton, "Sharon Balks at Giving Testimony on Details of Beirut Massacre," *Washington Post*, November 21, 1984, 7.

39. Tim Llewellyn, "The Bitter Legacy of Sharon's Unfinished Business," *Scotsman*, September 16, 2002, 11.

40. *The Beirut Massacre: The Complete Kahan Commission Report*, 67.

41. Gabriel Sheffer, *Moshe Sharett: Biography of a Political Moderate* (Oxford: Clarendon Press, 1996), 686.

42. Ibid., 686.

43. Benny Morris, *Righteous Victims: A History of the Zionist-Arab Conflict, 1881–1999* (New York: Alfred A. Knopf, 1999), 208.

44. See Howard M. Sachar, *A History of Israel from the Rise of Zionism to Our Time* (New York: Alfred A. Knopf, 1996), 215–216; Tom Segev, *One Palestine Complete: Jews and Arabs Under the British Mandate*, trans. Haim Watzman (New York: Metropolitan Books, 2000), 430–431; John Bierman and Colin Smith, *Fire in the Night: Wingate of Burma, Ethiopia, and Zion* (New York: Random House, 1999), 125.

45. Schiff and Ya'ari, *Israel's Lebanon War*, 14.

46. "Begin and Rabin Battle in Parliament over Lebanon," *New York Times*, June 4, 1981, 1.

47. *The Beirut Massacre: The Complete Kahan Commission Report*, 9.

48. See Ariel Sharon, TV interview, September 24, 1982, BBC Summary of World Broadcasts, September 27, 1982.

49. See Benny Morris, *1948 and After: Israel and the Palestinians* (Oxford: Clarendon Press, 1990).

50. See David K. Shipler, "The Massacre Brings on a Crisis of Faith for Israelis," *New York Times*, September 26, 1982, 1.

51. Anne Karpf, "Remember the Pain, Heal the Wounds," *Guardian*, March 26, 2002, G2, 5.

52. Morris, *1948 and After*, 75. See also John Bagot Glubb, *A Soldier with the Arabs* (London: Hodder and Stoughton, 1957).

53. Morris, *Righteous Victims*, 255.

54. Benny Morris, *Birth of the Palestinian Refugee Problem Revisited* (New York: Cambridge University Press, 2004), 621.

55. See James Ron, *Frontiers and Ghettos: State Violence in Serbia and Israel* (Berkeley: University of California Press, 2003), 179–187.

56. *The Beirut Massacre: The Complete Kahan Commission Report*, 12.

57. Ibid., 13.

58. "Obituary of Elie Hobeika," *Daily Telegraph*, January 25, 2002, 31.

59. Ze'ev Schiff in David Shipler, "Begin Agrees to Establish a Panel to Investigate the Beirut Massacre," *New York Times*, September 29, 1982, A1.

60. Jonathan Randal, *Going All the Way: Christian Warlords, Israeli Adventurers and the War in Lebanon* (New York: Vintage Books, 1984), 15.

61. Schiff and Ya'ari, *Israel's Lebanon War*, 211.

62. Ibid., 211.

63. Friedman, "The Beirut Massacre: The Four Days.".

64. Schiff and Ya'ari, *Israel's Lebanon War*, 246.

65. *The Beirut Massacre: The Complete Kahan Commission Report*, 54.

66. "Excerpts from Sharon's Address to Parliament in Defense of Army's Role," *New York Times*, September 23, 1982, 18.

67. *The Beirut Massacre: The Complete Kahan Commission Report*, 63.

68. Thomas Friedman, *From Beirut to Jerusalem* (New York: HarperCollins, 1998), 164.

69. *The Beirut Massacre: The Complete Kahan Commission Report*, 69.

70. Russell Watson, Scott Aullivan, John Walcott, and Ray Wilkinson, "Israel in Torment," *Newsweek*, October 4, 1982, 20; David K. Shipler, "Killings a Shock, Israeli Aides Say," *New York Times*, September 20, 1982, 1.

71. *The Beirut Massacre: The Complete Kahan Commission Report*, 44.

72. "Calls for Inquiry Mounting in Israel," *New York Times*, September 24, 1982, 8.

73. Schiff and Ya'ari, *Israel's Lebanon War*, 306.

74. Shipler, "Army's Anger at Sharon Said to Grow."

75. "Begin Makes Formal Request for Independent Probe of Massacre," *Washington Post*, September 30, 1982, 33.

76. Shipler, "Killings a Shock, Israeli Aides Say."

77. See Sharon, "Sharon's Knesset Address," September 22, 1982; "Excerpts from Sharon's Address to Parliament in Defense of Army's Role."

78. Watson et al., "Israel in Torment," 20.

79. Schiff and Ya'ari, *Israel's Lebanon War*, 277.

80. Shipler, "Evidence Suggests Israelis Were Aware of the Killings."

81. "Shatila and Sabra" Editorial, *Washington Post*, September 20, 1982, 14.

82. Edward Walsh, "Israel Denies Responsibility, Says It Prevented More Deaths," *Washington Post*, September 19, 1982, 1.

83. *The Beirut Massacre: The Complete Kahan Commission Report*, 45.

84. "Begin Calls Blaming of Israel for Killings Totally Despicable," *New York Times*, October 2, 1982, 1.

85. Schiff and Ya'ari, *Israel's Lebanon War*, 279.

86. *The Beirut Massacre: The Complete Kahan Commission Report*, 48.

87. "Begin's 22nd September Knesset Speech," BBC Summary of World Broadcasts, September 24, 1982.

88. Ibid.

89. Sharon, "Sharon's Knesset Address," September 22, 1982.

90. Ibid.

91. Sharon, TV interview, September 24, 1982.

92. Sharon, "Sharon's Knesset Address," September 22, 1982.

93. Edward Walsh, "Begin Makes Formal Request for Independent Probe of Massacre," *Washington Post*, September 30, 1982, A33; Shipler, "Begin Agrees to Establish a Panel to Investigate the Beirut Massacre," September 29, 1982, A1.

94. *The Beirut Massacre: The Complete Kahan Commission Report*, 64.

95. Ibid., 63.

96. Ibid., 12.

97. Ibid., 69.

98. Ibid., 71–73.

99. Ibid., 104.

100. Ibid., 80–81.

101. Ibid., 92.

102. Ibid., 96.

103. Schiff and Ya'ari, *Israel's Lebanon War*, 250.

104. *The Beirut Massacre: The Complete Kahan Commission Report*, 86.

105. Mark Whitaker and Tony Clifton, "And the Gunmen Go Free," *Newsweek*, February 21, 1983, 37.

106. Llewellyn, "The Bitter Legacy of Sharon's Unfinished Business," 11.

107. Thomas L. Friedman, "Israeli General in Beirut Says He Did Not Know of Killings," *New York Times*, September 27, 1982, A1.

108. Whitaker and Clifton, "And the Gunmen Go Free," 37.

109. Orly Halpern, "Who Else but Israel," *Jerusalem Post*, April 11, 2006, 5.

110. Robert Fisk, "Ghosts and Secrets at Mass Killer's Funeral," *Independent on Sunday*, January 27, 2002, 16.

111. Friedman, *From Beirut to Jerusalem*, 165.

112. Edward Walsh, "Criticized Israeli Officers Leave Posts," *Washington Post*, March 2, 1983, A16.

113. See Gary Bass, *Stay the Hand of Vengeance: The Politics of War Crimes Tribunals* (Princeton: Princeton University Press, 2000), 14.

114. Sharon, TV interview, September 24, 1982.

115. Russell Watson, Milan Kubic, and Joyce Barnathan, "Sharon Takes the Rap," *Newsweek*, February 21, 1983, 30.

116. Ibid.

117. "An Ailing Begin Submits His Formal Resignation," *New York Times*, September 16, 1983, A6.

118. Schiff and Ya'ari, *Israel's Lebanon War*, 284.

119. Martin Gilbert, *Israel: A History* (London: Black Swan Books, 1998), 515.

120. Schiff and Ya'ari, *Israel's Lebanon War*, 285.

121. Watson et al., "Sharon Takes the Rap."

122. Thomas B. Rosenstiehl, "Sharon Loses Libel Suit," *Los Angeles Times*, January 25, 1985, 1.

123. See, for discussion of opinion poll data, Walsh, "Begin Makes Formal Request for Independent Probe of Massacre."

CHAPTER EIGHT

1. "Female GI in Abuse Photos Talks," http://www.cbsnews.com/stories/2004/05/12/iraq/main616921.shtml.

2. See also *Marie Claire* interview, http://www.marieclaire.com/world/news/lynndie-england-1.

3. "Lynndie England Convicted in Abu Ghraib Trial," *USA Today*, September 27, 2005, http://www.usatoday.com/news/nation/2005-09-26-england_x.htm.

4. Taguba Report in Mark Danner, *Torture and Truth* (New York: New York Review of Books, 2004), 292.

5. Ibid., 294.

6. Ibid., 295.

7. Ibid., 315.

8. Ibid., 325.

9. See Center for Human Rights and Global Justice at New York University, School of Law, Human Rights Watch and Human Rights First, "By the Numbers," *Detainee Abuse and Accountability Project* (April 2006), 2, http://www.hrw.org/en/reports/2006/04/25/numbers.

10. Dana Priest and Barton Gellman, "U.S. Decries Abuse but Defends Interrogations," *Washington Post*, December 26, 2002, A1, http://www.washingtonpost.com/wp-dyn/content/article/2006/06/09/AR2006060901356.html.

11. Jon Elster, *Closing the Books: Transitional Justice in Historical Perspective* (Cambridge: Cambridge University Press, 2004), 162.

12. Ibid., 162.

13. U.S. Department of Justice, Office of Legal Counsel, Memorandum for John Rizzo, Acting General Counsel, Central Intelligence Agency, August 1, 2002, http://www.aclu.org/safefree/torture/torturefoia.html.

14. Committee on Armed Services, U.S. Senate, "Inquiry into the Treatment of Detainees in U.S. Custody," 110th Congress, Second Session, November 20, 2008, 55.

15. Counter Resistance Techniques Memorandum, Secretary of Defense, December 2, 2002 in Danner, *Torture and Truth*, 181–182.

16. Danner, *Torture and Truth*, 182.

17. Committee on Armed Services, "Inquiry into the Treatment of Detainees in U.S. Custody," 115.

18. Ibid., 156.

19. Ibid., 158.

20. Ibid., 120.

21. Thomas Ricks, *Fiasco: The American Military Adventure in Iraq* (New York: Penguin Press, 2006), 197.

22. Quoted in Priest and Gellman, "U.S. Decries Abuse but Defends Interrogations," A1.

23. Ricks, *Fiasco*, 198.

24. Committee on Armed Services, "Inquiry into the Treatment of Detainees in U.S. Custody," xxix.

25. Elise Ackerman, "Iraq Jailers Linked to Afghan Abuse," *Miami Herald,* August 21, 2004, 1.

26. Committee on Armed Services, "Inquiry into the Treatment of Detainees in U.S. Custody," 170.

27. Ibid., 190.

28. Ibid., 191.

29. Ibid.,195.

30. Ibid., 196.

31. Ibid., 197 and 208.

32. Jones/Fay Report, in Danner, *Torture and Truth,* 488–489.

33. Committee on Armed Services, "Inquiry into the Treatment of Detainees in U.S. Custody," xxix.

34. Priest and Gellman, "U.S. Decries Abuse but Defends Interrogations," 1, http://www.washingtonpost.com/wp-dyn/content/article/2006/06/09/AR2006060901356.html.

35. Dana Priest, "Torture: The Road to Abu Ghraib and Beyond," in Karen J. Greenberg (ed.), *The Torture Debate in America* (Cambridge: Cambridge University Press, 2006), 15.

36. Ibid., 17.

37. Ibid., 15.

38. Jonathan Alter, "Time to Think About Torture," *Newsweek*, November 5, 2001.

39. Steven Lukes, "Liberal Democratic Torture," *British Journal of Political Science* 36 (2005): 15.

40. Steven Lukes, "Torture and Liberal Democracy: Response to Levey," *British Journal of Political Science* 37 (July 2007): 571–572; see Levey, "Beyond Durkheim: A Comment on Steven Lukes's 'Liberal Democratic Torture, '" *British Journal of Political Science* 37 (July 2007): 567–570.

41. Campaign advertisements are available at http://pcl.stanford.edu/campaigns/campaign2004/archive.html.

42. Survey data are available at http://news.bbc.co.uk/1/hi/in_depth/6063386.stm.

43. See http://news.bbc.co.uk/1/hi/in_depth/6063386.stm (accessed July 25, 2007).

44. Mental Health Advisory Team, Operation Iraqi Freedom 05-07, Final Report, Office of the Surgeon, Multinational Force—Iraq, November 17, 2006.

45. Committee on Armed Services, "Inquiry into the Treatment of Detainees in U.S. Custody," 69–70.

46. Ibid., 78.

47. Ibid., 85.

48. Ibid., 106.

49. Ibid., 107.

50. Ibid., 109.

51. Rumsfeld testimony, Senate Armed Services Committee, http://www.washingtonpost.com/wp-dyn/articles/A8575-2004May7.html.

52. Ibid.

53. President George W. Bush, May 10, 2004, http://www.whitehouse.gov/news/releases/2004/05/20040510-3.html.

54. http://www.whitehouse.gov/news/releases/2004/05/20040505-5.html.

55. Rumsfeld testimony, Senate Armed Services Committee.

56. "Watergate: Documents and Sources," http://www.washingtonpost.com/wp-srv/politics/special/watergate/resources.html.

57. Quoted in Eric Schmitt, "Rumsfeld Mischaracterizes Findings of 2 Studies on U.S. Abuse at Iraqi Interrogations," *New York Times*, August 28, 2004, 6.

58. Ibid.

59. Ibid.

60. Rumsfeld testimony, Senate Armed Services Committee.

61. Ibid.

62. Committee on Armed Services, "Inquiry into the Treatment of Detainees in U.S. Custody," 136. The plan to interrogate Mahamadou Walid Slahi, held in Guantanamo, included making him bark and do tricks. Other prisoners had dog collars put on and were treated similarly.

63. Schlesinger Report, in Danner, *Torture and Truth*, 331.

64. Ibid.

65. Ibid., 367.

66. Ibid., 331.

67. Ibid., 349–350.

68. Jones/Fay Report, in Danner, *Torture and Truth*, 405.

69. Ibid., 489.

70. A. T. Church, "Review of Department of Defense Detention Operations and Detainee Interrogation Techniques," Department of Defense, March 7, 2005, 3.

71. http://physiciansforhumanrights.org/library/news-2005-03-14.html.

72. Church, "Review," 11.

73. Philip Gourevitch and Errol Morris, *Standard Operating Procedure: A War Story* (London: Picador, 2008), 55.

74. Ibid., 239.

75. "President Discusses Creation of Military Commissions to Try SuspectedTerrorists," September 6, 2006 http://www.whitehouse.gov/news/releases/2006/09/20060906-3.html.

76. Philip Shenon, "So Is Waterboarding Torture? Mukasey May Never Say," *New York Times*, January 26, 2008, 11.

77. Stephen Grey, *Ghost Plane: The Inside Story of the CIA's Secret Rendition Programme* (London: C. Hurst, 2006), 212.

78. Gonzalez nomination hearing, http://www.washingtonpost.com/wp-dyn/articles/A53883-2005Jan6_4.html.

79. The memorandum from the U.S. Department of Justice, August 1, 2002, to Alberto Gonzalez states that "physical pain amounting to torture must be equivalent

in intensity to the pain accompanying serious physical injury, such as organ failure, impairment of bodily function, or even death." It concludes that "because the acts inflicting torture are extreme, there is significant range of acts that though they might constitute cruel, inhuman, or degrading treatment or punishment fail to rise to the level of torture . . . finally even if an interrogation method might violate Section 2340 A, necessity or self-defense could provide justifications that would eliminate any criminal liability." In Danner, *Torture and Truth*, 115.

80. Committee on Armed Services, "Inquiry into the treatment of detainees in U.S. custody," 55.

81. "Lynndie England Convicted in Abu Ghraib Trial."

82. http://www.icrc.org/web/eng/siteengo.nsf/html/5YRMYC; ICRC Report, in Danner, *Torture and Truth*, 253.

83. ICRC Report, in Danner, *Torture and Truth*, 254.

84. Schlesinger Report, in Danner, *Torture and Truth*, 2004, 339; Jones/Fay Report, in Danner, *Torture and Truth*, 443–444.

85. Jones/Fay Report, in Danner, *Torture and Truth*, 443–444.

86. Ricks, *Fiasco*, 215.

87. Ibid., 379.

88. Doreen Carvajal, "Groups Tie Rumsfeld to Torture in Complaint," *New York Times*, October 27, 2007, 8.

89. Major General Taguba, Preface to Physicians for Human Rights, "Broken Laws, Broken Lives: Medical Evidence of Torture by U.S. Personnel and Its Impact," June 2008, http://brokenlives.info/.

90. George W. Bush, *Decision Points* (New York: Crown, 2010), 89.

91. Donald Rumsfeld, *Known and Unknown: A Memoir* (New York: Sentinel, 2011), 547.

92. Bush, *Decision Points*, 89.

93. Analysis finds only mixed evidence to support the contention that there was damage to Bush's approval ratings as a result of Abu Ghraib. Depending on the time period analyzed and the statistical technique used, Eichenberg, Stoll, and Lebo find a statistically significant relationship in only two of eight models. See Richard C. Eichenberg, Richard J. Stoll, and Matthew Lebo, "War President: The Approval Ratings of George W. Bush," *Journal of Conflict Resolution* 50 (December 2006): 783–808.

94. Rumsfeld, *Known and Unknown*, 547–551.

95. Ibid., 501.

96. Ibid., 550.

97. http://news.bbc.co.uk/2/hi/americas/4519199.stm.

98. "General Clears Army Officer of Crime in Abu Ghraib Case," *New York Times*, January 11, 2008, 9.

99. "Pentagon Justice," *Washington Post*, September 2, 2007, B6.

100. "Dishonorable Service," *New York Times*, August 3, 2006, 20.

101. Thom Shanker, "General in Abu Ghraib Case Retires After Forced Delay," *New York Times*, August 1, 2006, 13.

102. "Pentagon Justice." B6.

CHAPTER NINE

1. Charles Simic, "Connoisseurs of Cruelty," *New York Review of Books*, March 12 2009, 23.

2. Ibid.

3. See Michael O'Hanlon, "Iraq Index," Brookings Institution, http://www.brookings.edu/topics/iraq.aspx, and, for UK forces, http://www.mod.uk/DefenceInternet/Home/.

4. See Jeanette Oldham, "SAS Soldier Shot," *Sunday Mercury*, March 13, 2005, 2;Sean Rayment, "Soldiers Will Quit SAS over Trooper on Murder Charge," *Daily Telegraph*, March 7, 2005, 2.

5. Homer, *The Iliad*, trans. Robert Fagles (Harmondsworth, Middlesex: Penguin, 1990), 111.

6. While the death penalty is available in the United States and not in the United Kingdom, it has not been used for the unlawful killing of Iraqis. Only one soldier in the Iraq conflict faces the death penalty on murder charges. That is a case where the soldier killed two fellow American soldiers. The outcome of the court-martial is not known at this point (Ross Bynum, "Georgia Soldier Facing Death Penalty Seeks New Lawyer," Associated Press, March 10, 2011). In the rape and murder of a fourteen-year-old Iraqi girl, her parents, and her younger sister, the jurors could not agree on the death penalty and so the defendant was sentenced to life in prison.

7. Martin Gilbert, *Winston S. Churchill, 1917–1922* (London: Heinemann, 1975), 817.

8. David E. Omissi, *Air Power and Colonial Control: The Royal Air Force 1919–1939* (Manchester: Manchester University Press, 1990), 152.

9. Ibid., 154.

10. Ibid., 154.

11. Toby Dodge, *Inventing Iraq: The Failure of Nation Building and History Denied* (London: Hurst and Company, 2003), 154.

12. "Questions to Ministers," *Guardian* July 4, 1924, 12.

13. T. E. Lawrence "Colonel Lawrence's Views," Letter to the Editor, *The Times*, July 23, 1920, 15.

14. "The Assyrian came down like the wolf on the fold / And his cohorts were gleaming in purple and gold": Lord Byron, "The Destruction of Sennacherib" (1815).

15. Gertrude Bell, Letter to her father, May 28, 1924, http://www.gerty.ncl.ac.uk/letters/l1646.htm.

16. "The Outbreak at Kirkuk: Trial of Native Levies," *Times*, November 6, 1924, 1.

17. See Judith Kelley, "Who Keeps International Commitments and Why? The International Criminal Court and Bilateral Nonsurrender Agreements," *American Political Science Review* 101 (August 2007).

18. See Dana Priest and Barton Gellman, "U.S. Decries Abuse but Defends Interrogations," *Washington Post*, December 26, 2002, A1.

19. Ministry of Defense, "The Army Courts-Martial System," January 11, 2005. http://www.operations.mod.uk/telic/newsItem_id=3068.htm.

20. Estella Velez-Pollack, "Military Courts-Martial: An Overview," Congressional Research Service Report for Congress, Washington, DC: Library of Congress, May 26, 2004.

21. See Mark Sappenfield, "Line Between War, Murder Tough to Draw," *Christian Science Monitor*, June 22, 2006, 1.

22. Philip Alston, *Report of the Special Rapporteur on Extrajudicial, Summary or Arbitrary Executions, United Nations, General Assembly*, A/HRC/11/2/Add.5, May 28, 2009, 22–23.

23. Ibid., 24.

24. Josh White, Charles Lane, and Julie Tate, "Homicide Charges Rare in Iraq War," *Washington Post*, August 28, 2006, 1.

25. See for example Gary D. Solis, "Military Justice, Civilian Clemency: The Sentences of Marine Corps War Crimes in South Vietnam," *Transnational Law & Contemporary Problems* 10 (2000): 67, and Deborah Nelson, *The War Behind Me: Vietnam Veterans Confront the Truth About U.S. War Crimes* (New York: Basic Books, 2008).

26. The first stage of data collection was done through electronic searches of "major world publications" using Nexis electronic archives. The initial search terms were "killing" or "abuse," "court martial," "soldier," and "Iraq." Subsequent stages included specific place names or the name of a defendant. British court-martial records are available through Smith Bernal Wordwave Limited. Some U.S. records are available from the American Civil Liberties Union, http://www.aclu.org/natsec/foia/log2.html . These data do not contain records of killing and abuse done by private military contractors. The UN report states that "the failures of reporting and transparency by PCs employed by various Government and civilian agencies are even more dramatic than those for the military" (Alston, *Report of the Special Rapporteur*, 23). A valuable study by Major Mynda G. Ohman, "Integrating Title 18 War Crimes into Title 10," *Air Force Law Review* (December 22, 2005), collected open-source reports of U.S. military investigations, courts-martial, and administrative actions for the first two years of the conflict and provided a means of checking the data collection.

27. White et al., "Homicide Charges Rare in Iraq War," 1.

28. Ibid.

29. Robert Aitken, "The Aitken Report: An Investigation into Cases of Deliberate Abuse and Unlawful Killing in Iraq in 2003 and 2004." U.K. Ministry of Defense, January 25, 2008, http://www.mod.uk/NR/rdonlyres/7AC894D3-1430-4AD1-911F-8210C3342CC5/0/aitken_rep.pdf.

30. Ibid., 4.

31. See Sean Rayment, "Revealed: As Many as 50 British Soldiers Face Trial for Murder and Other Crimes in Iraq," *Sunday Telegraph*, February 27, 2005, 6.

32. Robert Fisk, "Who Killed Baha Mousa?," *Independent*, December 15, 2004.

33. Audrey Gillan, "Father Describes the Horror of Seeing Son's Body," *Guardian*, April 17, 2007, 9.

34. Audrey Gillan, "Diary of a Squaddie: Sunburn, Sore Feet and Three More Ali Babas Tossed in the River," *Guardian*, April 28, 2007, 15.

35. See Mynda G. Ohman, "Integrating Title 18 War Crimes into Title 10," *Air Force Law Review*, December 22, 2005.

36. Kevin Sites, "Open Letter to Devil Dogs of the 3.1: A Letter to Marines Involved in the 2004 Battle for Fallujah," http://hotzone.yahoo.com/b/hotzone/blogs995.

37. It is instructive to compare these conviction rates with the 66 percent conviction rate for murder in 2003 in the seventy-five largest counties in the United States in 2003; Bureau of Justice Statistics, *Sourcebook of Criminal Justice Statistics*, http://www.albany.edu/sourcebook/. The rate in the United Kingdom in 2007 was 78 percent; Ministry of Justice, *Criminal Statistics: England and Wales 2007* (London: Office for Criminal Justice Reform, 2008), Table S 2.1; http://www.justice.gov.uk/publications/docs/crim-stats-2007-tag.pdf.

38. Steven J. Brams, *Rational Politics: Decisions, Games, and Strategy* (Boston: Harcourt, Brace Jovanovich, 1985), 141.

39. Jean-Jacques Laffont and David Martimort, *The Theory of Incentives: The Principal-Agent Model* (Princeton: Princeton University Press, 2002), 3.

40. Aitken, "The Aitken Report," 24.

41. Gillan, "Father Describes the Horror of Seeing Son's Body."

42. Proceedings of Court-Martial, Military Court Centre Bulford, 7 September 2006—30 April 2007, in the case of 224841881 Corporal Donald Payne, 2nd Battalion, The Duke of Lancaster's Regiment (Kings Lancashire and Border), 5658.

43. Aitken,"The Aitken Report," 24.

44. "Profiles: Iraq Abuse Soldiers," BBC News February 25, 2005, http://news.bbc.co.uk/1/hi/uk/4294765.stm.

45. Paul von Zielbauer, "Marine Corps Squad Leader Is Guilty of Unpremeditated Murder in Killing of an Iraqi Man," *New York Times*, August 3, 2007, 10.

46. "Soldier Blues," *Economist*, May 15, 2004.

47. Doreen Carvajal, "Groups Tie Rumsfeld to Torture in Complaint," *New York Times*, October 27, 2007, 8.

48. Nelson, *The War Behind Me*, 142.

49. Solis, "Military Justice, Civilian Clemency, " 81; for the killing of Ali Mansur Muhammad see Joe Mozingo, "A Killing in the Desert," *Los Angeles Times*, September 14, 2009, 1, and Mark Schlachtenhaufen, "Edmond Soldier, Family Await Appeal Decision," *Edmond Sun* (Oklahoma), March 30, 2011, http://www.edmondsun.com/local/x300767414/Edmond-soldier-family-await-appeal-decision.

50. See Richard Norton-Taylor, "Officers in Quandary over Legality of Orders to Condition Prisoners" *The Guardian*, March 14, 2007, 4.

51. Aitken, "The Aitken Report," 12.

52. Norton-Taylor, "Officers in Quandary."

53. Proceedings of Court-Martial, Military Court Centre Bulford, 351.

54. Ibid., 352.

55. Ibid., 385.

56. Ibid., 375.

57. Proceedings of Court-Martial, Military Court Centre Hohne, 10–11 January 2005, in the case of Fusilier Gary Bartlam 1st Battalion, The Royal Regiment of Fusiliers, 14.

58. Ibid., 19.

59. Proceedings of Court Martial, Osnabruck, 18 January to 25 February 2005, in the case of Corporal Daniel Kenyon, Lance Corporal Darren Paul Larken, Lance Corporal Mark Paul Cooley, 1st Battalion Royal Regiment of Fusiliers, 147–148.

60. Thomas Ricks, *Fiasco: The American Military Adventure in Iraq*,(New York: Penguin Press, 2006), 284–287.

61. Court-martial documents received by the American Civil Liberties Union in response to a Freedom of Information Act request, http://www.aclu.org/natsec/foia/log.html, 10350–10351.

62. Ibid.

63. Ibid., 10204.

64. Jon Sarche, "Critics Say Light Sentence for Soldier in Iraqi Death May Tarnish U.S.," Associated Press, January 25, 2006, available at http://www.lexisnexis.com.

65. "U.S. Army Interrogator Convicted in Death," *St. Petersburg Times*, January 23, 2006, 2A.

66. White et al., "Homicide Charges Rare in Iraq War."

67. Ricks, *Fiasco*, 194.

68. "Danish Prosecutor Won't Appeal Acquittal of Officers Accused of Iraqi Prisoner Abuse," Associated Press Worldstream, July 10, 2006.

69. BBC News, http://news.bbc.co.uk/1/hi/uk/7500204.stm.

70. Adam Ingram, Testimony at the Baha Mousa Inquiry (June 2, 2010), 52, http://www.bahamousainquiry.org/baha_mousa_inquiry_evidence/evidence1.htm.

71. Ibid., 59–62.

72. House of Commons, *Parliamentary Debates*, May 10 2004, 421, c. 22.

73. Ibid., *c. 25.*

74. House of Commons, *Parliamentary Debates*, May 17 2004, 421, cc. 669–670.

75. Ibid., c. 670.

76. "Soldier Blues," *e Economist*, May 13, 2004, http://www.economist.com.

CHAPTER TEN

1. See Ruth Grant and Robert Keohane, "Accountability and Abuses of Power in World Politics," *American Political Science Review* (February 2005).

2. For an example of research in this area see Zeev Maoz, "Realist and Cultural Critiques of the Democratic Peace: A Theoretical and Empirical Reassessment," *International Interactions* 24 (1998): 3–89.

3. Although any failure of accountability could be attributed to the stability of France's political system at that time and the fear of provoking a coup—and so more easily dismissed as belonging to an outlier among democracies.

4. Larry May, *War Crimes and Just War* (New York: Cambridge University Press, 2007), 264.

5. Benny Morris, *Birth of the Palestinian Refugee Problem Revisited* (New York: Cambridge University Press, 2004), 621.

6. The description of type I and type II errors in hypothesis testing helps in thinking about these mistakes.

7. Kaare Strøm, "Parliamentary Democracy and Delegation," in Kaare Strøm, Wolfgang C. Müller, and Torbjörn Bergman (eds.), *Delegation and Accountability in Parliamentary Democracies* (Oxford: Oxford University Press, 2006), 95.

8. Quoted in Dan Froomkin, "Pack of Liars," *Washington Post*, April 22, 2009, A1.

9. For a systematic analysis of whether or not an inquiry is appointed, see Raanan Sulitzeanu-Kenan, "Reflection in the Shadow of Blame: When Do Politicians Appoint Commissions of Inquiry?" *British Journal of Political Science* 40 (July 2010).

10. Edward Walsh, "Begin Makes Formal Request for Independent Probe of Massacre," *Washington Post*, September 30, 1982, A33.

11. Richard Falk, "The Kahan Commission Report on the Beirut Massacre," *Dialectical Anthropology* 8 (1984): 319–324.

12. International Criminal Tribunal for the Former Yugoslavia, Case No. IT-95-5/18-PT, February 27, 2009, http://www.icty.org/x/cases/karadzic/ind/en/090227.pdf.

13. Samuel Berlinski, Torun Dewan, Keith Dowding, and Gita Subrahmanyam, "Choosing, Moving and Resigning at Westminster, UK," in Keith Dowding and Patrick Dumont (eds.), *The Selection of Ministers in Europe* (London: Routledge 2009), 71.

14. For applications of this line of analysis see George Stigler, "An Economic Theory of Regulation," *Bell Journal of Economics and Management Science* 2 (1971): 3–21, or James Q. Wilson, *American Government: Institutions and Policies* (Lexington, MA: D. C. Heath, 1980).

15. Glenn R. Parker, *Self-Policing in Politics: the Political Economy of Reputational Controls on Politicians* (Princeton: Princeton University Press, 2004), 1, 122.

16. For coverage of Watergate see the *Washington Post*, http://www.washington-post.com/wp-srv/onpolitics/watergate/chronology.htm.

17. Gerald C. Wright Jr., "Constituency Response to Congressional Behavior: The Impact of the House Judiciary Committee Impeachment Votes," *Western Political Quarterly* 30 (September 1977): 401–410. Whether congressional behavior related to Abu Ghraib had an impact—and Rove's assessment of the electoral impact of war crimes—might be investigated in a similar fashion.

18. Fyodor Dostoyevsky, *The Brothers Karamazov* (New York: Vintage Classics, 1991), 255.

19. Ernest Renan, "What Is a Nation?," Sorbonne Lecture, March 11, 1882, http://www.nationalismproject.org/what/renan.htm.

20. Sir James Frazer, *The Golden Bough: A Study in Magic and Religion* (1922; Ware, Herts: Wordsworth Editions Ltd., 1993), 539.

21. Ibid., 579.

22. Grant and Keohane, "Accountability and Abuses of Power in World Politics," 39.

23. House of Commons, *Parliamentary Debates*, March 6, 1945, 408, cc. 1899–1901.

24. John Stuart Mill, *Considerations on Representative Government* (1861; Rockville MD: Serenity Publishers, 2008), 26.

25. Robert Aitken, "The Aitken Report: An Investigation into Cases of Deliberate Abuse and Unlawful Killing in Iraq in 2003 and 2004." U.K. Ministry of Defense, January 25, 2008, http://www.mod.uk/NR/rdonlyres/7AC894D3-1430-4AD1-911F-8210C3342CC5/0/aitken_rep.pdf, 24.

26. Ibid., 24.

27. Ibid., 24.

28. Stanley Milgram, "Some Conditions of Obedience and Disobedience to Authority," *Human Relations* 18 (1965): 57–76.

29. General Sir Mike Jackson, *Soldier: The Autobiography* (London: Bantam Press, 2007), 344–345.

30. See George Eliot, *Middlemarch* (New York: Bantam Books, 1992), 219.

31. Mill, *Considerations on Representative Government*, 27.

32. The Russian journalist and human rights activist Anna Politkovskaya commented on the violations committed by Russian forces in Chechnya and on Putin's 2004 victory: "even if we knock off 20 per cent as window dressing, he still received enough votes to secure the presidency." See Politkovskaya, *Putin's Russia*, trans. Arch Tait (London: Harvill Press, 2004), 269.

33. Karl Rove, *Courage and Consequence: My Life as a Conservative in the Fight* (New York: Threshold Editions, 2010), 78.

34. Ibid., 389.

35. David Bromwich, "The Curveball of Karl Rove," *New York Review of Books*, July 15, 2010, 18.

36. Bruce Bueno de Mesquita, Alastair Smith, Randolph M. Siverson, and James D. Morrow, *The Logic of Political Survival* (Cambridge: MIT Press, 2005), 19.

37. Ibid., 37.

38. Ibid., 181.

39. Adam Smith, *The Wealth of Nations* (1776; New York: Bantam Dell, 2003), 572.

40. See John Zaller, *The Nature and Origin of Mass Opinion* (New York: Cambridge University Press, 1992).

41. W. Lance Bennett, Regina Lawrence, and Steven Livingston, *When the Press Fails: Political Power and the News Media from Iraq to Katrina* (Chicago: University of Chicago Press, 2007), xi.

42. Ibid., 127.

43. See ibid. on this point.

44. Ze'ev Schiff and Ehud Ya'ari, *Israel's Lebanon War* (London: Unwin Paperbacks, 1986), 306.

45. Quoted in Roger Anstey, *The Atlantic Slave Trade and British Abolition, 1760–1810* (London: Macmillan, 1975), 388; see Neil J. Mitchell, *The Conspicuous Corporation: Business, Public Policy, and Representative Democracy* (Ann Arbor: University of Michigan Press, 1997) for an analysis of this policy.

Bibliography

Abbott, Wilbur Cortez. *The Writings and Speeches of Oliver Cromwell*. Cambridge, MA: Harvard University Press, 1937–1947.

Aitken, Robert. "The Aitken Report: An Investigation into Cases of Deliberate Abuse and Unlawful Killing in Iraq in 2003 and 2004." U.K. Ministry of Defense, January 25, 2008.

Akerlof, George. "The Market for Lemons: Quality Uncertainty and Market Mechanism." *Quarterly Journal of Economics* 84 (August 1970): 488–500.

Alston, Philip. *Report of the Special Rapporteur on Extrajudicial, Summary or Arbitrary Executions, United Nations, General Assembly*. A/HRC/11/2/Add. 5 Vol., May 28, 2009.

Amnesty International. *Off the Record: U.S. Responsibility for Enforced Disappearances in the War on Terror*. 2007. http://www.amnesty.org/en/library/info/AMR51/093/2007/en

Anstey, Roger. *The Atlantic Slave Trade and British Abolition, 1760–1810*. London: Macmillan, 1975.

Arrow, Kenneth J. "The Economics of Agency." In *Principals and Agents: The Structure of Business*. Ed. John W. Pratt and Richard J. Zeckhouser. Boston: Harvard Business School Press, 1985.

Arthur, Paul. *Governance and Politics of Northern Ireland*. Burnt Mill, Essex: Longman, 1984.

Austin, John L. "A Plea for Excuses." *Philosophical Papers* (1961): 123–152.

Banks, Jeffrey S., and Barry R. Weingast. "The Political Control of Bureaucracies Under Asymmetric Information." *American Journal of Political Science* 36 (May 1992): 509–524.

Bardhan, Pranab. "Corruption and Development: A Review of Issues." *Journal of Economic Literature* 35 (1997): 1320–1346.

Bar-Siman-Tov, Yaacov. "Ben-Gurion to Sharett: Conflict Management and Great Power Constraints in Israeli Foreign Policy." *Middle Eastern Studies* 24 (1988): 330–356.

Bar-Zohar, Michael. *Ben-Gurion*. London: Weidenfeld and Nicolson, 1977.

Bass, Gary. *Stay the Hand of Vengeance: The Politics of War Crimes Tribunals*. Princeton: Princeton University Press, 2000.

Beevor, Anthony. *The Battle for Spain: The Spanish Civil War 1936–1939*. London: Weidenfeld and Nicolson, 2006.

"Begin's 22nd September Knesset Speech." BBC Summary of World Broadcasts, September 24, 1982.

Bennett, W. Lance, Regina Lawrence, and Steven Livingston. *When the Press Fails: Political Power and the News Media from Iraq to Katrina*. Chicago: Chicago University Press, 2007.

Bergman, Torbjörn, Wolfgang C. Müller, Kaare Strøm, and Magnus Blomgren. "Democratic Delegation and Accountability: Cross-national Patterns." In *Delegation and Accountability in Parliamentary Democracies*. Ed. Kaare Strøm, Wolfgang C. Müller, and Torbjörn Bergman. Oxford: Oxford University Press, 2006.

Biddle, Tami Davis. *Rhetoric and Reality in Air Warfare: The Evolution of British and American Ideas About Strategic Bombing, 1914–1945*. Princeton: Princeton University Press, 2002.

Bierman, John, and Colin Smith. *Fire in the Night: Wingate of Burma, Ethiopia, and Zion*. New York: Random House, 1999.

Bobb, Clifford. *The Marketing of Rebellion*. Cambridge: Cambridge University Press, 2005.

Boin, Arjen, Paul't Hart, Eric Stern, and Bengt Sundelius. *The Politics of Crisis Management: Public Leadership Under Pressure*. Cambridge: Cambridge University Press, 2005.

Bonner, Raymond. "The CIA's Secret Torture." *New York Review of Books* 54 (January 11, 2007): 28–31.

Brams, Steven J. *Rational Politics: Decisions, Games, and Strategy*. Boston: Harcourt, Brace Jovanovich, 1985.

Brehm, John, and Scott Gates. *Working, Shirking, and Sabotage*. Ann Arbor: University of Michigan Press, 1997.

Bromwich, David. "The Curveball of Karl Rove." *New York Review of Books* 58 (July 15, 2010): 18–20.

Brym, Robert J., and Yael Maoz-Shai. "Israeli State Violence During the Second Intifada: Combining New Institutionalist and Rational Choice Approaches." *Studies in Conflict and Terrorism* 32 (2009): 611–626.

Brysk, Alison. *The Politics of Human Rights in Argentina: Protest, Change, and Democratization*. Stanford: Stanford University Press, 1994.

Bueno de Mesquita, Bruce, George W. Downs, Alastair Smith, and Feryal Marie Cherif. "Thinking Inside the Box: A Closer Look at Democracy and Human Rights." *International Studies Quarterly* 49 (September 2005): 439–457.

Bueno de Mesquita, Bruce, Alastair Smith, Randolph M. Siverson, and James D. Morrow. *The Logic of Political Survival*. Cambridge: MIT Press, 2005.

Bush, George W. *Decision Points*. New York: Crown, 2010.

Carey, Sabine C. "The Use of Repression as a Response to Domestic Dissent." *Political Studies* 58 (February 2009): 167–186.

Carver, Michael. *Out of Step*. London: Hutchinson, 1989.

Cheibub, Jose Antonio, and Adam Przeworski. "Democracy, Elections, and Accountability for Economic Outcomes." In *Democracy, Accountability, and Representation. Democracy, Accountability, and Representation*. Ed. Adam Przeworski, Susan C. Stokes, and Bernard Manin. Cambridge: Cambridge University Press, 1999.

Churchill, Winston S. *Triumph and Tragedy*. Boston: Houghton Mifflin, 1953.

Cingranelli, David, and Mikhail Filippov. "Electoral Rules and Incentives to Protect Human Rights." *Journal of Politics* 72 (January 2010): 243–257.

Cohen, Stanley. *States of Denial: Knowing About Atrocities and Suffering*. London: Polity Press, 2001.

Collett, Nigel. *The Butcher of Amritsar: General Reginald Dyer*. London: Hambledon Continuum, 2005.

Collier, Paul, and Anke Hoeffler. "Greed and Grievance in Civil War." *Oxford Economic Papers* 56 (2004): 563–595.

Council of Europe Committee on Legal Affairs and Human Rights. *Secret Detentions and Illegal Transfers of Detainees Involving Council of Europe Member States: Second Report*. Council of Europe, June 7, 2007.

Danchev, Alex, and Daniel Todman (eds.). *Fieldmarshal Lord Alanbrooke, War Diaries 1939–1945*. Berkeley: University of California Press, 2001.

Danner, Mark. *Torture and Truth*. New York: New York Review of Books, 2004.

———. "U.S. Torture: Voices from the Black Sites." *New York Review of Books* 56 (March 12 2009) .

Datta, V. N. *Jallianwala Bagh*. Bhopal: Lyall Book Depot, 1969.

Davenport, Christian. *State Repression and the Domestic Democratic Peace*. New York: Cambridge University Press, 2007.

Davenport, Christian, and David A. Armstrong II. "Democracy and the Violation of Human Rights: A Statistical Analysis from 1976 to 1996." *American Journal of Political Science* 48 (July 2004): 538–554.

Dawson, Graham. *Making Peace with the Past? Memory, Trauma and the Irish Troubles*. Manchester: Manchester University Press, 2007.

Dodge, Toby. *Inventing Iraq: The Failure of Nation Building and History Denied*. London: Hurst and Company, 2003.

Donohue, Laura K. *The Cost of Counterterrorism: Power, Politics, and Liberty*. Cambridge: Cambridge University Press, 2006.

Dostoyevsky, Fyodor. *The Brothers Karamazov*. Trans. Richard Pevear and Larissa Volokhonsy. New York: Vintage Classics, 1991.

Dowding, Keith, and Patrick Dumont, eds. *The Selection of Ministers in Europe*. London: Routledge, 2009.

Dowding, Keith, and Won-taek Kang. "Ministerial Resignations 1945–1997." *Public Administration* 76 (Autumn 1998): 411–429.

Downes, Alexander B. "Desperate Times, Desperate Measure: The Causes of Civilian Victimization in War." *International Security* 30 (Spring 2006): 152–195.

Eichenberg, Richard C., Richard J. Stoll, and Matthew Lebo. " War President: The Approval Ratings of George W. Bush." *Journal of Conflict Resolution* 50 (2006): 783–808.

Eliot, George. *Middlemarch*. New York: Bantam Books, 1992.

Elster, Jon. *Closing the Books: Transitional Justice in Historical Perspective*. Cambridge: Cambridge University Press, 2004.

Falk, Richard. "The Kahan Commission Report on the Beirut Massacre." *Dialectical Anthropology* 8 (1984): 319–324.

Fearon, James D. "Domestic Political Audiences and the Escalation of International Disputes." *American Political Science Review* 88 (September 1994) 577.

Fearon, James D. "Electoral Accountability and the Control of Politicians: Selecting Good Types Versu Sanctioning Poor Performance." In *Democracy, Accountability, and Representation*. Ed. Adam Przeworski, Susan C. Stokes, and Bernard Manin. Cambridge: Cambridge University Press, 1999.

Fearon, James D., and David D. Laitin. "Ethnicity, Insurgency, and Civil War." *American Political Science Review* 97 (2003): 75–89.

Fein, Helen. *Imperial Crime and Punishment: The Massacre at Jallianwala Bagh and British Judgement 1919–1920.* Honolulu: University Press of Hawaii, 1975.

Finer, S. E. "The Individual Responsibility of Ministers." *Public Administration* 34 (Winter 1956): 377–396.

Fiorina, Morris P. "Group Concentration and Delegation of Legislative Authority." *Regulatory Policy and the Social Sciences.* Ed. Roger G. Noll. Berkeley: University of California Press, 1985.

Flinders, Matthew. "The Enduring Centrality of Individual Ministerial Responsibility Within the British Constitution," *The Journal of Legislative Studies* 6 (2000):73-92.

Franklin, Mark, and Matthew Ladner. "The Undoing of Winston Churchill: Mobilization and Conversion in the 1945 Realignment of British Voters." *British Journal of Political Science* 25 (1995): 429–452.

Fraser, Antonia. *Cromwell: The Lord Protector.* New York: Alfred A. Knopf, 1973.

Frazer, Sir James. *The Golden Bough: A Study in Magic and Religion.* Ware, Herts: Wordsworth Reference, [1922] 1993.

Friedman, Marilyn. "How to Blame People Responsibly" (unpublished manuscript).

Friedman, Thomas. *From Beirut to Jerusalem:One Man's Middle Eastern Odyssey.* New York: HarperCollins, 1998.

Furneaux, Rupert. *Massacre at Amritsar.* London: George Allen and Unwin, 1963.

Gay, Oonagh, and Thomas Powell. *Individual Ministerial Responsibility—Issues and Examples.* 04/31 Vol. House of Commons Research Paper, April 5, 2004.

Gibney, Mark, Rhoda E. Howard-Hassmann, Jean-Marc Coicaud, and Niklaus Steiner, eds. *The Age of Apology: Facing Up to the Past.* Philadelphia: University of Pennsylvania Press, 2007.

Gilbert, Martin. *"Churchill: A Life."* New York: Henry Holt, 1991.

———. *Israel: A History.* London: Black Swan, 1998.

———. *Winston S. Churchill, 1917–1922.* London: Heinemann, 1975.

———. *Winston S. Churchill, 1945–1965.* London: Heinemann, 1988.

Glubb, John Bagot. *A Soldier with the Arabs.* London: Hodder and Stoughton, 1957.

Gourevitch, Philip, and Errol Morris. *Standard Operating Procedure: A War Story.* London: Picador, 2008.

Grant, Ruth, and Robert Keohane. "Accountability and Abuses of Power in World Politics." *American Political Science Review* 99 (February 2005): 29–43.

Grayling, A.C. *Among the Dead Cities.* London: Bloomsbury Publishing, 2006.

Greenberg, Karen, ed. *The Torture Debate in America.* Cambridge: Cambridge University Press, 2006.

Grey, Stephen. *Ghost Plane: The Inside Story of the CIA's Secret Rendition Programme .* London: C. Hurst, 2006.

Hafner-Burton, Emilie M., and Kiyoteru Tsutsui. "Human Rights in a Globalizing World: The Paradox of Empty Promises." *American Journal of Sociology* 110 (2005): 1373–1411.

Hamill, Desmond. *Pig in the Middle: The Army in Northern Ireland 1969–1984.* London: Methuen, 1985.

Harris, Arthur T. *Bomber Offensive.* London: Collins, 1947.

Hastings, Max. *Bomber Command.* New York: Dial Press, 1979.

Hayner, Priscilla B. *Unspeakable Truths:Facing the Challenge of Truth Commissions.* New York: Routledge, 2001.

Heath, Edward. *The Course of My Life.* London: Hodder and Stoughton, 1998.

Hegarty, Angela. "Truth, Law and Official Denial: The Case of Bloody Sunday." *Criminal Law Forum* 15 (2004): 199–246.

Homer. *The Illiad.* Trans. Robert Fagles. Harmondsworth Middlesex: Penguin Books, 1990.

Hood, Christopher. "The Risk Game and the Blame Game." *Government and Opposition* 31 (Winter 2002): 15–37.

———. "What Happens When Transparency Meets Blame-Avoidance." *Public Management Review* 9 (2007): 191–210.

Alistair. *A Savage War of Peace: Algeria 1954-1962.* New York: New York Review of Books Classics, 2006.

Horowitz, Michael, and Dan Reiter. "When Does Aerial Bombing Work? Quantitative Empirical Tests, 1917-1999." *Journal of Conflict Resolution* 45 (2001): 147–173.

House of Commons. *Parliamentary Debates.* http://hansard.millbanksystems.com/ commons

House of Lords. *Parliamentary Debates.* http://hansard.millbanksystems.com/lords

Hume, David.. *Hume's Moral and Political Philosophy.* Ed. Henry D. Aiken. New York: Hafner Press, 1948.

Hume, David. "Of the First Principles of Government." In *Hume's Moral and Political Philosophy.* Ed. Henry D. Aiken. New York: Hafner Press, 1948.

"Israel: The Rise of Ariel." *Economist,* August 8, 1981, 27.

Jackson, Mike. *Soldier: The Autobiography.* London: Bantam Press, 2007.

Jescheck, Hans-Heinrich. "The General Principles of International Criminal Law Set Out in Nuremberg, as Mirrored in the ICC Statute." *Journal of International Criminal Justice* 2 (2004): 38–55.

Jordan, Grant. *The British Administrative System: Principles Versus Practice.* London: Routledge, 1994.

Kahan Commission. *The Beirut Massacre: The Complete Kahan Commission Report.* New York: Karz-Cohl, 1983.

Keck, Margaret, and Kathryn Sikkink. *Advocacy Beyond Borders.* Ithaca: Cornell University Press, 1998.

Kelley, Judith. "Who Keeps International Commitments and Why? The International Criminal Court and Bilateral Nonsurrender Agreements." *American Political Science Review* 101 (August 2007): 573–589.

King, Gary, Robert O. Keohane, and Sidney Verba. *Designing Social Inquiry: Scientific Inference in Qualitative Research.* Princeton: Princeton University Press, 1994.

Laffont, Jean-Jacques, and David Martimort. *The Theory of Incentives: The Principal-Agent Model.* Princeton: Princeton University Press, 2002.

Lafree, Gary, Laura Dugan, and Raven Korte. "The Impact of British Counter-Terrorist Strategies on Political Violence in Northern Ireland: Comparing Deterrence and Backlash Models?" *Criminology* (February 2009): 17–45.

Landman, Todd. *Protecting Human Rights: A Comparative Study.* Washington, DC: Georgetown University Press, 2005.

Landman, Todd and Anita Godhes. "Principals, Agents, and Atrocities: The Case of Peru 1980-2000." Unpublished manuscript.

Landman, Todd, and Marco Larizza. "Inequality and Human Rights: Who Controls What, When, and How." *International Studies Quarterly* 53 (September 2009): 715–736.

Lash, Joseph P. *Roosevelt and Churchill 1939–1941: The Partnership That Saved the West.* London: Andre Deutsch, 1977.

Levey, Geoffrey Brahm. "Beyond Durkheim: A Comment on Steven Lukes's 'Liberal Democratic Torture." *British Journal of Political Science* 37 (July 2007): 567–570.

Lijphart, Arend. *Patterns of Democracy: Government Forms and Performance in Thirty-Six Countries.* New Haven: Yale University Press, 1999.

Lukacs, John. *Five Days in London: May 1940.* New Haven: Yale University Press, 2001.

Lukes, Steven. "Liberal Democratic Torture." *British Journal of Political Science* 36 (January 2006): 1–16.

———. "Torture and Liberal Democracy: Response to Levey." *British Journal of Political Science* 37 (July 2007): 571–572.

Machiavelli, Niccolo. T*he Prince.* Trans. Robert M. Adams. London: Norton, 1977.

Maoz, Zeev. "Realist and Cultural Critiques of the Democratic Peace: A Theoretical and Empirical Reassessment." *International Interactions* 24 (1998): 3–89.

May, Larry. *War Crimes and Just War.* Cambridge: Cambridge University Press, 2007.

McCann, Eamon. *Bloody Sunday in Derry: What Really Happened.* Dingle, Co. Kerry, Ireland: Brandon, 1992.

McCormick, James M. *American Foreign Policy and Process.* Itasca, IL: F. E. Peacock, 1992.

McCormick, James M., and Neil J. Mitchell. "Human Rights and Foreign Assistance: An Update." *Social Science Quarterly* 70 (December 1989): 969–979.

McCubbins, Matthew, Roger G. Noll, and Barry R. Weingast. "Administrative Procedures as Instruments of Political Control." *Journal of Law Economics and Organization* 3 (1987): 243–277.

McGraw, Kathleen. "Managing Blame: An Experimental Test of the Effects of Political Accounts." *American Political Science Review* 85 (December 1991): 1133–1157.

McKittrick, David, and David McVea. *Making Sense of the Troubles.* London: Penguin Books, 2001.

Meron, Theodor. "Shakespeare's Henry the Fifth and the Law of War." *American Journal of International Law* 86 (1992): 1–45.

Milgram, Stanley. "Some Conditions of Obedience and Disobedience to Authority." *Human Relations* 18 (1965): 57–76.

Mill, John Stuart. *Consideration on Representative Government.* Rockville, MD: Serenity Press, [1861] 2008.

Milton, John. "The Tenure of Kings and Magistrates." In *Complete Prose Works of John Milton.* Ed. Don M. Wolfe, III: 205–206. New Haven: Yale University Press, 1962.

Mitchell, Neil J. *Agents of Atrocity: Leaders, Followers and the Violation of Human Rights in Civil War.* New York: Palgrave Macmillan, 2004.

———. *The Conspicuous Corporation: Business, Public Policy, and Representative Democracy.* Ann Arbor: University of Michigan Press, 1997.

———. "Resisting Machiavelli: Reducing Collective Harm in Conflict." In *The Greater Good.* Ed. Donnelson Forsythe. New York: Palgrave Macmillan, 2011.

Morris, Benny. *Birth of the Palestinian Refugee Problem Revisited.* New York: Cambridge University Press, 2004.

———. *1948 and After: Israel and the Palestinians*. Oxford: Clarendon Press, 1990.

———. *Righteous Victims: A History of the Zionist-Arab Conflict, 1981–1999*. New York: Alfred A. Knopf, 1999.

Morrow, James. "When Do States Follow the Laws of War?" *American Political Science Review* 101 (August 2007): 559–572.

Müller, Wolfgang C., Torbjörn Bergman, and Kaare Strøm. "Parliamentary Democracy: Promise and Problems." In *Delegation and Accountability in Parliamentary Democracies*. Ed. Kaare Strøm, Wolfgang C. Müller, and Torbjörn Bergman. Oxford: Oxford University Press, 2006.

Nelson, Deborah. *The War Behind Me: Vietnam Veterans Confront the Truth About U.S. War Crimes*. New York: Basic Books, 2008.

Newman, Frank, and David Weissbrodt. *Selected International Human Rights Instruments*. Cincinnati, OH: Anderson, 1996.

Norpoth, Helmut. *Confidence Regained*. Ann Arbor: University of Michigan Press, 1992.

Nye, Joseph S. Jr. *The Powers to Lead*. Oxford: Oxford University Press, 2008.

Ohman, Mynda G. "Integrating Title 18 War Crimes into Title 10." *Air Force Law Review* 57 (December 22, 2005)

Omissi, David E. *Air Power and Colonial Control: The Royal Air Force 1919–1939*. Manchester: Manchester University Press, 1990.

Ó Siochrú, Micháel. *God's Executioner: Oliver Cromwell and the Conquest of Ireland*. London: Faber and Faber, 2008.

Overy, Richard. *Why the Allies Won*. London: Pimlico, 2006.

Parker, Glenn R. *Self-Policing in Politics: The Political Economy of Reputational Controls on Politicians*. Princeton: Princeton University Press, 2004.

Physicians for Human Rights. *Broken Laws, Broken Lives: Medical Evidence of Torture by U.S. Personnel and Its Impact*. June 2008. http://brokenlives.info/?page_id=69

Poe, Steven C., Sabine C. Carey, and Tanya C. Vazquez. "How Are These Pictures Different? A Quantitative Comparison of the U.S. State Department and Amnesty International Human Rights Reports, 1976–1995." *Human Rights Quarterly* 23 (2001): 650–677.

Politkovskaya, Anna. *Putin's Russia*. Trans. Arch Tait. London: Harvill Press, 2004.

Poth, Stephan, and Torsten Selk. "Principal Agent Theory and Artificial Information Asymmetry." *Politics* 29 (June 2009): 137–144.

Pringle, Peter, and Philip Jacobson. *Those Are Real Bullets, Aren't They?* London: Fourth Estate, 2000.

Randal, Jonathan. *Going All the Way: Christian Warlords, Israeli Adventurers and the War in Lebanon*. New York: Vintage Books, 1984.

Rawls, John. *Law of the Peoples*. Cambridge, MA: Harvard University Press, 2001.

Report of the Committee Appointed by the Government of India to Investigate the Disturbances in the Punjab. Cmd. 681, London: His Majesty's Stationery Office, 1920.

Richards, David L., and Ronald D. Gelleny. "Good Things to Those Who Wait? National Elections and Government Respect for Human Rights." *Journal of Peace Research* 44 (July 2007): 505–523.

Ricks, Thomas E. *Fiasco: The American Military Adventure in Iraq*. New York: Penguin Press, 2006.

Risse, Thomas, Stephen C. Ropp, and Kathryn Sikkink, eds. *The Power of Human Rights: International Norms and Domestic Change*. Cambridge: Cambridge University Press, 1999.

Robertson, Geoffrey. *Crimes Against Humanity: The Struggle for Global Justice*. London: Penguin Press, 1999.

Ron, James. *Frontiers and Ghettos: State Violence in Serbia and Israel*. Berkeley: University of California Press, 2003.

———. "Savage Restraint: Israel, Palestine and the Dialectics of Legal Repression." *Social Problems* 47 (November 2000): 445–472.

Rose, Richard. "A Model Democracy?" In *Lessons from America: An Exploration*. Ed. Richard Rose. New York: Wiley, 1974.

Rove, Karl. *Courage and Consequence: My Life as a Conservative in the Fight*. New York: Threshold Editions, 2010.

Rumsfeld, Donald. *Known and Unknown: A Memoir*. New York: Sentinel, 2011.

Sachar, Howard M. *A History of Israel Trom the Rise of Zionism to Our Time*. New York: Alfred A. Knopf, 1996.

Sayer, Derek. "British Reaction to the Amritsar Massacre 1919–1920." *Past and Present* (May 1991): 130–164.

Schiff, Ze'ev. "The Green Light." *Foreign Policy* 50 (1983): 73–85.

Schiff, Ze'ev, and Ehud Ya'ari. *Israel's Lebanon War* (London: Unwin Paperbacks, 1986).

Schiller, Friedrich. *The History of the Thirty Years' War in Germany*. Trans. A. J. W. Morrison. Boston: Francis A. Nicolls, [1793] 1901.

Segev, Tom. *One Palestine Complete: Jews and Arabs Under the British Mandate* . Trans. Haim Watzman. New York: Metropolitan Books, 2000.

Sharon, Ariel. TV interview, September 24, 1982. BBC Summary of World Broadcasts, September 27, 1982.

Sharon, Ariel. "Sharon's Knesset Address." September 22, 1982. BBC Summary of World Broadcasts, September 24, 1982.

Sheffer, Gabriel. *Moshe Sharett: Biography of a Political Moderate*. Oxford: Clarendon Press, 1996.

Shively, W. Philips. *Power and Choice*. New York: McGraw-Hill, 2003.

Simic, Charles. "Connoisseurs of Cruelty." *New York Review of Books* 56 (March 12, 2009).

Simmons, Beth. *Mobilizing for Human Rights*. Cambridge: Cambridge University Press, 2009.

Smith, Adam. *The Theory of Moral Sentiments*. New York: Prometheus Books, [1759] 2000.

———. *The Wealth of Nations*. New York: Bantam Dell, [1776] 2003.

Solis, Gary D. "Military Justice, Civilian Clemency: The Sentences of Marine Corps War Crimes in South Vietnam," *Transnational Law & Contemporary Problems*, 10 (2000):59-84.

Stigler, George. "An Economic Theory of Regulation." *Bell Journal of Economics and Management Science* 2 (1971): 3–21.

Strøm, Kaare. "Parliamentary Democracy and Delegation." In *Delegation and Accountability in Parliamentary Democracies*. Ed. Kaare Strøm, Wolfgang C. Müller, and Torbjörn Bergman. Oxford: Oxford University Press 2006.

Strøm, Kaare, Wolfgang C. Müller, and Torbjörn Bergman, eds. *Delegation and Accountability in Parliamentary Democracies*. Oxford: Oxford University Press, 2006.

Sulitzeanu-Kenan, Raanan. "Reflection in the Shadow of Blame: When do Politicians Appoint Commissions of Inquiry?" *British Journal of Political Science* 40 (July 2010): 613–634.

———. "'Scything the Grass: Agenda Setting Consequences of Appointing Public Inquiries in the UK. A Longitudinal Analysis." *Policy and Politics* 35 (2007): 629–650.

Taylor, Frederick. *Dresden: Tuesday 13 February 1945*. London: Bloomsbury, 2005.

Thatcher, Margaret H. *The Downing Street Years*. London: HarperCollins, 1993.

Thornton, Rod. "Getting It Wrong: The Crucial Mistakes Made in the Early Stages of the British Army's Deployment to Northern Ireland (August 1969 to March 1972)." *Journal of Strategic Studies* 30 (February 2007): 73–107.

Timmerman, Jacobo. *Prisoner Without a Name, Cell Without a Number*. New York: Vintage Books, 1982.

Trollope, Anthony. *Phineas Redux*. London: Penguin Books, 2003.

U.S. Senate, Committee on Armed Services. *Inquiry into the Treatment of Detainees in U.S. Custody*. Washington, DC, November 20, 2008.

Velez-Pollack, Estella. *Military Courts-Martial: An Overview*. Congressional Research Service Report for Congress. Washington, DC: Library of Congress, May 26 2004.

Voltaire. *Candide* . Trans. Burton Raffel. New Haven: Yale University Press, [1759] 2005.

Walsh, Lawrence E. "Political Oversight, the Rule of Law, and Iran-Contra." *Cleveland State Law Review* 42 (1994): 587–597.

Walzer, Michael. *Arguing About War*. New Haven: Yale University Press, 2004.

Waterman, Richard W., Amelia A. Rouse, and Robert L. Wright. *Bureaucrats, Politics and the Environment*. Pittsburgh: University of Pittsburgh Press, 2004.

Weaver, Kent. "The Politics of Blame Avoidance." *Journal of Public Policy* 6 (October 1986): 371–398.

Webster, Charles, and Noble Frankland. *The Strategic Air Offensive Against Germany, 1939–1945*. London: Her Majesty's Stationery Office, 1961.

Weinstein, Jeremy M. *Inside Rebellion: The Politics of Insurgent Violence*. Cambridge: Cambridge University Press, 2007.

Wilson, James Q. *American Government: Institutions and Policies* . Lexington, MA: D. C. Heath, 1980.

Wright, Gerald C. Jr. " Constituency Response to Congressional Behavior: The Impact of the House Judiciary Committee Impeachment Votes." *Western Political Quarterly* 30 (1977): 401–410.

Zaller, John. *The Nature and Origin of Mass Opinion*. New York: Cambridge University Press, 1992.

Ziegler, Philip. *Edward Heath: The Authorised Biography*. London: Harper Press, 2010.

Index

About the Author

NEIL JAMES MITCHELL is Professor of International Relations in the School of Public Policy at University College London and the author of *Agents of Atrocity: Leaders, Followers, and the Violation of Human Rights in Civil War.*